D0454947

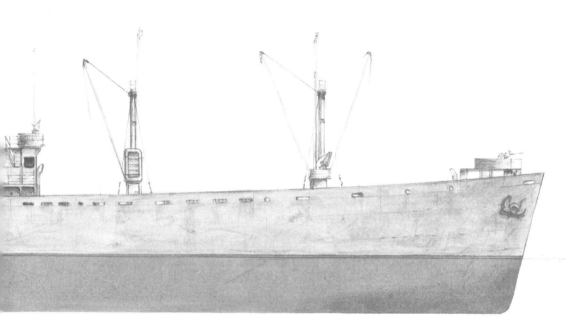

THE
FORGOTTEN
HEROES

THE
FORGOTTEN
HEROES

THE HEROIC STORY OF THE
UNITED STATES MERCHANT MARINE

Brian Herbert

A TOM DOHERTY ASSOCIATES BOOK
NEW YORK

*To the forgotten heroes of the U.S. Merchant Marine
who served America so valiantly in wartime,
this book is dedicated with great respect
and admiration.*

*This book is also for the loyal, supportive families
of these brave merchant seamen.*

CONTENTS

CONTENTS

ACKNOWLEDGMENTS

Special acknowledgments to:

Lieutenant Dean E. Beaumont of the United States Merchant Marine, for inspiring this work with his own remarkable story, and for promoting the worthy cause of his fellow merchant mariners.

Janet Herbert, my loving wife, for granting me the time and space to complete this important project.

Pat LoBrutto, editor extraordinaire, whose perceptive suggestions greatly improved this manuscript.

With appreciation, I also acknowledge the generous assistance and advice of the following individuals:

Carol A. Beaumont, Phyllis Beaumont-Evans and the family of Arthur Beaumont, Margaret Bennett, Matt Bialer, Ronald Blanquie, Kathleen Favot-Blanquie, Dominique Blanquie, Thomas R. Bowerman, Buck Braden, John C. Burley, Cheryl Capitani, Jack Carver, Carolyn Cella, Captain Peter Chelemedos, John Clatworthy, Colonel Harold E. "Hal" Cook, Captain William C. Crozier, Sean Dodds, Tom Doherty, Lieutenant Jack W. Faulkner, Doug Fleming, William B. "Bill" Flury, Charles Dana Gibson, Robert Gottlieb, Misha Hall, Howard J. "Howie" Hansen, Robert L. Heitzinger, Margaux Herbert, Pamela

Horn Lingbloom, Lieutenant Bill Hower, Captain Harold Huyke, Joyce Justice, Captain Alan H. Knox, Bruce Magnuson, Don Marcus, Carolyn Marr, Sheila McIntyre, Captain Frank Medeiros, Penny Merritt, Ronald Merritt, Jan Michaelis, Ian A. Millar, Les Modell, Captain Arthur R. Moore, James P. Morrison, Jim Mossman, Darren Noble, Bill Shanks, Kathleen Sidjakov, Nicholas Sidjakov Sr., Nicholas Sidjakov Jr., John Silbersack, Bob Simpson, Brian Sobel, Paul Stevens, Richard M. "Dick" Swift, Valentine Swagel, Wilson J. Taylor, Edwin Urstadt, John George "Jack" Urstadt V, Theodore "Ted" Weller, and Gary Wilt.

In addition, I am grateful for the contribution of resources by the following organizations:

U.S. Merchant Marine Veterans of World War Two
Naval Undersea Marine Library—Keyport, Washington
Puget Sound Maritime Historical Society—Seattle, Washington

Braving the wind, braving the sea,
Fighting the treacherous foe . . .

—FROM THE U.S. MERCHANT MARINE ANTHEM[1]

THE UNITED STATES MERCHANT MARINE OF TODAY IS ONLY A SHADOW OF ITS FOR-
mer self, with fewer merchant ships afloat than those currently sailing under the flag of the tiny Mediterranean republic of Malta, which
occupies only 124 square miles. Since the end of World War Two,
the U.S. fleet has undergone a steady decline of ships, and now
operates just 1.7 percent of the merchant vessels in the world.[2]

Few Americans know that civilian seamen were among the
greatest heroes of World War Two, and were even the first casualties
of the war: A Japanese submarine torpedoed the transport ship SS
Cynthia Olson seventeen minutes before the attack on Pearl Harbor. All thirty-three civilian seamen and two U.S. Army passengers
aboard the vessel perished.[3]

Because of a pressing need for crews to man cargo ships during
the war, the Merchant Marine sent a number of cadets directly into
action, instead of requiring that they graduate first. None of the
armed forces did this to their undergraduates, not West Point nor
Annapolis, nor any of the other academies—and 142 Merchant

Marine cadets were eventually killed in action. So many boys were sent into the heat of battle, where they became men. It is no surprise, then, that the motto of the Merchant Marine Academy is *Acta Non Verba*: "Deeds, Not Words."[4]

Under precarious conditions these merchant seamen performed extraordinary acts of bravery; they were the lifeline of the Allied forces, making victory not only possible, but inevitable. Hardly anyone realizes this, or that merchant seamen formed the first Navy of the United States in colonial times. In fact, more seamen died in the Revolutionary War than did soldiers in George Washington's Continental Army.[5]

Our Merchant Marine has an outstanding tradition, one that has come to the forefront in every war the United States has fought over a period of more than two hundred years. There are many stories of self-sacrifice and heroism, and none are so remarkable as the exploits of the civilian seamen of World War Two. It is, however, one of the saddest and most outrageously unfair chapters in all of American history.

The Merchant Marine Act of 1936 enabled the government to declare Merchant Marine ships as auxiliary military vessels. During World War Two the men of the Merchant Marine were sent into war zones, ordered to transport troops, bombs, tanks, planes, aviation fuel, torpedoes, munitions, and other dangerous war matériel.

The public also does not know that the fight, for these seamen, did not end with the war. It continues to this day, as they seek respect and recognition for their great efforts. At the vanguard of the effort is Dean E. Beaumont of Scottsdale, Arizona, who has struggled for years to obtain military benefits for himself and his comrades. I met him on board the *Queen Elizabeth II* ocean liner, out in the middle of the Pacific Ocean, in a region where he had risked his life more than half a century earlier. He began to tell me incredible stories, and prompted me to do my own research.

An impartial analysis of World War Two reveals significant events that were omitted from the history books read by American schoolchildren, such as the fact that the U.S. Merchant Marine suffered more deaths per capita in that war than any of the American armed forces. (See chapter 10, "The Submarine Parade," page 101.) The losses were so high, and the deaths those men suffered so horrible, that casualty rates were kept secret during the war, to avoid creating a shortage of volunteers, and to prevent the enemy from knowing how successful their attacks had been.[6]

The jobs of the merchant seamen were so perilous that some resigned and went into military service, which they thought might be more safe. For the most part, the men of the United States Merchant Marine were not fighters—not with weapons. But they had a fighting spirit that permitted them to overcome tremendous obstacles and to persevere. Through the most hazardous and dangerous of conditions they delivered war supplies to our overseas troops, and transported the soldiers themselves to battle zones.*

With their essential cargoes, it is no wonder that Merchant Marine ships were the targets of German U-boats, surface raiders, and Japanese kamikaze planes. Merchant petroleum tankers were blown up, incinerating men to death or burning them severely. Torpedoes fired at merchant ships carrying ammunition caused explosions so immense that no traces of the vessels or their crews were ever found.

Despite the attempt to keep such losses secret, survivors told harrowing stories, and the men who sailed on United States merchant ships knew how dangerous it was. Even so, there never was a shortage of volunteers. Ships always had crews, and went out again and again. One of those volunteers later said: "The ships were being sunk so rapidly by German submarines, I knew one seaman who was torpedoed twice in two weeks."[8] Remarkably, these brave men put only five-eights of an inch of steel—the thickness of a typical hull—between themselves and a torpedo.

Stanley Hildbreth of Oregon was a volunteer. Injured on a Lib-

---

*Virtually all of the Merchant Marine sailors in World War Two were men. Only in recent years have significant numbers of women been accepted into the industry's training programs. (See endnote for additional information on the women who served on Allied merchant ships in World War Two.)[7]

erty ship in the invasion of Sicily, he was hospitalized, but connived a way to get out so that he could take part in the Normandy invasion. "I didn't want to miss the big one," he said.[9]

At the end of the war, the men and women who had served in the armed forces were honored with parades, veterans' benefits, and the G.I. Bill, which gave them educational assistance as well as low-interest business, farm, and home loans. But the members of the United States Merchant Marine received none of that. Instead they were shunned and ridiculed: They were called "draft-dodgers," "slackers," "bums," and a long list of other uncomplimentary names. Many former seamen became derelicts without homes after the war, left to wander the cold streets of America like stray, unwanted animals. Some of them committed suicide.

Even though the U.S. Merchant Marine was on the winning side in World War Two, forming a vital part of the Allied war effort, it was also one of the big losers in the conflict. Inexplicably, the military losers in the war, particularly Germany and Japan, were treated better by the American government than the men of the Merchant Marine were. The vanquished foes received billions of dollars in reconstruction aid; the Merchant Marine got little more than cardboard medals which they had to request by mail.

Following World War Two, no victory parades or WELCOME HOME signs awaited the men who had served so valiantly in the maritime service. They never received the respect and adoration of a grateful nation. Even though they served in war zones and suffered huge casualty rates, merchant seamen received no veterans' benefits whatsoever until 1988—more than forty years after the end of the war—and by that time those benefits were extremely limited, of little use to most of the aged survivors. For the merchant seamen who died between 1945 and 1988, the benefits were completely worthless to them—and to their families, who also had suffered immensely.

What went so terribly wrong? How could this possibly occur in a nation that prides itself on justice? The answer lies in a complicated cesspool of American politics and bitter relationships that remain to this day.

It is one of the great calamities of American history that these valiant seamen, who were so vital to our victory against the Axis forces, have never received the recognition or the benefits they deserve. Surviving Merchant Mariners from World War Two are in their seventies and eighties now; they are dying every day, reducing their number. In the years since the war, more than 125,000 have died.

For those who are still with us, and for the families of those who perished during and after the war, the government of the United States—and the people of this great nation—need to redress a terrible wrong. This book tells the story of the forgotten heroes of the United States Merchant Marine, and also serves as a plea for justice.

—Brian Herbert
Seattle, Washington

THE
FORGOTTEN
HEROES

ONE

DREAMS OF GLORY

In no other trade or calling can you discover such men who have been tempered and formed by their daily environment, the sea.

—DOUGLAS REEMAN[1]

ONE OF THE YOUNGEST OFFICERS TO SERVE IN THE U.S. MERCHANT MARINE DUR-ing World War Two was Dean E. Beaumont—a remarkable man, who inspired this work and contributed many of the stories. In his late seventies today, he can invariably be seen wearing his blue-and-gold Merchant Marine cap. A tireless promoter of the cause of neglected merchant seamen, he will tell you of the sacrifices of his fellows in the war, and how they were abandoned and scorned afterward. He is working to get national legislation passed on their behalf, and is in touch with some of the most important political leaders in our country. But it is a difficult, uphill battle.

Dean has a ready smile and an outgoing, engaging personality that is surprising, considering the political obstacles he has faced, and the personal hardships he went through in World War Two, when he almost lost his life more than once. He will tell you about those perilous times, but the words come with difficulty, filled with emotion and sincerity.

He is also quick to say, "I am not a hero. Others did more than I did, had it worse than I did." That may be true, but his story is one of personal valor and sacrifice—not only for what he did during the war, but for his leadership today on political battlefields, beyond the age when most people retire.

Like Will Rogers, Dean always tries to see the good in people. He is the son of the renowned artist Arthur Beaumont (1890–1978), who is widely considered the unofficial "Artist Laureate" of the United States Navy. I also am the son of a very famous man, Frank Herbert (1920–1986), who wrote the most-admired novel in science-fiction history, *Dune* (1965).* Both Dean and I inherited artistic legacies, and we continue to work hard to promote the works and concepts of our fathers. While I write best-selling *Dune* series novels (with Kevin J. Anderson), Dean promotes his father's works by speaking about him all over the world and by arranging to donate the valuable paintings to worthy individuals and institutions.

Arthur Beaumont's paintings are exhibited at the U.S. Naval Academy, the Pentagon, the White House, and the Smithsonian Institution.[2] They are also on display at the Merchant Marine Academy in Kings Point, New York. His extraordinary paintings have been praised by Prince Charles of England, President Franklin D. Roosevelt, Mrs. Dwight D. Eisenhower, and Her Majesty Queen Fredrika of Greece—to list just a few. Arthur Beaumont was named one of the greatest watercolor artists of all time, and has been listed in *Who's Who in America*.

Born near Norwich, England, in 1890, Arthur Beaumont was the son of a British Army surgeon. Emigrating to Canada in 1909, and to the United States the following year, Arthur, who assumed the nickname "Beau," always retained his strong British accent. He was six foot two and slender, with black hair and brown eyes. He had a

---

*Throughout the writings of Frank Herbert, there is a recurring ocean theme. In *Dune*, it takes the form of vast deserts with dunes like the waves of a great sea, and monsters beneath the sand that are worse than anything Ahab ever faced in *Moby-Dick*. In an early novel, *The Dragon in the Sea* (1955), Frank Herbert even "invented" containerized shipping; thus my family had a connection with the Merchant Marine long before I met Dean Beaumont and undertook the fascinating story of U.S. merchant seamen.

warm, generous personality and a strong moral sense—character traits that were passed on to his son, Dean. Beau studied at the Mark Hopkins School of Art at Berkeley, and at the Los Angeles School of Art and Design. His talents would eventually lead him to advanced studies in London and in Paris, where he became a member of the distinguished Académie Julian.

As a youth Beau worked for the Miller and Lux cattle ranch in central California, one of the largest spreads in the world. In two and a half years of rugged outdoor work, he rose to the position of "assistant superintendent of ranch hands." That career ended when he was shot and left for dead by cattle rustlers, resulting in a long period of hospital recuperation.[3] Before that horrendous event, Arthur Beaumont had painted numerous scenes of cowboys and horses reminiscent of the work of Frederic Remington, and he had been gaining considerable notice as an artist.[4]

During the 1920s, Arthur Beaumont made a modest living doing artwork for magazines and teaching the craft. He and his wife Dorothy had two of their eventual four children in that decade: Phyllis (1922) and Dean (1924). The family rented an old house at 1809 Oak Street in Los Angeles, near Figueroa Street and Washington Boulevard. Dean would remember the address for the rest of his life, because "1809" was the same year Abraham Lincoln was born.

Dean remembers his mother, Dorothy, as a sweet, intelligent woman with blonde hair and blue eyes. On a par intellectually with her erudite husband, Dorothy studied at UCLA during the early years of her marriage and earned a master's degree in education; afterward, she taught English at John Burroughs Junior High School, and then at Los Angeles High School. A devout Christian, Dorothy frequently used biblical stories to counsel her children. Over a career spanning forty years, she never took a day off from work, and eventually became a superintendent for the city school system.

By 1932, Arthur Beaumont was beginning to make a name for himself as a portrait and naval artist. That year, Admiral William D. Leahy of the U.S. Navy granted him a commission as a "reserve lieutenant," a position in which Beau would regularly provide paintings for the naval service. Such an appointment was a new concept, but Leahy was a man of wide-ranging vision, and felt that the pictures would be valuable to historians in the future, after the ships went out of commission, as all of them inevitably did.

In 1933 a very unusual event occurred. While the artist worked at his easel, which he had set up on a dock where he could get a good view of a naval vessel, he was approached by a tall man in baggy clothes. The fellow appeared to be a young derelict, with long hair and an unshaven face. Upon seeing the quality of the painting, the man offered several thousand dollars for it. Beaumont smiled and replied, "Sure. We have a deal." As they shook hands, he expected the man to go away and never come back again. Later in the day, however, just as Beau was putting his supplies away, the man came back and handed over a thick wad of cash for the painting. They shook hands again, and this time the man provided his name: Howard Hughes.

Unfortunately, money management was not one of Arthur Beaumont's strengths. He was, like my own father, Frank Herbert, highly creative, but paid little attention to finances. Dean Beaumont's family was not living in a very good neighborhood at the time and his father didn't want him to go to the public school. But it was all they could afford.

Even with all of his later fame, Arthur Beaumont never would become a wealthy man, though he did learn how to trade his paintings for valuable services. In 1934 he made a deal with the Harvard School, a military academy in Los Angeles. Every year he would paint a picture of the school president, and in exchange was given a year's tuition for Dean to attend the prestigious school. At the age of ten, the boy began to attend the academy. He had to dress up every day in a blue or tan uniform, with a tie and hat.

A short while later, the Beaumonts moved to a larger house, at 816 South St. Andrews Place, near Wilshire Boulevard and Western Avenue. This was a large old house in a much nicer neighborhood, and was closer to Dean's school.

The young man enjoyed hearing the stories his father told about growing up in England and working on a cattle ranch. Dean especially liked to accompany the tall, studious man on weekends, when his father went to the U.S. Navy base at Long Beach, where ships were anchored near the breakwater. There, Arthur Beaumont painted watercolors of naval ships and oil portraits of officers. Frequently they went aboard big battleships, including the USS *Arizona*.

Eventually Dean could identify ships from a distance. Many battleships (such as the USS *West Virginia*, the *Colorado*, and the *Tennessee*) had basket masts. In contrast, the USS *New Mexico* and *Idaho* had been modernized and were completely different. The *Arizona* and its sister ship, the USS *Oklahoma*, had big tripod masts; the *Arizona* had an upper mast above the fire-control station that was painted black, while the *Oklahoma*'s was painted gray instead. Dean soon knew all of the ships' unique features.

The old house on South St. Andrews Place was spacious, with a maids' quarters in the rear—what might be called a "granny flat" today. Normally, the Beaumont family could not afford a housecleaner, and Dean's mother Dorothy did most of the work, in addition to holding down her full-time job as a teacher. On the one occasion when they did use an outside service, the hired woman was cleaning Arthur's art studio and accidentally stuck a broom handle through a 4- by 5-foot oil painting of the Navy cruiser USS *Los Angeles* that was sitting on an easel. The painting—99 percent complete at the time—was needed for the opening of the Los Angeles Maritime Museum, so Beau had to perform quick repairs to finish it in time for the ceremonies.*

Despite his inherent good nature, Dean's father could be grumpy on occasion, when interrupted in his studio. One time,

---

*Years later, the piece would grace the rotunda of Los Angeles City Hall. Somehow it disappeared after two decades there, when a thief cut it neatly out of its frame and spirited it away. While he was heartsick over the incident, Arthur Beaumont still managed to quip, "Well, there aren't that many artists that have a painting stolen from them. It must be a sign that I'm getting famous, if people want to steal my work."

Arthur Beaumont answered the phone and told the caller, "This is the world's greatest artist and you've called at just the wrong moment."[5]

As a child Dean developed asthma, which he blamed on a couple of factors: At the age of two, he'd had a large white cat that he loved. He used to hold the animal and rub his face in its fur. In addition, the family moved a number of times, invariably into large, dusty houses.

During his formative years, the boy's medical condition worsened until it bothered him severely two or three days a week. Dean lost sleep, and, when the attacks got really bad, he missed school, sometimes one day a week. This chronic debility would adversely affect him when the Second World War began, making him ineligible to join the armed forces and leaving him with only one option to serve his country—as a civilian volunteer in the United States Merchant Marine.

ALL THE SHIPS
AT SEA

You can't win the war without us.

—MERCHANT MARINE SAYING

IN 1935, ARTHUR BEAUMONT MADE ONE OF HIS TRADEMARK BARTERING AR-rangements, this time with the Pacific Coast Club in Long Beach, which was associated with a big hotel chain. In exchange for one painting a year, the organization provided him with a nice two-level penthouse at the top of the club building, where Beau established a neat, well-organized studio. He lived and worked there most of the time, going back to the family home in Los Angeles a couple of times a week.

The club penthouse had a large bedroom downstairs, along with two bedrooms upstairs, and provided Beau with easier access to the big warships he needed to paint, since so many of them were at the Navy base in Long Beach. Dean went to stay with his dad a couple of times a month. When they weren't visiting ships together, they liked to walk on the nearby beaches.

One day Dean's father took him to meet Admiral William D. Leahy.* Arthur Beaumont was painting the famed naval officer's

---

*In 1937, Admiral Leahy would become Chief of U.S. Naval Operations. During World War Two he also served as ambassador to Vichy, France, and as President Roosevelt's Chief of Staff.[1]

portrait. As a lieutenant in the naval reserve, Arthur Beaumont wore his own Navy livery on such occasions, while little Dean would be nattily attired in his military academy uniform. They had lunch in San Diego with Leahy and a couple of captains on the admiral's flagship, the destroyer tender USS *Dobbin*.

During the meal, Arthur Beaumont told the admiral about an idea he had for an "acoustic torpedo," which would use an electronic unit in its nose to home in on the propeller noise of an enemy ship. In order to protect American vessels, they needed adjustments in order to make sounds that were different, to keep from attracting the acoustic sensors themselves. The admiral said the idea sounded very interesting, and he asked Beau to draw up some plans, to the extent that he could.

Beaumont set to work and drew his idea up for submission to a U.S. Navy experimental department. Unfortunately, the Navy decided not to investigate the idea any further, and it was shelved.* One evening, however, Dean's father put on a party in the penthouse, where important military and political people were present, including British, German, and French consuls. That night, the plans disappeared out of a desk drawer.

Subsequently, the German Navy came up with what they called a "T-5 Zaunkönig acoustic homing torpedo," and it matched Arthur Beaumont's concept. In late September 1943, the Germans sank a disturbingly high number of destroyers and merchant ships (including the refrigerated ship SS *Oregon Express*).† But the Allies countered quickly with what they called "foxers": hollow-tube noisemakers that were much louder than a ship's propellers. The devices (which had little holes in them and resonated with pitch-pipe–type noises)

---

*In the early 1940s, the actress Hedy Lamarr—who was quite brilliant and was once married to a German munitions dealer—developed an idea for a radio-controlled torpedo. Under her married name of Hedy K. Markey, she patented it with George Antheil (patent number 2,292,387, filed June 10, 1941). They called it a "Secret Communication System," and presented the idea to the U.S. Navy. Unfortunately, the idea, like that of Arthur Beaumont, for his own torpedo, was rejected by officers who did not think that good ideas could come from sources outside the Navy.[2]

†On an earlier voyage, the crew of the SS *Oregon Express* rescued ninety-six crew and passengers from the sunken British ship *Waiwera*, and took them to safety in New York City.[3]

were towed behind the ships, and drew the torpedoes to them, to be destroyed in harmless detonations. Ironically, the Allies later came up with their own acoustic torpedo called "the Cutie," which was copied from the "German" designs![4]

As a young student Dean did not pay much attention to the news of labor unrest in the merchant maritime industry, and hardly noticed when the Merchant Marine Act was passed in 1936. This congressional act, signed by President Roosevelt, inaugurated a new shipbuilding program under the direction of the newly formed U.S. Maritime Commission, to make up for the decline of merchant shipping since the end of World War One. The act set an ambitious goal of producing five hundred new ships over the next decade, and established labor standards for merchant seamen.[5]

Early in 1941, Arthur Beaumont painted a picture of two fishing boats at Pearl Harbor and showed them to a U.S. Navy admiral. The artist said to the admiral, "Those are not fishing poles on top. That's a spy ship with aerials." (Beau's commission was in the intelligence service of the U.S. Navy—a formality in order to get him in—but he took his position seriously.)[6] The admiral said he would look into the matter.

Dean Beaumont delayed starting college after high school, since he wanted to join the Navy instead but he wasn't old enough yet. In December 1941, at the age of seventeen, Dean was with his father in Washington, D.C., where Arthur Beaumont was producing paintings of tanks, guns, and airplanes for the U.S. Army. The two of them were living outside of the city at the Chevy Chase Country Club, along with military officers, including a number of Navy admirals.

When news of the Pearl Harbor attack came in on December 7, Dean was walking by the White House on Pennsylvania Avenue, and saw the commotion of security personnel and the fear and shock on the faces of people on the street. At the country club, officers had been wearing civilian clothing before the sneak attack, but that changed immediately. The boy was struck by how many of them wore uniforms afterward.

His father was out of town on that fateful day, and returned the following morning. Like Dean, he was enraged at the actions of the Japanese empire, and deeply saddened, for the two of them had been on many of the ships that were damaged or destroyed, including the most famous of all, the USS *Arizona*. "Our lives will never be the same again," Arthur Beaumont told his son.

For the rest of his life, Beau was upset that the U.S. Navy had not taken prompt action concerning the apparent evidence of spying that the artist had uncovered in Hawaii. (Neither this bit of advice nor his "acoustic torpedo" idea was acted upon in time to prevent the harm done.)

Now Dean wanted to join the Navy more than ever. He would be eighteen in a few months, but there were doubts about his medical eligibility, since his asthma was worsening.

Young Dean Beaumont had heard about the United States Merchant Marine, but only peripherally. He knew about the massive shipbuilding program that been under way since 1936, and that many privately owned merchant vessels were being declared "naval auxiliary craft," to aid in the war effort. Dean also heard about unarmed or lightly armed commercial ships on the high seas, torpedoed and sunk by German U-boats.

Unbeknownst to young Beaumont, the brave, enterprising crews of some merchant vessels had rigged up telephone poles to look like guns. The MS *Cape Henry*, a brand new C-1–class cargo ship, sailed into the Gulf of Mexico with its cargo holds full of ammunition—and fake guns fore and aft. Second Mate Alan H. Knox told me years later that they used 8- by 8-inch timbers with covers over them.

Dean had seen the merchant service blasted in the press, particularly by Hearst newspaper columnists Walter Winchell and Westbrook Pegler. Winchell's attacks also reached fifty million Americans in his radio broadcasts to "Mr. and Mrs. America and all the ships at sea." In a June 1940 program, Winchell accused the

National Maritime Union (representing merchant seamen on the East Coast) of sabotaging American ships, asserting that seamen in the union were communist sympathizers who were putting mercury and emery dust into the engines.

In response, the union filed a million-dollar lawsuit against the fiery columnist—and received money for damages, albeit only a few thousand dollars. Undeterred, Winchell asserted that merchant seamen were overpaid.[7] His claims, while totally unfounded, were in the tradition of the "yellow journalism" and "Hearsteria" of the Hearst press machine, and inflamed the minds of American citizens and their military and political leaders. This would prove damaging to American merchant seamen during the war, and for more than fifty years afterward.

It was one of many nails in the coffin of the U.S. Merchant Marine.

THREE

STORMY WATERS

Politics are almost as exciting as war, and quite as
dangerous. In war you can only be killed once, but
in politics many times.

—SIR WINSTON CHURCHILL[1]

THE UNITED STATES MERCHANT MARINE, WHILE NOT A MILITARY SERVICE, FOUGHT
a war on many fronts. The private companies that owned and operated merchant ships (as auxiliary naval vessels under wartime law)
not only had enemies in every ocean . . . they had enemies at home.
The companies were strong enough to fight for their rights, but the
merchant seamen were left to the protection of their unions, and—
despite some short-term legal and contractual successes—history
showed that the unions did not have the political power necessary
to adequately advance the interests of their membership.

In the spring of 1942, the U.S. Navy attempted to take control
of the Merchant Marine. To justify this move, they charged that
"there has been a failure by cargo-vessel crews and officers to obey
Navy orders and . . . the discipline of the crews, afloat and ashore, is
inadequate."[2]

With the assistance of the seamen's unions, the merchant shipping companies thwarted this attempt, thus protecting their lucra-

tive government contracts. The unions, representing seamen who wanted to keep the union contracts they had struggled so hard to obtain, thought their interests and those of the companies were parallel.[3] But the unions were shortsighted, accepting increased wages for membership and gaining only a short-term advantage; this bargain would eventually exact a price higher than anyone ever imagined. It would cost American seamen dearly in terms of benefits, for they would not qualify for the educational or home loan benefits of the G.I. Bill after the war, and would not receive the medical coverage they so desperately needed. Even worse, the increased wages they thought they were receiving were not really higher at all, as I will show in chapter 19, "They Earned Our Respect," page 180.

It was also a critical strategic mistake for the unions to draw the ire and political fire of armed-forces leaders. This blunder would come back to haunt union membership after the war, when military people would belittle the contributions of merchant seamen during the war and actively lobby against benefits for them.

Even after failing to incorporate the Merchant Marine into their ranks, the United States Navy, skilled at maneuvering through political waters, still managed to exert de facto authority over the merchant service during the war. The Navy also gained control of the U.S. Coast Guard, and the USCG became responsible for the inspection of merchant ships' seaworthiness, and for the examination, licensing, and certification of Merchant Marine personnel.[4]

Through destroyers and other escort ships, the Navy also controlled merchant-ship convoys, and directed the placement of merchant ships in invasion forces and other dangerous operations. In addition, the administrator of the War Shipping Administration (and of the U.S. Maritime Commission) was Emory S. Land, a retired U.S. Navy rear admiral. All evidence shows, however, that Mr. Land ran the WSA effectively, and that he and his management staff defended merchant seamen against unfair political attacks.

Stormy political waters swirled around the Merchant Marine before, during, and after World War Two. At Midway, in 1942, there was a report that each member of the crew of the SS *Nira Lucken-bach* had received a $1,000 bonus and had refused to unload war materials from a ship on a Sunday unless they were paid overtime wages. The truth was that the facilities and manpower necessary for unloading hazardous cargo—in this case, bombs and barrels of gasoline—were not available at Midway Island. Nonetheless, with only his small crew, the captain proceeded to unload anyway, doing the best he could. The charges were proven false. In reality, the merchant crew had not refused to unload, and had not received a bonus.[5]

Yet another tall tale originated from Kuluk Harbor, Alaska, and involved the SS *Thomas Jefferson*, a Liberty ship. Reportedly, a U.S. Navy destroyer had approached a docked merchant ship and asked for a line to be thrown to them. Allegedly, no one responded on the merchant ship, since they had already done their eight hours of work and had gone ashore. This story proved to be false as well. The trouble stemmed from animosity between the master of the merchant ship and an officer on the Navy destroyer, after the master demanded a receipt for fuel oil the destroyer had received.[6]

Such stories began as rumors, were further distorted along the way, and eventually found their way into the press, causing the public to think of them as facts, when they were not. Newspaper articles, with banner headlines critical of the Merchant Marine, ran all over the United States. Some accounts, like the "Midway" story cited above, referred to "bonuses" that merchant seamen received in war zones, an unfortunate choice of words. Members of the armed forces, such as the U.S. Navy, also received additional payments for hazardous duty.[7]

The public, always emotional during wartime, and highly susceptible to the power of suggestion, also began to perceive merchant seamen as "hiding" in the safety of their ships, while members of the armed forces were putting their bodies on the line. Civilian seamen were unfairly called "draft-dodgers" even though they were often in more physical danger than most military servicemen, as proven by the casualty statistics.

The roots of some of these problems went back to the labor unrest of the 1930s, when merchant seamen won better wages and working conditions through the efforts of their unions. Prior to that, conditions aboard many ships had been deplorable, with underpaid men crowded into tight, filthy quarters where diseases spread quickly. After struggling so hard to obtain improvements, these men wanted to hold on to their gains. But world events would put them on a collision course with powerful forces, at home and abroad.

Neutrality acts passed by the U.S. Congress between 1935 and 1937 banned trading with belligerent nations or giving loans to them, and required that any military items sold to other countries had to be paid for before they could be taken out of the United States. In 1939 the laws were changed to permit belligerents such as Great Britain and France to obtain military supplies if they first paid for them in full.[8]

On December 29, 1940, President Franklin Delano Roosevelt delivered one of his most famous speeches, in which he said that the United States "must be the great arsenal of democracy." Under that doctrine, he vowed to provide Great Britain with armaments and food supplies, so they could not be isolated and starved into submission by the Germans, which had almost occurred two decades earlier, during World War One. To accomplish this ambitious goal, it was necessary to dispatch a steady stream of merchant-ship convoys across the Atlantic Ocean. This would put the sailors of the U.S. Merchant Marine in harm's way.

Convoys, while providing additional security for merchant ships, were still dangerous. Ships at the four corners of the formation, the "coffin corners," could be picked off most easily by German U-boats. Another favored German tactic involved "wolf packs" of several U-boats, which would surface in the middle of a convoy and pick off merchant ships like ducks in a shooting gallery, before the military escort ships could intervene. Yet an additional danger involved the close proximity of ships transporting hazardous war cargoes. A collision between two merchant vessels in one North Atlantic convoy resulted in an explosion and fire that killed most of

the men in both crews. Their ships had been carrying aviation gasoline, cotton, oil, and other highly flammable materials.[9]

Another story remains shrouded in mystery. Reportedly, an
American merchant ship was running without lights in a North
Atlantic convoy. The crew suddenly heard a horrendous grinding
noise, and the ship shuddered to a stop. The crew found wreckage
and bodies floating in the water. It turned out they had struck a
French submarine—evidently operated by "the Free French"—and
that all hands were lost. The crew of the merchant ship was sworn
to secrecy, but word of the collision leaked out after the war. It was
reported to be one of the biggest submarines in the world, perhaps
the largest.

John George Urstadt IV, an apprentice seaman in 1944, later
described to his family what it was like on convoy duty. His son Jack
wrote to me:

> Their convoys were extremely large, sometimes over
> 200 ships, but were spaced out so that enemy subs
> could not sink too many. He said that in daylight you
> could not even see other ships because of the curve of
> the earth, but at night he . . . witnessed explosions and
> ships ablaze on the horizon . . . Their only real deterrent
> was a "can" or a depth charge type mine that was
> launched off the stern and floated at a certain depth
> until hopefully a U-boat stalking them struck it. . . . My
> Dad . . . heard the concussion of those explosions often.

The American shipbuilding program, begun with the establish-
ment of the U.S. Maritime Commission in 1936, went ahead full-
bore after the outbreak of hostilities in Europe. Around the time of
Roosevelt's "Arsenal of Democracy" speech, the commission granted
contracts to the West Coast industrialist Henry J. Kaiser and his
partner, Todd Shipyards, to build Liberty ships. A short while afterward the program was stepped up, with additional contracts
awarded to Bethlehem Shipbuilders and Newport News.[10]

The flamboyant, independent Henry Kaiser (who had helped build Hoover Dam) soon severed his partnership with Todd and went on to become the most famous builder of Liberty ships even though he had never built a ship before. Nicknamed "Hurry-Up Henry," he used mass-production methods to construct 442-foot vessels at a pace never seen or imagined before.[11] One of his Liberty ships, the SS *Robert E. Peary*, was built in four days, fifteen hours, and twenty-nine minutes.[12]

Of great concern to a number of quality-control experts, Kaiser decided not to build the hulls of his ships with rivets. He welded them instead, which was much faster but did not allow the hulls to flex in heavy weather. There were instances of welded ships (in a variety of designs, not just Liberty ships) breaking in half at sea and making "a deafening noise like a gunshot" as they did so. One Liberty ship split in half during a rough North Atlantic storm, but the stern section kept floating; the entire crew huddled in there for more than thirty-six hours before a corvette rescued them.

A naval board of inquiry determined that welding these ships was in fact satisfactory, because of the number of cargo ships needed by the Allies. The board pointed out as well that most instances of broken hulls were due to poor welding practices and hulls that were too rigid. To rectify these problems, the naval board initiated a procedure of reinforcing the welds on all existing and future ships, and of providing straps for some of the key structural points where the hulls needed to flex when at sea.[13]

One of the merchant seamen I interviewed for this book, Jack Faulkner, boarded a brand-new Liberty ship in Portland, Oregon, where it had been built in the Kaiser Shipyard. It was late 1942 or early 1943, and Faulkner was on board for several days while the vessel was loaded with military cargo. Just before it went to sea, however, the order came in to reinforce the welds on the ship. Everything had to be unloaded, and the crew was transferred to other vessels.

Despite the improvements in welding practices, Henry Kaiser received the brunt of any bad publicity that arose from the quality-control issue, some of it coming from shipbuilding competitors who were envious of his success. His Liberty ships were derisively referred to as "Kaiser coffins."

To a degree, this had to do with Kaiser's lack of ship-manufacturing experience and his methods, but unsubstantiated stories also were circulated about him. Alluding to a lack of shipbuilding experience—not only his own, but also his workers'—he was rumored to have placed one advertisement offering to hire twenty thousand additional shipyard workers. Another tale said that he referred to "the front" and "the back" of ships under construction, instead of "fore" and "aft." Such accounts may have been apocryphal, but it was known that he hired thousands of inexperienced shipbuilders and trained them.[14]

It must be realized, too, that Kaiser was working with plans provided to him by the U.S. Maritime Commission. Based upon a British design for a cargo ship with reciprocating steam engines, it was modified by the Americans. President Roosevelt approved the design, but only for its functionality. He referred to Liberty ships as "dreadful-looking objects" and "ugly ducklings." The vessel would have a top speed of only 10 to 11 knots, which made it an easy target for the faster German U-boats. "Ugly duckling" or "sitting duck," the Liberty ship was a dangerous craft traveling through dangerous waters, but this cannot be blamed on Henry J. Kaiser alone. It was designed to be expendable: Each ship was considered a success by the U.S. Maritime Commission if it delivered a full load of war matériel and then was sunk afterward.[15]

Administrator Emory S. Land of the War Shipping Administration initially wanted to build faster C-type cargo ships instead of Liberties. After investigating the matter in detail however, he determined that the manufacturing facilities for the more sophisticated diesel-powered vessels were not available.

Liberty ships were named for the famous American speech in which Patrick Henry proclaimed, "Give me liberty or give me death!" Fittingly, the first vessel to be launched was the SS *Patrick Henry*. By September 27, 1941, declared "Liberty Day" by President

Roosevelt, fourteen new Liberties were launched from shipyards around the country.[16]

Ships were being built so rapidly, in fact, that there were not enough crew members to man them. Through posters and other forms of advertisement, the U.S. Maritime Commission called for civilian volunteers, and men answered the call by the tens of thousands. In 1941 the federal government established the Merchant Marine Academy at Kings Point, New York, and a number of state-operated schools and boot camps were opened as well. Men were allowed to serve in the Merchant Marine in lieu of military duty. Under the law, volunteers had to ship out again within thirty days of the completion of their most recent voyage. They were also permitted to turn down assignments on two ships, but had to take the third.

Because of the need for manpower, the standards of recruitment into the Merchant Marine were not as stringent as those of the armed forces. People with moderate medical conditions were permitted to join, along with independent sorts who did not want to wear uniforms or salute officers. Virtually all applicants were welcomed into the merchant service, along with a number who had drinking problems—a situation that caused even more criticism of merchant seamen by outsiders, who referred to them as "drunks." In all fairness to the Merchant Marine, it should be pointed out that drinking was not permitted aboard most ships.* The seagoing vessels—their interiors, at least!—were essentially dry. In this strict environment, many alcoholics sobered up after a couple of weeks at sea.

In September 1942, Dean Beaumont enrolled as a freshman at Occidental College in Los Angeles. At eighteen he was of draft age, but

---

*The masters of some ships did allow beer on board. Merchant seaman John C. Burley reported to me that half of a cargo hold on one Liberty ship was filled with beer, and each man was allotted three bottles a day.

his family convinced him to wait awhile before attempting to join the Navy. Overall, his asthma seemed to be improving, perhaps from living away from the dusty old house on South St. Andrews Place. Sometimes, however, he still experienced unexpected attacks.

Dean had earned his Eagle Scout merit badge several years earlier, and had continued his involvement with the scouts afterward. In the early months of the war, he also joined the California State Naval Guard and dressed in khakis, a tie, and an armband while performing wartime patrols and first-aid duties. Additionally, he performed volunteer work for the Navy League, with his father. All the while, Dean's friends were being drafted, and he never stopped wanting to join the fight himself. Until that day came, he would do what he could.

Needing to earn money for his studies, Dean and a couple of his Phi Gamma Delta fraternity brothers went to the central-casting office in Hollywood, and asked if they needed any young people in motion pictures. A man in the office gave them a business card and told them to telephone every afternoon at three o'clock, and he would announce how many extras were needed the next day. Quite often the casting office needed ten, eighteen, or twenty people.

One day they needed five hundred extras for two weeks, for the movie *Five Graves to Cairo*, starring Erich von Stroheim. Dean earned a commission for finding extras for that film, but couldn't go to the movie set himself, since he had to stay in college and finish a term paper. The extras were supposed to go to the Salton Sea lake in California and wear the uniforms of German soldiers. College students were able to earn good money doing this. If an extra played a dying British soldier and let a tank run over him, for example, he earned a $100 bonus; to accomplish this, the extra was "shot" and would fall into a hole, which a tank then drove over. A number of Dean's fraternity brothers earned enough money to buy cars doing this.

Dean himself worked as an extra on forty movies, including *Reveille With Beverly* (starring Ann Miller) and *Stage Door Canteen* (with a cameo by Edgar Bergen). Both were popular patriotic films, released during the war. In the latter movie, Dean was featured in the opening scene, shortly after the credits. He was one of two soldiers walking down a stairway into the "Stage Door Canteen," where the movie's USO-style entertainment was staged for servicemen.

In February 1941, German admirals recognized the threat presented by the Allied convoys of merchant ships that were crossing the Atlantic Ocean to England. To counter this, the German admirals convinced Adolf Hitler to direct all available air and sea power against the convoys, which he said was essential if the Axis ever hoped to defeat the British.[17]

The Germans assigned surface warships to the Atlantic sea-lanes, along with air support, to the extent possible. They even built disguised raider ships that looked like innocent merchant vessels flying neutral flags, but were in reality armed predators. Some of the most notorious Nazi raiders during the war were the *Atlantis*, the *Thor*, the *Michel*, the *Pinquin*, and the *Stier*. Known as "ghost ships," because they slipped easily past British cordons into the Atlantic Ocean and back to port again, these German ships sank hundreds of thousands of tons of Allied shipping. The Axis raiders had telescoping smokestacks and masts, false deckhouses, and a variety of national flags. Like pirate ships of yore, they had side ports that slid open to expose guns. Some of them had torpedo boats, and even scout planes, cleverly concealed inside hatches.[18]

But the brunt of the German strategy in the Atlantic would fall upon U-boats, initially operating alone and later in the "wolf packs." During the early months of the war, in a period U-boat captains called "the Happy Time," their submarines experienced great success against Allied cargo ships. In part, this had to do with the fact that some of the German submarines were commanded by men who had been merchant tanker captains in this area before the war, so they knew these waters very well. U-boats attacked Merchant

Marine convoys crossing the ocean, and also found prime hunting grounds in the Atlantic coastal waters of the United States, from Maine to Florida—where American merchant ships operated without the protection of convoys, or any other form of military escort.[19] In order to intensify the pressure on the shipping industry, the Germans substantially increased the production of U-boats: an effort to defeat the Allied strategy of building more cargo ships than the Germans could sink.

In early 1942, more than a thousand merchant seamen died in American coastal waters, within sight of land on the East Coast. In some cases, sunbathers on the beaches saw explosions and fires offshore. The men on those ships were civilian volunteers, but they suffered casualty rates much higher than those of the United States armed forces. So many Allied ships went down, that the Nazi submarine crews were hailed as heroes in Germany when they returned to port.[20]

The American government managed to keep a lid on publicity about these terrible losses. The maritime historian Ian A. Millar wrote:

> It would not do to reveal that our own country through interservice discord and political ignorance had set up our ships and merchant seamen as sitting ducks for the German Kreigsmarine's torpedoes and deck guns. Speak with the seamen who survived and the people who lived on the Outer Banks of North Carolina. They will tell you this holocaust was a tragic reality. They saw the ships hit, saw the men who choked and retched from swallowing oil. They saw the bodies of dead merchant seamen washed up in the tangle of cargo on the beaches.[21]

On the night of March 13, 1942, the tanker SS *John D. Gill* was torpedoed off Cape Fear, North Carolina, en route to an oil refinery in Pennsylvania. Within minutes the ruptured ship was surrounded by a sea of burning oil. Herbert Gardner, a twenty-two-year-old wiper, dove in and swam under the oil. He came up several times in the midst of flames, burning his arms and head. Finally, having suffered severe burns, Gardner crawled aboard a life raft with other survivors. For two hours afterward, he vomited from all of the oil and the salt water he had swallowed.

Edwin F. Cheney Jr., a young seaman on the *Gill*, took heroic actions throughout the emergency, which resulted in his receiving one of the few Merchant Marine Distinguished Service medals during the war. He was the first to swim under the burning oil to the life raft, and then saved at least six of his crewmates by diving back into the water and guiding them to the raft, even though he himself had badly burned his hands, and his body had been seared.

That night, the men on the raft used oars to propel the raft. Since there were no oarlocks, however, some of the men had to bend over and grip the bottom of the raft, so that their cupped, badly burned hands could form makeshift oarlocks. One man, Gary Potts, sustained internal injuries in this manner. A Coast Guard cutter finally rescued them, but many of the men were very seriously injured. One of the medical workers who aided them said, "They were burned so badly their flesh would come off in your hands."[22]

After the Texaco tanker the SS *Connecticut* was torpedoed in early 1942, Chief Officer Bill Carroll made it to a lifeboat, and ended up at the tiller. The boat was clear of the tanker—almost a thousand feet away—when another torpedo struck. Carroll looked back at flames shooting high into the air. The distance was not enough. Carroll lost all of his hair and his eyebrows, and suffered blistering on his entire face.[23] Had he been any closer, perhaps on the tanker itself, it would have been far worse. The heat generated in petroleum fires, with so much flammable, explosive fuel, is astronomical.

Even small merchant ships did not escape the attention of the German U-boats. When the little tanker MT *William C. McTarnahan* was torpedoed by *U-506*, Bosun Thomas W. Murray suffered severe burns on his arms and hands, to the extent that the skin "peeled off like a long pair of gloves and was hanging from his fingertips." While Murray did make it to shore, he died anyway from his grievous wounds.[24]

Some of the greatest successes won by the U-boats were in the Caribbean Sea and in the Gulf of Mexico, where the Germans sought to cut off supplies of petroleum products. The men who served on Allied tankers in those waters had extremely dangerous jobs. On July 9, 1942, the SS *Benjamin Brewster*, with a cargo of aviation gas and petroleum, was torpedoed and erupted in flames, causing oil to burn all around the vessel on the surface of the water. It happened so quickly that the crew did not have time to launch lifeboats, and many of them died horribly, or were maimed. Of the crew of thirty-five merchant seamen and five Navy Armed Guardsmen, twenty-four civilian seamen and one bluejacket were lost.[25] A survivor described the "screams of the dying, some being boiled alive, others fried on the steel decks. . . ." One of the surviving engineers was "a charred and misshapen figure" laid out on a stretcher. Another lost his right hand, from the terrible burns.[26]

FOUR

REPORTING
FOR DUTY

*More facts come up every day about how the
Merchant Marine was jumped on by our own
armed forces and political leaders.*

—LIEUTENANT DEAN BEAUMONT,

UNITED STATES MERCHANT MARINE

PRIOR TO WORLD WAR TWO, THERE WERE ONLY 55,000 SEAMEN IN THE AMERI-
can Merchant Marine, a figure that would nearly quadruple at the
height of the war.[1] United States industry—the "sleeping giant" that
had been awakened by the sneak attack on Pearl Harbor, on December 7, 1941—built the largest fleet of merchant ships in history
between 1941 and 1945. This generated a need for crews, and the
War Shipping Administration was constantly looking for recruits.
The men who joined the Merchant Marine came from all parts of the
country, from all walks of life, with varying levels of education.
Some didn't want to go into military service, while others could not
pass military physical examinations.

Many of these men fit into another category: they loved the
romance of the sea. Jack Faulkner was only seventeen years old
when he started sailing on merchant oil tankers, working in engine
rooms during his summer breaks from school. He studied in

machine shop, and in 1942 went to work as a machinist for the Boeing Company in Seattle. He soon grew tired of "filing metal burrs on a bench," and thought of shipping out again. From his rooming house on a hill he saw merchant ships coming and going in Elliott Bay. At the first opportunity he signed on to a freighter bound for Alaska, carrying military cargoes and troops. Later Faulkner would get involved in the invasion of Sicily, and would transport bombs to an American air base in the Pacific. Starting out as a wiper, he rose to the rank of lieutenant.

Another man with a romantic view of the sea was Frank Medeiros, who eventually became a captain in the Merchant Marine. At the tail end of the Depression, Medeiros was a teenager experiencing a tough time making ends meet. For a while he worked for the 1939 World's Fair in San Francisco, but that was no career. He thought about going into merchant shipping instead, where he had heard that he could make a good living. But seamen's papers were hard to come by in those days, because of labor disputes in the larger port cities. To get around this obstacle, a Merchant Marine officer suggested that Medeiros go to one of the smaller ports, where he could obtain papers easily and find a ship that would hire him. But the fellow recommended the port of Albany, New York, more than three thousand miles away.

Undeterred, young Medeiros hitched rides on trains for the whole trip, standing or sitting in dangerous places on the framework beneath railcars, a practice known as "riding the blinds." It was a risky way to travel; he had to constantly worry about falling asleep and tumbling beneath the train. Sometimes Medeiros rode on top of the water tender, which was coal-fired. All by himself, he made it to Albany in five days, and shipped out on a vessel which would later be damaged by a delayed-action bomb at Port Said, Egypt. Fortunately he escaped injury in that event, but in 1942 he would sail another ship on the Murmansk Run, the most dangerous waters in the world (see chapter 9, "The Russian Gauntlet," page 92).

Another veteran merchant seaman, eighty-year-old Peter Chelemedos, rode freight trains around the United States during the Great Depression. Hoboes taught him how to ride inside unre-frigerated reefer-cars with dry groceries or potatoes, or in boxcars, or on the locomotive tender, sheltered from the wind behind the coal chute. Sometimes he even rode on top of coal piles. Chelemedos also described "riding the blinds" to me, and said he was unable to fall asleep there, out of fear that he would fall to his death beneath the wheels of the train. "I hung on for dear life," he recalled.

One time, while riding the blinds in Calfornia, Chelemedos got off early, in San Luis Obispo, because he was freezing. Also, he didn't want to get smothered from the train's thick black smoke in the tunnels that were just ahead, to the south. As he stepped off the train, however, he could hardly walk on his frozen feet, and ended up in a public hospital for a month.

At the age of seventeen, he signed on to work the banana boat *Southern Lady* for two bits a month—just 25 cents—plus meals. After riding trains, Chelemedos told me with a chuckle, that sounded pretty good to him. But a short while later, when the war started, the young adventurer would have two ships shot out from under him.[2]

Young Dean Beaumont found his way onto a merchant ship by a different route.

Shortly after the D-Day invasion of June 6, 1944, news reports described the intense fighting on the beaches of Normandy, and the thousands of American soldiers who were dying as Allied forces continued to attack the Germans. In a patriotic fervor, enlistments for all of the armed forces increased across the United States.

Occidental College in Los Angeles was no exception. Dean Beaumont and his fraternity brothers, with their semester coming to an end, went to the Army and Navy recruiting offices and signed up. Everyone was accepted for military duty, excluding Dean. His asthma, perhaps worsened by stress, was particularly bad the day of the medical examination, and he failed it.

That summer, Dean was home with his parents. A friend of his dad's, Larry Kent, happened to stop by the house. Kent, whose father-in-law had founded the American Mail Lines Steamship Company, was now the personnel manager. They had forty-two merchant ships at the time.*

At dinner, Kent asked Dean, "How would you like to join the Merchant Marine?"

"Naw, I don't think so. I tried to join the Navy, and they rejected me."

"Your father told me. But with the Merchant Marine, your asthma doesn't matter, and you could serve your country *now*, instead of waiting. We need men for new Liberty ships that are being built."

Dean asked several questions about the service, but didn't commit himself. He picked at his food. The young man knew almost all of the capital ships in the U.S. Navy; he used to go on those with his father. Some of them, such as the USS *Arizona* and USS *Oklahoma*, had been sunk in the devastating attack on Pearl Harbor. Dean had always wanted to join the Navy, but had never even considered the Merchant Marine.

"It might not be a bad idea," his father said reassuringly. Dean had always been close to his dad and, after failing the physical, had worried about letting him down.

"Do you know how to type?" Kent asked.

"Yep."

"Do you know how to run an adding machine?"

"Yep."

"Do you know anything about first aid?"

---

*American Mail Lines (AML) also owned one of the most famous Liberty ships in the war, the SS *Samuel Parker*. It was one of the few merchant ships to be given the Gallant Ship Award by the War Shipping Administration.

"Sure, I was in the Boy Scouts, and I worked as a volunteer with the California State Naval Guard."

"Well, we need a purser on a ship that's leaving soon. I think we can get you on as an officer. You would do typing for the captain, check passports, and light medical stuff."

"An *officer*?" Dean's eyes lit up.

"Well, an ensign. That's the lowest officer. But after a few months at sea you can take a test and make lieutenant JG, and you can keep getting regular promotions. The pay is good, too."

They reached an agreement, and shook hands across the table.

A short while later, Kent took Dean, by train, to the U.S. Coast Guard office in San Francisco for testing. Dean passed, and said he received his commission as a Merchant Marine officer "faster than anyone in the history of the service"—bypassing the normal training program. He received a certification card, a uniform, and a hat, and was on a train back to Los Angeles to catch his ship, the SS *Brander Matthews*. The whole process took only four days.

He reported to the ship the next day in San Pedro, and within hours he was under way on an ugly gray ship, heading out the channel into the Pacific Ocean, bound for the island of Saipan in the Marianas. It was a pleasant, blue sky day in the early fall of 1944. The Japanese-controlled island had been invaded and conquered by two U.S. Marine divisions and one U.S. Army division a few months earlier, and the Japanese had been making retaliatory air attacks ever since.[3]

The five large cargo holds of the brand-new Liberty ship were filled with thousands of 8- by 8-foot steel boxes with brackets on all corners. These were sturdy dock-pieces, since the Saipan port had been destroyed by bombing attacks. As the vessel crossed the sea, Dean felt thrilled that he was finally able to contribute to the war effort, and was proud to be an officer. He didn't feel that the position had been handed to him at all. He was qualified for it, having spent five years in a military academy as well as time he'd spent in the Boy Scouts and in the state naval guard. He had been an honor student and had earned awards for his work. In addition, he'd had all those experiences with his father on U.S. Navy ships, so he knew signaling and other skills that many of his young shipmates did not.

The casual air on the SS *Brander Matthews* seemed odd to him, however. When men walked up the gangway to board the ship, they did not ask, in the Navy fashion, "Permission to come aboard, sir?" Instead, they merely said, "Hi, how are you?" Ordinary seamen didn't have to salute officers or wear uniforms. They just waved instead of saluting, or didn't acknowledge the officer at all.

Even Merchant Marine officers didn't wear their uniforms very often. On warm days the entire ship's company was attired in grubby old T-shirts, shorts, or swimming trunks, and dirty tennis shoes or boots as they performed their duties. Gradually, so that he would not be ridiculed, Dean began to dress like that himself. In the next port he would purchase a pair of casual shoes, the "loafer" kind that you could slip your feet into. It was all quite a contrast with the spit-and-polish U.S. Navy, where the crew had to line up on deck for inspection in sparkling uniforms, wearing ribbons.

Independent by nature, merchant seamen didn't care about formalities or decorations. As the young purser soon learned, however, this did not mean they didn't perform their work. On the contrary, the ship was well kept up, in a clean, operating condition. It was a priority for the men to do this. It was not only a matter of pride to keep a vessel shipshape; it was a necessity at sea. A few experienced men on the ship taught the young recruits how to do things properly, and the job got done; it was this way throughout the entire U.S. Merchant Marine.

Some of the civilians who volunteered to serve in the Merchant Marine were physically handicapped, since this service accepted them, while the armed forces did not. One radio officer had a deformed torso from a birth defect; a chief pumpman had a wooden leg; and a Chief Mate only had one arm.[4]

Dean Beaumont learned that merchant seamen such as himself were called "Z-men" because of the "Z-books" they carried around with them, containing their identification papers. He grew close to other officers on the Liberty ship, too, especially to the elderly Captain Vincent F. Nielsen, who had been a port captain and a pilot in New York Harbor until being called to duty. Twice a week they played cards in the officers' lounge with the chief engineer and the Chief Mate, both in their mid-forties. Usually it was a game of bridge, and as they played, the older men often told stories of their adventures at sea, or tales they had heard from other sailors.

Lacing their language with colorful terms and profanity, the officers may have described boozing seamen and dogs that drank beer with them . . . or women that were sneaked on board . . . or prankish cooks who baked soap into pies.[5] Dean might have heard stories such as the one about Captain Phillip V. Shinn of the tanker SS *Yamhill*, who purchased a hand-carved elephant-design end table in India and later wished he had purchased two of them. One of the merchant seamen under his command, Bill Jopes, had a matching table of his own, and for some time the captain had been offering to buy it from him. In the midst of a battle with a submarine, Jopes relieved the tension—enemy shells were falling closer and closer to the tanker—by offering to sell his table to the captain at a low price. A short while later Jopes began to raise the price when the submarine retreated, and he ending up keeping the table.[6]

To a large extent the men used humor to relieve the tension of being in situations where they could be blown out of the water at any moment—and also to relieve the frustration of not being able to fight back effectively. Lincoln R. Masur, a seaman on the SS *William Dawes*, wrote the following in a letter after he narrowly escaped death:

> On July 22nd (1942) I had an unusual experience off the coast of Australia. At five A.M. our ship received a message from General Tojo in the form of a torpedo.[7]

The seamen also told tales of good fortune, which provided hope to men who so desperately needed it in a hostile, dangerous environment. Harold L. Myers, a clerk on the Esso tanker *E. G. Seubert*, jumped into the sea with his dog after the ship was torpedoed in the Gulf of Aden. The dog, a Persian deerhound he had purchased in an Arabian port, swam through oily water while the seaman swam along behind, with the long leash wrapped around his wrist. It was nighttime, and Myers could not see anything, through the darkness and thick fuel oil that stung his eyes. His leg throbbed with pain, an injury he'd sustained when he was thrown out of his bunk. Fuel oil filled his ears, also, plugging up his hearing. Finally his fellow crewmen heard the dog panting, and pulled the animal into a lifeboat. Myers felt the leash tighten, and he called out. The lucky man was rescued, having been saved by his dog.[8]

But stories of hardship and tragedy were more prevalent. The men on merchant ships exchanged yarns of torpedoed ships and long journeys in open lifeboats, of men dying of exposure. They referred to torpedoes as "tin fish," and used other colorful terminology Dean Beaumont had never heard before.

The clean-cut young ensign might have heard, too, about the tanker SS *Jack Carnes*, which made three voyages from the island of Aruba in the Caribbean Sea to Swansea, Wales. It was one of the new, fast tankers early in the war, and made the trips without escort, transporting highly volatile aviation gas that was needed by the Royal Air Force for their Spitfire fighter planes. The ship carried a merchant crew of forty men plus twelve Armed Guardsmen, consisting of U.S. and British Navy personnel.

Coming back empty in August 1942 after its third trip to Wales, the *Jack Carnes* engaged in a running sea-battle with a U-boat. The Germans fired deckguns containing exploding antiaircraft shells, trying to take out the tanker's bridge and radio room. But the merchant ship's Armed Guard, firing their 5-inch aft gun, almost hit the submarine, causing it to dive and disappear. (Submarines were known to be fragile vessels, and could be sunk by one well-placed shot.)

Unfortunately, the sub came back that evening and struck them with two torpedoes at midships, causing the tanker to stop dead in the water. It was around eleven P.M., shortly before William C. Crozier, a young Third Assistant Engineer, was supposed to report for his graveyard shift in the engine room. Crozier told me that he and the rest of the crew made it safely into two lifeboats, each of which held twenty-eight men. Before abandoning ship, however, the radio operator got off a distress call. For a while the submarine did not surface and the tanker appeared stable. . . . So the crew was about to reboard her, when suddenly three more torpedoes hit the *Jack Carnes*. It split in half and went down.

The crewmen were fortunate to make it into the lifeboats at all. This was possible only because the empty ship had virtually no gas fumes in its tanks, thanks to a special venting system with big sails on the deck which gathered wind and funneled it down into the tanks, cleansing them. (Fumes were also reduced by saltwater ballast, which was pumped into the tanks.)

Shortly after getting into the lifeboats, however, the men were caught in a big storm. One lifeboat—with the captain, three officers, and twenty-four other men aboard—capsized, and all were drowned. On Crozier's boat, the bosun improvised a "drouge," or sea anchor, by cutting a ballast tank from the boat and pitching it over the side on a line. This gave them stability in the high winds and pitching seas, preventing them from flipping over.

An American destroyer at a refueling station in the Azores heard the distress call and rushed out to sea on a rescue mission. In the raging storm, the crew of the warship could not find any sign of the wreckage or the survivors, and eventually gave up the effort.

Crozier and his companions spent six days in the lifeboat, and finally came within sight of Terceira Island in the Azores. Just before reaching shore they fired flares, causing fishermen to come out and help them. All of the men on that boat survived.[9]

Some trips in open boats were even longer. After the freighter *Prusa* sank in 1941, Captain George H. Boy saved the lives of twelve men by leading them on an incredible thirty-one-day voyage in a lifeboat, covering a distance of nearly three thousand miles.[10]

Men often died of exposure in open lifeboats, or lost one or more of their extremities to frostbite. Dying of thirst, some of them drank seawater, which caused them to go insane and jump into the sea. Those who survived were fortunate to have more experienced or resourceful men on board with them.

When the Liberty ship SS *Richard Hovey* was torpedoed and sunk by a Japanese submarine, thirty-nine American crewmen escaped in a lifeboat, barely eluding the deadly intentions of the enemy commander, who tried to slaughter them with machine-gun fire. A junior engineer on the merchant vessel, Arthur John Drechsler, would receive the Merchant Marine Distinguished Service medal for saving his companions: The murderous gunfire had punctured the freshwater tanks on the lifeboat, leaving the men low on water. According to Drechsler's citation:

> With no other tools than an axe, pliers, a screwdriver, and a steel punch, Drechsler, utilizing metal brackets from a foot rest, two empty food containers, the metal cone from a storm oil bag, and the rubber hose from a lifeboat pump, improvised an ingenious still which produced a ration of eleven ounces of potable water per man throughout the sixteen days before rescue.[11]

Sometimes the men only had a life raft. Harold J. McCormick, chief of a Navy gun crew, described the aftermath of the sinking of the Liberty ship SS *William Gaston* in 1944:

> For the next several hours we huddled on the raft, clinging to the deck boards to keep from being swept overboard. The deck of the raft was about the size of a 9 by 12 rug, wholly inadequate for 14 men. The top, bottom, and sides were wooden lattice work, holding a number of steel drums which provided buoyancy. Being aboard was like riding a combination rollercoaster-flume ride, rising repeatedly to the crest of a wave and then sliding

down into a deep trough, with seas breaking over us from all sides.[12]

When the freighter SS *Puerto Rican* was torpedoed at night off the coast of Iceland, the men had trouble releasing the lifeboats and rafts, which were encrusted with ice. Firemen August Wallenhaupt finally made it onto a raft, with others. He reported later that the men tried to pray aloud, but frigid waves kept filling their mouths with water, and they had to pray silently. A 1944 story in *Reader's Digest* described the ordeal:

> Every few minutes a particularly heavy wave would send [them] tumbling in a heap, clawing at the lines, clutching at each other in the darkness.

Men were washed overboard. Finally only two were left on the raft, and Wallenhaupt realized that the other man was dead, lying facedown on the raft, frozen solid to it. In order to protect himself from the icy waves and wind, Wallenhaupt lay down next to the body, on the leeward side.

> I didn't think of him as a dead human. He was something frozen, like a piece of earth. He was covered with a foot of solid ice.

Wallenhaupt was the only survivor of the SS *Puerto Rican*. When he was finally rescued, he had dropped from his usual weight of 170 pounds to less than a hundred. Doctors had to amputate both legs, and all of his fingers down to his knuckles, with the exception of the thumb of his right hand and two fingers on his left hand.[13]

FIVE

WAR
CRIMES

The list of bad things that can happen to a seaman
is much longer in wartime than in peacetime,
especially when you're dealing with a fanatical enemy.
Davy Jones's locker is filled with terrible secrets.

—HOWARD J. HANSEN,
UNITED STATES MERCHANT MARINE

TO AVOID DETECTION AT NIGHT, THE SS *BRANDER MATTHEWS* SAILED IN BLACK-out conditions beneath a blanket of stars, cabin windows covered tightly and no running lights on the decks or masts. The officers joked that the ship could not sink anyway, since the dock boxes in its cargo holds had air sealed inside them. But some of the war stories Dean heard raised the hackles on the back on his neck.

The men had spoken of Liberty ships breaking apart in rough water, of attacks by enemy aircraft, and of atrocities committed against merchant seamen by German and Japanese submarine captains. In these tales the men did not always know the names of the ships involved, the dates, or other specifics. But documentation was developed during the war; some from survivors, and some from Axis submarine logs and other records obtained after the Allied victory. One substantiated case involved the unarmed freighter the SS

David H. Atwater, which was shelled by a German U-boat on April 2, 1942, causing it to sink off the coast of Virginia. The crew was not given any chance to abandon ship, and when they tried to do so, their lifeboats were riddled by machine-gun fire. Only three out of twenty-eight crew members survived.[1]

Another unarmed ship, the converted tanker SS *Carrabulle*, was heavily shelled by a U-boat on May 26, 1942, in the Gulf of Mexico. Almost the entire crew escaped in two lifeboats. Then the submarine drew close to them, and the German captain asked if all hands had abandoned ship. The crew answered no. The officer then laughed and fired a torpedo at the SS *Carrabulle*. The explosion sank the ship and blew up one of the lifeboats, killing twenty-two of twenty-four men aboard.[2]

In yet another incident, a German submarine torpedoed the Greek freighter *Peleus* near Liberia. Two survivors were taken aboard the sub for questioning and then returned to their raft, after removing their life jackets. The commander of the submarine, Kapitänleutnant Heinz Eck, ordered his men to throw hand grenades at all the rafts, and to riddle them with machine-gun fire. After the war, Eck was found guilty of committing a war crime and was executed by firing squad.[3]

The SS *Brander Matthews* went to Honolulu first, where Dean took a brief shore leave. At Pearl Harbor he saw the devastating results of the sneak attack by Japan: the Navy battleships that had been damaged or sunk. He had been on those ships with his father, had loved them: the USS *Arizona*, the *Oklahoma*, the *Nevada*, the *Maryland*. Seeing the devastation saddened him, and reinforced his will to contribute to the Allied war effort.

After that, Dean's Liberty ship made its way to an anchorage at Eniwetok in the Marshall Islands, where they joined half a dozen other merchant vessels already there. This anchorage was one of the biggest in the western Pacific, inside the protection of a coral reef that could be blocked off at the ends to keep enemy submarines out.

The next day, the American fleet arrived: two aircraft carriers, three cruisers, ten destroyers, and smaller vessels—twenty-five ships in all. Dean was particularly impressed when the aircraft carrier USS *Kearsage* came steaming into the anchorage, an immense warship with fighter planes arrayed on the deck, and a crew of three thousand sailors. It anchored three hundred yards off the port bow of the SS *Brander Matthews*. In the words of Dean Beaumont: "Our ship, with its little guns, was like a peashooter in comparison."

Throughout the rest of the war, Dean's attitude would gradually darken from experience, as he risked his life repeatedly but still felt the unfair sting of criticism and derision from members of the armed forces, at all levels. Many years later, Dean wrote a note to me in which he said,

> I was excited—thrilled to be in the U.S. Merchant Marine, not one bit afraid. . . . I felt proud to be part of the great Navy fleet. But little did I know they would later disown us—as being *nothing* but Merchant Marine civilians.

As a young ensign in 1944, Dean had no inkling of the troubles that would follow, of the perilous, confusing political waters that merchant seamen would sail through. Such troubles remained ahead of him, beyond the visible horizon. . . .

The *Brander Matthews* waited at Eniwetok for a Navy escort ship to accompany it to Saipan, a journey of one thousand nautical miles. A couple of days later, the escort showed up. A converted tugboat, it had machine guns mounted on its decks, and mine-sweeping equipment. On a cloudy morning, the unusual craft led the way out of the anchorage, followed by three Liberty ships.

Dean Beaumont had heard stories of atrocities committed by German U-boat crews, but most of those incidents had occurred far away, in the Atlantic Ocean or in the Gulf of Mexico. There were no

known U-boats in the Pacific, only a smaller fleet of Japanese submarines, known as I-boats. But the Japanese could be even more
ruthless, if they found their prey. In 1943, two Allied merchant vessels, the SS *Daisy Moller* and the SS *British Chivalry*, were torpedoed in separate incidents by Japanese submarines in the Indian
Ocean. When the crewmen tried to escape in lifeboats, the submarines rammed them and Japanese sailors machine-gunned the
occupants.

A similar act of carnage was committed the following year by
Tatsunosuke Ariizumi, predatory commander of the Japanese submarine *I-8*. After torpedoing the Dutch merchant ship *Tjisalak* just
south of Colombo, Ceylon (Sri Lanka), Ariizumi ordered the survivors to board his sub. The Japanese then stole the men's valu-
ables, and tortured them, hitting them with sledgehammers,
beheading them with swords, and machine-gunning them. Ariizumi
massacred ninety-eight seamen, in all.

James Blears, one of the few survivors who managed to escape,
later recalled,

> They were laughing. They'd just go up and hit a guy on
> the back and take him up front, and then one of the guys
> with a sword would cut off his head *Zhunk!* One guy,
> they cut his head halfway off and let him flop around on
> the deck. The others I saw, they just lopped 'em off with
> one shot and threw 'em overboard. They were having
> fun, and there was a cameraman taking movies of the
> whole thing![4]

In 1944 there were at least three additional horrendous incidents of Japanese aggression, all against Liberty ship crews. One
involved the SS *Richard Hovey*, whose crew narrowly escaped
Japanese torpedoes, and survived sixteen days in a lifeboat. As the
merchant ship was sinking, the Japanese submarine surfaced and
its men on deck began firing machine guns and high-velocity rifles
at the seamen in the lifeboats. The submarine drew closer and

rammed one lifeboat, causing it to flip over. On the deck of the sub, Japanese sailors in khaki uniforms and caps laughed and shouted. One of them recorded the events with a motion-picture camera. The captain of the merchant ship, Hans Thorsen, was taken prisoner and died in captivity.[5]

I spoke with a survivor from another 1944 atrocity, Peter Chelemedos. He had served as a young Chief Mate on the SS *John A. Johnson*, en route from San Francisco to Honolulu, with a cargo of food, 500-pound bombs, ammunition, trucks, and tractors. In an emotion-filled voice, Chelemedos recalled he had been in the chart room on that fateful evening, writing in his log and listening to the radio. The ship's running lights were off on a moonlit night, with clouds alternately obscuring and revealing the moon. During the eight P.M. news, Admiral "Bull" Halsey announced that the U.S. Navy controlled the entire Pacific Ocean, since the Americans had won the battle for the Philippine Sea.

Chelemedos had been suffering a bad cold for several days. Captain Arnold H. Beekin saw him working and gave him three fingers of whiskey, with this advice: "Go down and get some hot tea. Drink the whiskey with the hot tea, take a hot shower, and pile the blankets on and stay in bed. I'll stand your morning watch for you."

The youthful Chief Mate did as he was told. But just as he reached up to turn off the bunk lamp, an explosion rocked the ship—it had been torpedoed. Chelemedos grabbed his life jacket and ran upstairs. He stopped in the chart room to get a sextant and a chronometer, for navigating in a lifeboat. Then he helped Radio Officer Gordon Brown replace the radio set on a bulkhead, since it had been jarred loose and wasn't working. Chelemedos then aided in the evacuation of the vessel.

All members of the crew and the military personnel aboard—seventy people in all—made it into lifeboats and onto rafts. Beneath a bright moon, the submarine surfaced, a Japanese emblem on the side, and with the designation *I-12*. Laughing crew members appeared on the deck. They fired machine guns and pistols at survivors, shouting, "Banzai!" whenever they hit the defenseless men.

Terrified merchant seamen dove out of the boats and off the rafts into the water, but the submarine came close and rammed the lifeboats—true to Japanese sub tactics—crushing to death a man who was clinging to the side. Other crewmen tried to avoid being seen. Navy Armed Guard gunner Raymond A. Booth described his own desperate struggle to stay alive, along with his shipmates:

> [All] of us, with the exception of three nonswimmers, went over the port side (of the lifeboat), nearly swamping the boat. I remember swimming through the oil and debris, thinking, *They will surely shoot at us. I must swim away from all these men.* After doing this, and with the submarine about fifty or sixty feet away, I began to make deep dives. I will never forget the loudness of those diesels underwater, and it was taking forever to pass. I would come to the surface, take a look, grab a gulp of air, and dive again. There were numerous bags (about 10-pound size) of flour amid the debris, and I remember looking around one of these at the sub.

Nearby, Peter Chelemedos had ordered the men in his lifeboat into the water, where they hid behind floating sacks of flour, boxes, and other debris. Fortunately for them, a cloud was passing over the moon, so the men could not be easily seen by the Japanese fighting from the deck of the submarine.

But the submarine managed to tear another Armed Guard gunner—Booth's friend, named Christensen—to pieces in its propellers. Chelemedos recalls seeing the Japanese try to murder one of the stewards, a black man, by catching him in the screws as he hung on to the side of the lifeboat with other men. Afterward, the steward had only a scratch on the palm of his hand from pushing the sub away; he said to Chelemedos, "Man, that's as close as I ever want to be to one of those darn things." They were among the lucky ones.

But one of Peter's friends, a ship's carpenter, was not so fortunate, and fell under the murderous hail of bullets. The young man had been recently married, with his whole life ahead of him. Peter Chelemedos wrote this touching piece about him:

> *Back aft, in the carpenter shop,*
> *young Jim Brady proudly*
> *showed me his new tool kit.*
> *He had put it together while*
> *on his way to join the ship,*
> *his first trip to sea.*
> *He didn't know the machine gun bullet*
> *that cut him down*
> *would have his name on it.*

At the time, another survivor, Radio Officer Gordon Brown, was on his first voyage, and he suffered severe mental anguish from the trauma of the experience, in which ten of his shipmates were murdered in cold blood. Officer Brown was later killed in a kamikaze attack while serving on a merchant ship.[6]

The worst World War Two atrocity against American merchant seamen, though, had occurred in the Indian Ocean,* shortly before Dean Beaumont embarked on his first-ever voyage. Much like the SS *Brander Matthews*, the Liberty ship SS *Jean Nicolet* left San Pedro, California, carrying a military cargo: in this case, mooring pontoons and unassembled landing-barges lashed to the decks, as well as important war supplies in the cargo holds, including two landing craft. Aboard the *Nicolet* were forty-one merchant crew members, twenty-eight Navy Armed Guard, a U.S. Army medic, and thirty U.S. Army passengers.

In June 1944, the vessel laid over at Fremantle, Australia, for a day, then set sail across the Indian Ocean toward Colombo, Ceylon.

---

*This was the worst *known* atrocity. Other American ships and their crews disappeared without a trace, leaving us to only speculate upon the horrors of their final moments.

On July 1, the crew spotted an empty lifeboat drifting in the water, with no sign of anything else. It filled the men with a sense of foreboding, but did not increase their fear—since each of them already knew how dangerous it was to transport war matériel across the oceans of the world. The captain, David Nilsson, did increase the lookouts, and put the gun crews on duty at dawn and dusk, when many of the submarine attacks occurred. The *Nicolet* was just south of the equator.

Shortly after midnight on July 2, 1944, the ship was torpedoed and shelled by the Japanese submarine *I-8*. Fires broke out on the ship, and it listed so heavily— to at least 35 degrees—that the captain feared it might capsize. All the passengers and crew, a hundred people, successfully abandoned ship in four lifeboats and two rafts. At this point only one man had a significant injury: a broken arm.

Then a strong searchlight shone and a submarine became visible, with Japanese seamen standing on the deck, dressed in their khaki uniforms with red Imperial Navy markings on the shoulders. At gunpoint the survivors were ordered to board the submarine by its commander, the notorious Captain Ariizumi who had massacred the crew of the Dutch merchant ship *Tjisalak* earlier in the year (see page 57).

The first to be taken on board the *I-8* was a seventeen-year-old mess-hall boy, William M. Musser, who was shot in the head and then kicked into the barracuda- and shark-infested waters. The next victim was an ordinary nineteen-year-old seaman, Richard L. Kean. The other Americans had their hands bound tightly with cords or wire, and personal articles were stolen, including watches, rings, and shoes.

Only five crewmen from the Liberty ship SS *Jean Nicolet* escaped, on a small balsa-wood raft, or swam away in the darkness. All four lifeboats were destroyed, and the captives on the submarine were subjected to beatings and torture. One man was hit in the face with a lead pipe, breaking his nose and knocking out his front teeth. Two of the tied-up men were washed overboard by a bow wave and left to drown. In the middle of the night, others were forced to run a gauntlet on the deck of the submarine, where Japanese seamen beat them with clubs, stabbed them with swords and knives, and hooked them into the water with fixed bayonets, brutally murdering more than half of the captives.

Just before dawn the following morning, thirty survivors were remaining on the deck of the Japanese submarine. Spotting an Allied plane—a Catalina—the Japanese guards disappeared into their hatches, then the captain crash-dived the sub, drowning half of the prisoners on deck. One of the surviving merchant seamen, Bill Flury, was among those on the deck of the submarine at the time. The young man managed to tread water without a life jacket, his hands bound behind his back, until one of his shipmates untied him. In the darkness, Flury heard the terrified screams of the other crewmen as sharks attacked them. He saw the burning *Jean Nicolet* sink and then disappear. He swam all night, and eventually was rescued by a British submarine-chaser.

Another seaman, Harold R. Lee, escaped the Japanese gauntlet, and dove into the water. He saved a member of the Navy Armed Guard, but also witnessed the horrors inflicted by sharks. One man was decapitated, and another lost his leg. In all, seventy-five died, including thirty members of the civilian crew. Faced with a war crimes trial at the end of the armed conflict, Captain Ariizumi disappeared, and is believed either to have swum ashore at one of the Japanese ports, or to have committed hara-kiri.[7]

Recently, I interviewed Bill Flury. A soft-spoken, polite man now in his seventies, he had been only eighteen at the time of the atrocity, working in the steward's department of the *Jean Nicolet* as a second cook and baker. Prior to volunteering for the Merchant Marine, he had worked in bakeshops since he was fourteen years old. He does not like to talk much about the horrors of what happened to him and his shipmates anymore, but lives with the nightmarish, traumatic events every day of his life, unable to forget.

Back in 1944, as young Dean Beaumont crossed the Pacific

Ocean on his first Merchant Marine voyage, he was running a gauntlet himself, trying to pass safely through waters that swam with steel sharks—enemy submarines. He and his fellow crewmen on the SS *Brander Matthews* would need a lot of luck to survive.

SIX

THE BATTLE
OF SAIPAN

*The fact that cargo made it through to America's G.I.s
was a story in itself. America's wartime cargo from
the homeland to the Pacific and Europe totaled more
than 268 million long tons. In the last year of the war
the delivery rate reached 8,500 tons every hour of
every day.*

—NORMAN Y. MINETA,
U.S. SECRETARY OF TRANSPORTATION[1]

EARLY IN WORLD WAR TWO, ARTHUR BEAUMONT BECAME AN ARTIST/WAR CORRE-
spondent for the *Long Beach Press-Telegram* and for the *Los
Angeles Evening Herald and Express.* As details of battles came
in over the wires, Beaumont created thrilling, highly realistic action
paintings that appeared on the front pages of newspapers all over
the United States.

After Colonel Jimmy Doolittle bombed Tokyo, using the aircraft
carrier USS *Hornet* as a base for his B-25s, the Navy asked Mr. Beaumont to revise his painting of the carrier that would appear in the
press. In order to confuse and frighten the Japanese even more, the
Navy wanted Arthur Beaumont to depict a carrier with two gun-
tubs ahead of the bridge, and two aft, which he did. This was totally

different from the actual configuration on the *Hornet*, which had guns on the sides.

Arthur Beaumont also had a subtle, very British sense of humor, which sometimes showed up in his work. The cognoscenti recognized something amiss with his watercolor painting of the destroyer *Everett F. Larson* (DD-830), which displayed signal flags that read, SPEED 60 KNOTS. Another destroyer in the painting was signaling back, INTERROGATIVE: SPEED 60 KNOTS. The artist did this intentionally, knowing full well that no warship could go that fast, in any Navy.[2]

Beaumont always did his research meticulously, even obtaining the original plans of the ships from the U.S. Navy Archives in Washington, D.C., and studying them carefully before beginning to paint.[3] In the manner of Mark Twain—who also performed extensive research before changing anything in his stories—Beau then adjusted details if he wanted to do so. His paintings were widely admired not only for their composition—the way he portrayed seagoing vessels in exciting situations—but also for the technical accuracy of the renditions, down to the tiniest elements of naval architecture.

He once said that he *had* to go to such lengths, since he had more than a million-and-a-half critics . . . in the United States Navy.

A number of Arthur Beaumont's works became very famous. One of these was the 4- by 5-foot painting he did in the 1930s, of the cruiser USS *Los Angeles*. The Navy used the painting for a big promotional campaign, and gave lithographs of it—signed by the artist—as gifts to anyone purchasing a war bond of $500 or higher. They raised an astounding $10,000,000—a huge sum for World War Two. A companion war-bonds program raised an additional $71,000,000. In all, it was enough to build a new cruiser and two destroyers.

In 1942, the U.S. Navy initiated a program to produce postage stamps with renditions of naval vessels on them, hoping this would promote interest in the Navy during the war. The Secretary of the

Navy, Frank Knox, along with President Franklin D. Roosevelt and Admiral William D. Leahy, approved the project. Arthur Beaumont was selected to create four paintings of Navy ships, including a destroyer, a cruiser, a battleship, and an aircraft carrier. The artist painted them in full color, and prints were reduced to postage-stamp size.

When they were ready, the stamp designs were sent off to the postmaster general in Washington, D.C. He liked them, but killed the project, citing a regulation that any picture painted by an artist could not be made into a postage stamp until ten years after the death of that artist. Because of this bureaucratic foul-up, the idea was abandoned. It was easier to fight World War Two than to butt heads with the American bureaucracy.

During his lifetime Arthur Beaumont produced more than four thousand paintings, a number of them valued at between $50,000 and $350,000 apiece. His work was featured in *National Geographic* magazine.[4] At the tail end of World War Two, the U.S. Navy thought so highly of him that they offered him the rank of "honorary admiral." Beau was one of only three men to be so honored at the time (along with famed movie director John Ford), but turned it down. Arthur didn't want all of the pomp and circumstance that went along with it, and preferred to wander around ships in his old khakis carrying his art supplies and dining with whomever he pleased—even the common sailors he referred to as "white-hats."[5]

Beau became so well known that Hollywood motion-picture companies started asking him to paint portraits of their major stars in the 1940s: including Joan Crawford, Rita Hayworth, and Lucille Ball. Flattered, Mr. Beaumont did dabble in those waters, but only briefly. He found the movie stars too picky, that they wanted changes on the paintings to make them look better. Beau was told the star wanted her hair to look more golden, or that she needed to look younger. The artist had too much integrity to go along with such requests, so he decided to stick to his portraits of military officers and paintings of ships. On occasion he did create backdrop paintings for motion pictures, but that was as close as Beau wanted to get to the film industry.

He and his wife Dorothy had written to their son at every opportunity, and worried about him. In Hawaii, Dean had picked up their letters and sent one of his own back to them, describing his dismay at what he had seen in Pearl Harbor.

Out on the Pacific Ocean, the SS *Brander Matthews* proceeded west with two other Liberty ships, following the lightly armed escort boat. Men stood on the decks of the vessels with binoculars, constantly on alert for signs of the enemy. Captain Vincent Nielsen had mentioned the possibility of steering a zigzag course to create difficulties for submarines, but thus far the tactic had not been employed. Liberty ships were painfully slow, chugging along at 10 knots per hour or less, and the captains were concerned that such a tactic would only leave them in harm's way for a longer period of time.

The ocean was choppy, but Dean—like his father—had good sea legs and didn't experience much trouble getting around. Some of the younger crew members on the SS *Brander Matthews* struggled with seasickness, but not Dean. The salt air felt good washing through his lungs, and he seemed to be breathing easier, but his asthma had a way of appearing at unexpected times.

Young Dean was off on an adventure aboard a merchant ship, bringing to my mind the Howard Pease novels I read as a boy—about young men sailing on tramp steamers to romantic, distant lands: *The Jinx Ship*, *The Hurricane*, *Shipwrecked* . . .

A peculiar medical situation came up during the voyage, and Dean had to handle it. Describing the event to me years later, he said, "I was the purser on board, and also the doctor, but only because I knew how to put on a bandage."

One morning the Chief Mate came to Dean and said a deckhand was seriously ill and unable to perform his work. Dean said to bring him to the clinic on the ship. A few minutes later the crewman was led into the clinic, a small room with two bunk beds. The bottom bunk was very low and they had been using the upper bunk as a table.

The patient bent over and moaned, saying something was seriously wrong his stomach, maybe cancer. Dean and the mate helped him onto the bed. Then Dean prodded the man's stomach and watched the wincing reaction on his face.

Dean took the mate aside and conferred with him, out in the corridor. "He might have appendicitis," Dean suggested, "or he might be faking. If he really is sick, this could be very serious."

"What are you going to do?" the mate asked.

"Let's pretend we're going to operate," Dean said, "and see what happens. You strap him down and I'll get the surgical equipment ready."

The mate smiled and nodded.

The two of them went back inside the clinic. While the mate strapped the crewman down to the bed, Dean started fooling around with medical utensils, boiling them, dropping them on the floor, and not boiling them again.

"What are you doing?" the crewman asked. He couldn't move his arms or legs, but stretched his neck around to try to see.

"It looks like you have appendicitis," Dean replied. "If it bursts, you'll be dead, so we gotta take it out."

The eyes widened. "Take it out? You mean *operate*?"

"Yep."

"Well, aren't you going to boil those instruments again?"

"They're clean enough."

Dean was holding his deadpan expression very well, but the mate didn't have as much control. He had to look away to keep from blowing the gag, and slipped out into the corridor.

"Do you know how to do this?" the man on the bed asked, with increasing concern.

"Well, I've never actually performed surgery before, but there's nothing to worry about. I told the radio operator to call Pearl Harbor and ask a doctor for instructions. The mate is going over to get their answer now."

"Wait," the man said. "I'm not sure about this."

But Dean wasn't listening. He went out of the room, leaving the man strapped to the bed. Five minutes later, Dean and the mate returned. Dean had a marking pen. He lifted the patient's shirt up and started drawing on his stomach, while the man struggled unsuccessfully to free his arms from the restraints.

"Now what are you doing?" the crewman demanded. His face was purple, and moist with perspiration.

"They told me how to mark where we're going to cut," Dean said calmly. "They said to make a line ten or eleven inches long right here"—Dean made a streak on the man's side—"for the first incision. After I get inside and look around, I might have to make a bigger cut."

"Look, I'm feeling a lot better," the crewman said. "I don't want an operation, so just let me out of here, okay?"

Dean looked at the mate, who nodded. The two of them released the man, and he jumped up and ran out of the room. Fifteen minutes later he was back at work on the deck, not saying anything.

When the small convoy reached their destination, the big battle of Saipan was over, but there were still Japanese air raids in the area, and reports of dead Japanese soldiers, sailors, and pilots still on the ground. The Japanese had lost the island, and it was a military embarrassment of such magnitude that the premier of Japan, the notorious General Hideki Tojo, was forced to resign on July 20, 1944, along with his entire cabinet.[6]

All three Liberty ships anchored out at the town of Garapan on the western shore of Saipan, with the SS *Brander Matthews* close to the beach. The entire town had been leveled and there were no port facilities remaining. Army crews began unloading the steel boxes from the holds and bolting them together to form a long dock that was twenty-four feet wide and more than a hundred feet long. The dock was set up so that trucks could drive on top of it to unload other ships.

The weather was warm, with no breezes or air-conditioning, so Dean needed to keep the porthole of his cabin open. He was located right over the galley, though, and got a lot of fumes and cooking odors. So, that day he made arrangements to switch to another cabin. This one was bigger, with two portholes and a bunk bed, instead of the single bed he'd had before. He opened the portholes and was breathing better, then went to sleep that night in the upper bunk.

At three A.M., the General Quarters alarm went off, and Dean jumped out of the bunk, shouting, "Here we go to war!" He had intended to run for the door, but forgot that he was in an upper berth and tumbled onto the steel deck, injuring his knees.

Dean threw on clothing, boots, and a helmet, then ran limping down the corridor and up the companionway steps, heading for the 20-millimeter Oerlikon antiaircraft gun where he had volunteered to be a loader—the equivalent of a gunner's mate in the U.S. Navy. The door to the outside deck was open, but as Dean roared through it, he stubbed his foot on the one-inch coaming of the threshold, and went skidding across the steel deck on his face—creating an injury from his hairline to the bottom of his jaw, from which he still bears scars, more than half a century later.

Finally making it to the gun-tub, Dean climbed in and loaded the antiaircraft gun for the Navy man who arrived seconds later. The ship still had its booms out, since they had been unloading that day. The booms were attached to the masts with guy-wires that were about an inch-and-a-half thick.

Illuminated in crisscrossing searchlight beams from the shore, three Japanese fighter planes swooped down at the ships, bullets flying from machine guns. American shore batteries opened up, and the sky grew bright with the orange embers of tracer fire. Dean saw one of the aircraft diving toward the *Brander Matthews*, peppering the superstructure and decks with bullets. As the plane strafed the Liberty ship, Navy gunners on the side decks fired antiaircraft guns, while men on the fore and aft decks fired 3- and 5-inch guns.

On one side of the 20-millimeter gun-tub, Dean leaned over and picked up an ammo box, without noticing, in all the commotion, that a two-ton boom was falling straight toward him. A young Navy gunner on the other side of the ship had shot the main mast and the wires holding up the boom. The sailor had missed a battle-phone command from an officer on the bridge, who was telling the gunners on one side or the other—port or starboard—to hold fire or open fire.*

Dean straightened his body as he stood up with a load of ammunition. At that very moment the boom slammed into the exact spot where he had been only seconds before, and smashed in the side of the gun-tub, bending the boom over the edge of the ship. Dean had his helmet on, but it wouldn't have done him much good. He had missed death by mere inches.

The shore batteries and Armed Guard crews kept firing at the planes, and finally the attackers soared up and away into the night sky. None of the American vessels was seriously damaged, although there were injuries to a dozen men.

"It was really close and the Lord was good to me," Dean said. "God saved my life."

The marine corps and the Army were in charge of the island of Saipan, and the next evening they announced that the merchant seamen could come ashore and watch movies. The crew of the SS *Brander Matthews* couldn't figure out how they were going to do

---

*This was a common occurrence. Alan H. Knox was second mate on the MS *Cape Henry*, a C-1 cargo ship. Off the eastern coast of South America, their Navy gun crew spotted a Vichy French spotter plane, which would report their location to any German U-boats in the area. Knox told me that the gunnery officer on the merchant ship ordered his men to "fire at will." Unfortunately, the ship's machine guns did not have keepers to restrict their turning radius, and the gunners fired bullets across the deck, past the wheelhouse. At the wheel, Knox saw bullets whiz by him—too close. Moments later, the gunnery officer got on the battle-phone and changed his command to: "Gunners on starboard side, shoot starboard; gunners on port side, shoot port."

that, since nothing was left of the town, but they walked across the new dock and went ashore. After the big battle, the rubble had been bulldozed; just dirt and dust and sand remained.

"Where's the theater?" Dean asked one of the soldiers.

"We'll bring it to you," the man responded cryptically. "Just sit on that mound of sand over there." He pointed. Then he marched off, toward an encampment of tents and trucks.

Dean and his companions shrugged, then went and sat down to wait. Pretty soon, a big Army truck came up. It turned around, then backed up and stopped.

Soldiers opened the back of the truck and slid an interior curtain aside, revealing a movie screen. A projector was on the other side of the screen, behind the driver's seat. It was done this way to conceal the lights from enemy planes that might fly over.

"We have two movies for you," a corporal announced. "*Reveille With Beverly* and *Stage Door Canteen*."

"You're kidding," Dean said. "I'm in both of those." He explained how he and his fraternity brothers had worked as extras in films to earn college money, and pointed out his moment in the opening scene of *Stage Door Canteen*. This gave him instant status around the makeshift theater.

The following day, the SS *Brander Matthews* took water ballast into its holds, and departed for San Pedro.

SEVEN

VALOR
AT SEA

*I have often wondered why we are told to read the
biographies of the famous when we need only turn
to the experiences of the common man for lessons
which sustain us in . . . life and death situations.*

—IAN A. MILLAR[1]

UNITED STATES MERCHANT SHIPS WERE ONLY LIGHTLY ARMED IN WORLD WAR
Two, but their gun crews fought valiantly against superior fire
power. Members of the Navy Armed Guard assigned to those ships
suffered more deaths and injuries than any other department of the
Navy. Civilian seamen worked as volunteers beside Navy personnel,
sometimes firing the guns themselves when the gunners were
injured or killed, and sometimes offering to stand watch for enemy
submarines or warplanes. In many of the battles, merchant ships
and their crews lost.

But there were notable exceptions. In 1942 the Liberty ship SS
Virginia Dare shot down seven German planes in Convoy PQ-18
on the way to Murmansk, Russia. In honor of this conquest, the
proud crew painted seven swastikas on the smokestack of the ship,
and received one of the few Gallant Ship Awards of the war. In the

same waters, the SS *Bellingham* won an argument with a German bomber by shooting it down.

Early in 1945, near the end of the war, the Liberty ship SS *Henry Bacon* was returning from Murmansk in another convoy. The weather in that area was particularly harsh and unpredictable, and when it worsened suddenly, the ship fell out of the convoy. A short while later, a squadron of more than twenty German torpedo planes attacked the Liberty ship, firing at least two torpedoes apiece. Remarkably, none hit the mark, as the *Bacon*'s helmsman steered the ship expertly to avoid them. During the fierce battle, the naval gun crew shot down five planes before a torpedo finally hit the ship below the waterline at the number 5 cargo hold. The *Henry Bacon* did eventually go down, but not without a heroic fight.[2]

I interviewed Alan H. Knox, who was on the Liberty ship *W. W. McCracken* when its gun crew shot down a Japanese "Betty" bomber off the coast of Australia. Mr. Knox, who was eighty-six years old when I spoke with him, described the battle in detail. He then paused, and said in a soft voice, "I'm amazed I remembered all that." It had all come back to him, as if he were in the midst of the battle again.

Thousands of other merchant seamen also had stories to tell, and some of them made it into print.

In 1943, the Liberty ship SS *Solomon Juneau* shot down two German planes in the Mediterranean Sea, and assisted nearby ships in shooting down three more. In 1944 the MS *Cape Romano* was attacked by Japanese bombers. Suddenly, a kamikaze plane streaked toward them, but the Armed Guard shot 20-millimeter machine guns at it, hitting the pilot. The plane swerved and hit the ship with only a glancing blow on the port side that did not sink it. That same year, the SS *John Evans* was attacked by a Japanese plane, which strafed it with machine-gun fire. The Armed Guard returned fire and killed the pilot. The plane hit the top mast and cargo booms before crashing into the water, but the ship was able to continue the mission under its own power. Yet another event involved the SS *Morrison R. Waite*, which shot down a Japanese zero in the Philippines in November 1944. Over the course of a forty-day period, the valiant crew of this ship went through no fewer than 135 air-raid alerts.[3]

A number of Armed Guard crews claimed to have sunk German U-boats or Japanese submarines. Among those with such stories were the men working in the gun-tubs of the SS *William H. Berg*, the SS *Liberator*, the SS *Frederick R. Kellogg*, the SS *Lihue*, the SS *Charles C. Pinckney*, and the SS *Edgar Allan Poe*. At the end of the war, however, the United States Navy and the British Admiralty discounted all of these claims, saying that the logs of captured submarines and other records did not support them.[4] It is a known fact, however, that German submarines were not heavily armored vessels, and were vulnerable to severe damage from even a 3-inch gun—and merchant ships typically carried 4- or 5-inch guns aft. This is why U-boats usually remained submerged when they attacked armed ships.[5]

The most legendary example of merchant seamen sinking a ship—a story that is well documented—concerns the SS *Stephen Hopkins*, a brand-new Liberty ship, built at the Kaiser Shipyard in Richmond, California.* The vessel was in ballast, on the way to Dutch Guiana to pick up a load of bauxite ore for the American war industry.

Captain Paul Buck, an experienced United Fruit Lines skipper, made certain that the civilian seamen and Navy Armed Guard worked together, and told them he would not give up the ship if an enemy submarine or surface ship got them in its crosshairs. Each day at dawn and dusk, the master called General Quarters drills, in

---

*The SS *Stephen Hopkins* was named after the chairman of the first Naval Committee of the United States and the brother of the first commodore, Esek Hopkins.[6] A story could be written about each of the heroic merchant seamen aboard the ship: including Captain Paul Buck, Cadet-Midshipman Edwin J. O'Hara, Radio Officer Hudson A. Hewey, Bosun Phelps, Chief Engineer Rudolph A. Rutz, Second Assistant Engineer George S. Cronk, Second Mate Joseph E. Layman, mess boy Herbert Love, Chief Mate Richard Moczkowski, and Chief Steward Ford Stilson. All of them, with the exception of Cronk and Stilson, died defending their ship. U.S. Navy Ensign Kenneth M. Willett also fought heroically, and lost his life. (See also chapter 8, "Torpedo Run," page 86, regarding Rutz and Cronk; and chapter 15, "Hurricane at Sea," page 152, regarding Hewey).

which he organized combined gunnery operations between civilian and naval personnel.

On a rainy morning in September 1942, the lookout saw two vessels emerge from a mist in the south Atlantic, heading directly toward the *Stephen Hopkins*. Moments later, the *Hopkin*'s officers determined that the interlopers were German raiders, and a general alarm was sounded. The crew of one of the approaching ships—the auxiliary cruiser *Stier*—had been in the process of painting camouflage on the hull of the vessel when the raiders had come upon what they thought would be a sitting duck, the *Stephen Hopkins*. The auxiliary cruiser, which had six 5.9-inch guns, was accompanied by a supply ship, the *Tannenfels*. (In another engagement, a sister ship of the *Stier*, the *Kormoran*, sank a first-line Australian warship, the cruiser *Sydney*.)

The Germans raised their battle flags and, at one thousand yards, opened fire. One of their salvos hit a main boiler of the merchant ship, killing men in the engine room and slowing the *Hopkins* to a speed of only 1 knot.

Navy Ensign Kenneth M. Willett ran aft and manned the 4-inch gun, but shrapnel hit him in the stomach. He kept going, firing shells only a third as heavy as those from the *Stier*. Willett operated the gun until the magazine blew up, killing him. Navy Armed Guard sailors had also been killed in the forward gun-tub of the *Stephen Hopkins*, so Second Mate Joseph E. Layman took their place at the 37-millimeter gun, aided by mess boy Herbert Love, who passed shells to him. They were hitting the *Stier*, but then the *Tannenfels* fired, killing both of the merchant seamen.

Seeing the *Stier* on fire and listing, Captain Paul Buck brought the *Stephen Hopkins* around, so that its aft gun could fire at the *Stier* more directly. Having been hit in several places, the merchant ship was also afire, and sinking, but even so, it still had some fight left.

One of the civilian seamen aboard, an eighteen-year-old engine cadet named Edwin J. O'Hara (serving as a Merchant Marine Academy cadet-midshipman), helped several injured Navy sailors to safety, then ran back to the unmanned aft gun. He loaded one of the five remaining shells into the gun and fired it; then fired another and another, hitting the *Stier* repeatedly. Both German raiders then opened fire on O'Hara with their bigger guns, killing him instantly. (See also chapter 23, "Healing the Wounds," page 228.)

This brave young seaman had been an undergraduate of the U.S. Merchant Marine Academy at Kings Point, New York. Because of the need to man these ships on an emergency basis, O'Hara had been pressed into service as a seaman before receiving his degree.

A short while after O'Hara died, the *Stier* finally sank—followed by the SS *Stephen Hopkins* with its United States flag, the Stars and Stripes, still flying. A lifeboat from the merchant ship made its escape across misty, choppy seas, carrying nineteen men. Captain Buck was in fact seen on another life raft, but was never heard from again. Four of the men in the lifeboat died before it eventually made the coast of Brazil a month later, without the aid of navigation instruments or charts.

Years afterward, Hans Grunert (one of the *Tannenfels*'s crewmen) told a German newspaper they had searched for American survivors in the rough seas, without success. Then he said, "With our flag at half-mast we made a full circle around the spot where the Liberty ship had sunk, thus rendering the last honors to our brave adversary."

The SS *Stephen Hopkins* subsequently received the Gallant Ship Award from the War Shipping Administration, one of the few merchant ships to receive such a high honor.[7]

American merchant seamen deserve much of the credit for sinking the German warship *Stier*. (In addition, as I will discuss in chapter 23, "Healing the Wounds," page 228, Cadet Edwin J. O'Hara should be awarded the Congressional Medal of Honor posthumously—an acknowledgment denied him by armed-forces officials.)

Even though some German submarine crews were nearly as bad as the worst among the Japanese—machine-gunning helpless merchant seamen—many of the German sailors still held a high degree of honor and respect for their enemies. This had to do in part with the Germans' awareness that a common fate could await them all:

> *There are no roses on a sailor's grave,*
> *No lilies on an ocean wave,*
> *The only tribute is the seagull's sweeps,*
> *And the teardrops that a sweetheart weeps.*
>
> —German song [8]

There are many, many more stories of Merchant Marine valor that will never be told, because so many of their ships disappeared without a trace during the war.

EIGHT

TORPEDO RUN

Show me a hero and I'll prove he's a bum.

—F. SCOTT FITZGERALD

MORE THAN 8,300 U.S. MERCHANT MARINE SEAMEN DIED AS A RESULT OF enemy actions in World War Two, and thousands more were injured, many of them maimed. Hundreds of American merchant ships were sunk. As described earlier, terrible burns were common among petroleum tanker crews, and other civilian seamen suffered disproportionately severe losses as well. The "Black Gang" engine-room crews on Liberty ships and various merchant vessels were among the hardest-hit—and the most dedicated of all.

They took their critical jobs very seriously, and as a result of their efforts the engines kept running, enabling the ships to deliver their essential war cargoes. The procedure followed in the engine room of just one Liberty ship illustrates how dedicated and diligent these men were in their duties. During the war, oil products were in short supply; they were so scarce and so vital that cans of oil on this ship were kept locked up, with two keys required for access—much like the system used on modern nuclear submarines before a missile can be fired. On the Liberty ship, the chief engineer had one key, and the oiler had the other.

The bravery of engine-room crews was unmatched. They served in oppressively warm compartments belowdecks, unable to see the surrounding sea or to seek limited protection from incoming torpedoes or aircraft. Men working the engine rooms were unable to hear over the throbbing noise of the engines until an explosion occurred, often taking the men with it.

Merchant seaman John C. Burley told me how unnerving it could be below decks, hearing noises outside and wondering what they were. In one convoy, Burley heard explosions nearby, rattling the bolts of the ship; then one of the officers told him it was U.S. Navy destroyers going after enemy submarines that had been sighted in the area.

Many engine rooms took direct hits by torpedoes, killing the crewmen instantly. Those who did not die at once were frequently trapped in fires below decks. In fact, the captains of enemy submarines and surface raiders frequently targeted engine rooms, in order to stop the ships and make them easier to finish off.

This is what had happened to the engine room of the SS *Stephen Hopkins*, when one of its main boilers was hit. In the ferocious heat of the battle, described in chapter 7, "Valor at Sea," Chief Engineer Rudolf A. Rutz of the *Hopkins* sacrificed himself in order to save others. Even though he was badly burned, had a serious shrapnel injury to his arm, and flames all around him, he took heroic actions, and gave up his life to save others. His friend, Second Assistant Engineer George S. Cronk, wrote these touching words afterward, in a letter to the gallant seaman's sister:

> He and I were together all the time the battle was going on, carrying wounded men out of the engine room and off the decks and out of their quarters where they were shelled in their beds. When the "abandon ship" signal was given, he was putting life preservers on the wounded men. He told me to go to the boat deck, and that is the last anyone saw of him.[1]

Bill Bailey, a merchant seaman with much experience in engine rooms, and as a labor organizer said:

> It's a big difference from standing up on the bridge, to coming down four or five stories . . . to the floor plates of the ship, knowing that if a torpedo hits and they get the engine room, you're never going to see the 'up' deck. You're finished with the engine.[2]

Among the men in the *Hopkins* engine room who survived a first torpedo, the story of Third Assistant Engineer Philip C. Shera is particularly telling. For his actions he received the Merchant Marine Distinguished Service medal from the U.S. Maritime Commission. His citation read, in part:

> At the time the first torpedo struck his ship, he ordered the engine-room crew on deck, and alone remained to answer the bridge signals. A second torpedo hit the engine room, fracturing the steam pipes and killing Shera in the act of answering the bridge telegraph for full astern.[3]

Another merchant seaman, Charles Blackston, described what happened after a torpedo hit the engine room.

> A number of (men) about fourteen . . . were killed, never got off the ship. . . . The merchant crew had it bad because of the fact that the quarters were around the engine-room area, and (the torpedo) hitting in the engine-room area, it trapped them in their (quarters) and they were literally incinerated, cremated.[4]

Entertainer Bob Hope, who had a serious side, was a big supporter of the armed forces of the United States, and in one of his

1944 radio broadcasts he spoke of the brave civilians who manned our merchant ships:

> Listen, it takes nerve to go down to work in a hot engine room, never knowing when a torpedo might smash the hull above you and send thousands of tons of seawater in to snuff out your life. It takes courage to sail into the waters of an enemy barbaric enough to tie your hands and feet and submerge you so you can drown like a rat, without a fight. It takes courage to man an ammunition ship after you heard how Nazi bombers blew up seventeen shiploads of ammunition at Bari and not a man was ever found of the crews.[5]

I interviewed one of the lucky survivors of the terrible Battle of Guadalcanal. Civilian seaman Wilson J. Taylor served as deck engineer on the SS *George Himes*, a Liberty ship that was attacked by a Japanese torpedo boat at Guadalcanal in October 1943. It was one A.M. and U.S. Marines were on board, unloading aerial torpedoes and barrels of aviation gasoline. The ship was in shallow water, at Tenaru Beach. Taylor had just relieved a fireman in the engine room, so the fellow could eat. "I wasn't even supposed to be there," Taylor recalled.

Suddenly a torpedo hit, only thirty feet from him, at the number 4 cargo hold. Thinking quickly, Taylor turned off the fires in the boilers and shut down the generators, killing all electricity on the ship. Using a flashlight, he ran up the stairway onto the deck, where he put on a helmet and a life jacket, which the men called a "Mae West." Then he reported to his assigned battle station at the stern, where he "pushed" ("loaded") ammunition for the Navy gun crew.

Another seaman, Jack Faulkner, told me he worked as a wiper on the SS *Frank B. Kellogg*, a Liberty ship that had been involved in the invasion of Sicily in July 1943. He was only eighteen years old at the time. "Sometimes I wondered if I was going to make it," he said, as he recalled being in the engine room when German torpedo planes were attacking. "But I was young and didn't think about it much."

Faulkner also served on other ships during the war, transporting military cargo and troops to war zones. One of those runs was to Adak in the Aleutian Islands; another was on board an old freighter that took a full cargo of 100-to 2,000-pound bombs from San Pedro, California, to Kwajalein Atoll in the Marshall Islands. The Allies had an important naval and air base there, and the planes had run out of bombs. The ship went all the way over and back without any escort.

The crews of ships carrying bombs, torpedoes, and ammunition faced additional hazards. The risk of explosion was extremely high, and strict safety standards had to be followed. An incident at the U.S. Navy ammunition depot in Port Chicago, California, demonstrated the severity of the danger. There, on July 17, 1944, the Liberty ship SS *E. A. Bryan* was being loaded with ammunition, but it exploded with the force of a five-kiloton atomic bomb, destroying five ships and killing seventy merchant seamen and forty members of the Navy Armed Guard. The blast nearly destroyed the entire town of Port Chicago and was heard more than two hundred miles away.

I interviewed one man, Gary Wilt, who as a child was living in the town of Benicia at the time, about five miles away. He recalled looking across the flats at night and seeing the sky lit up with fires, and how frightened everyone was. Even at that distance, windows of homes were broken, and the outside doorknobs of Mr. Wilt's family home were blown off.

In all, more than three hundred people were killed in the Port Chicago accident. It was one of the worst Allied disasters of the war and slowed the delivery of military supplies to Saipan, where Dean Beaumont's Liberty ship went a short while later.

The titanic Port Chicago explosion led to a strike by U.S. Navy ammunition loaders, who claimed the U.S. Navy was discriminating against them because they were black. The men, who became known in the press as "the Port Chicago 50," said they were not being trained properly and that white Navy personnel were not engaged in the extremely dangerous job of loading ammunition.

While "the 50" were convicted of mutiny in a military court, then dishonorably discharged and sentenced to fifteen years of hard labor, the rulings were all overturned two years later, and the men were given honorable discharges.[6]

An even bigger disaster occurred in April of that year, when a cargoload of cotton aboard the freighter *Fort Stikine* caught fire at port in Bombay, India, and soon got out of control. Flames spread to other holds, containing ammunition, fertilizer, and kerosene oil. The ship, docked in the inner harbor of the city, exploded, creating an earth tremor so huge that it was felt in the Himalaya Mountains, a thousand miles away.

The ship also carried a secret cargo of 124 gold ingots that were being transported from the Bank of England to a reserve bank in India, in order to stabilize the Indian currency. Like manna from heaven, ingots rained from the sky in Bombay, many of them taken up by poor people. Half an hour later, a second, even larger explosion occurred, generating a tidal wave that lifted another freighter in the air and dropped it on top of a four-story building. All told, around fifteen hundred people were killed, and six hundred buildings were destroyed.[7]

Dean Beaumont told me of another incident, in Hawaii, which also underlined the danger of working on such vessels. An ammunition ship blew up in a back bay of Oahu during the war—an event that may have been sabotage. Dean's own ship, the SS *Brander Matthews*, would soon take on a very dangerous cargo of its own.

With water ballast in its holds, the Liberty ship headed back across the Pacific Ocean toward home, unescorted. Again they stopped at Eniwetok in the Marshall Islands. Inside the sheltered anchorage, Dean spotted the aircraft carrier USS *Ticonderoga* one of the new Essex-class carriers. Jimmy Carroll, a classmate of Dean's from Occidental College, was a petty officer second class on the warship.

Dean could read and transmit light signals, remembering the lessons from his Boy Scout days, to send messages between vessels, something the young radio operator on the SS *Brander Matthews* could not do. The radio man was so green that he couldn't even read signal flags.

Sending messages back and forth between their respective bridge decks, Dean and Jimmy Carroll arranged to meet ashore. They went to a big swimming party on the beach. The water of the atoll was incredibly clear, with sunlight showing all the way through to the bottom. Armed U.S. Marines were posted to watch for sharks. A lot of beer was flowing at the event, but Dean didn't drink; he had Coca-Colas instead. During the party, the marines shouted for swimmers to get out of the water—a shark had been spotted. They then shot it with high-powered rifles, causing the water to run red with blood.

The next morning the SS *Brander Matthews* continued its trip back to America. Out in the middle of the Pacific Ocean, the crew spotted sharks, and decided they would catch one for dinner, or perhaps a marlin or tuna. In a locker the chief engineer found a length of new rope, secured a big hook to it, and snagged a chunk of roast beef onto the hook. The vessel could only make 10 knots, and the lure-and-hook contraption bounced through the water in the ship's wake. The men left it there for two days, but no shark ever took the bait. They decided that the rope probably wasn't long enough; since water was frothing up from the propeller. The next time the crewmen used a very long line, stretching half a mile behind the ship, and it worked! One of the men had caught a good-sized tiger shark.

(Other merchant seamen were not so fortunate. Roy Purdy, now deceased, used to tell his friend Howard J. Hansen about the time an American ship was torpedoed and went down in those same waters. Sharks were tearing the men to pieces—troops and merchant seamen alike—until Purdy's ship came to the rescue, and saved the men in the water who were still alive.)

Back In San Pedro, California, Dean signed on as purser for the next voyage, while some of his crew members—upon learning that the ship would be carrying ammunition—switched to other vessels. Still, there was no shortage of merchant seamen willing to join the crew of the *Brander Matthews*. A new, more experienced radio officer signed on, but most of the other officers remained.

With a couple of days off, Dean visited Occidental College and saw several of his former classmates. He was wearing a khaki uniform with an ensign's bar on the collar, and explained to them that he was an officer in the U.S. Merchant Marine.

They said, "What are you really doing, Dean? Are you making another movie?" They remembered him and other members of his fraternity wearing uniforms home from movie sets, to don on the set the next day.

"No, I'm an officer—a purser. I was almost killed by a kamikaze at Saipan."

Dean's friends were in the Navy now, just apprentice seamen who did a lot marching back and forth in white uniforms. Some of them would never get off the college campus during the war, while Dean was already an officer who had seen duty in a war zone.

Two of his pals refused to believe he was an ensign or even in the service, so Dean invited them to have lunch with him on board the *Brander Matthews*. He told them the ship was being loaded and would be ready to go soon. Upon taking them down to the dock in San Pedro, however, Dean could not find his ship. His companions laughed, and one of them said, "Now we *know* you're kidding."

Then Dean saw the big gray cargo vessel at the end of a long dock. The dock was marked with NO SMOKING signs, red flags, and blinking red lights. The SS *Brander Matthews* had been moved to the ammunition depot at the end of the Pico Street landing.

Suddenly his friends were nervous, but they accompanied him onto the dock anyway. He explained to them how the ship had come back from Saipan with water ballast in its holds, and that the ballast was being pumped out to make room for the new military cargo.

As they were eating lunch in the officers' dining room of the *Brander Matthews*, they could see a great big sling outside, through the portholes, lifting large round objects from the dock. The loads would be held up over the deck of the ship, then would go down into the holds and crash around, shaking the entire vessel. Moments later, the sling would come up empty and go back down toward the deck.

"Twenty tons a load," Dean commented, as he continued eating. "What are those round things?"

"Oh, I don't know," Dean said calmly. "Five-hundred pound bombs. We're taking them over to India to be loaded on B-24s."

"*Bombs?*" one of his friends said, rising to his feet. "Let's get out of here!"

"Aw, don't worry about it," Dean said. "There's no pins in the bombs, so they can't go off." He smiled. "At least, that's what I hear."

The sling went by again, making a *whoosh* and a *thunk* as the bombs were loaded into the hold and the men below spread the cargo out. At the table, drinks sloshed in glasses as the ship shook.

Dean's nervous friend sat back down, but didn't seem very hungry anymore. The fellow soon made an excuse about an appointment he'd forgotten, and left. Dean's other friend did stay, and said how impressed he was that Dean was an officer, and that he had not realized how much the Merchant Marine was doing for the war effort.

The *Brander Matthews* loaded ten thousand tons of bombs—weighing twenty million pounds!—into the five cargo holds, plus eight U.S. Army trucks on deck. Just before departure, a seaman boarded the ship, a man in his forties, smoking a cigarette as he walked up the gangway. Dean and another young officer were at the gangway, and told him that smoking was not allowed on the ship. They informed him this was an ammunition ship, and strict controls had to be enforced.

Warning signs were all over the place, but the newcomer apparently hadn't noticed them, or didn't care to comply. He had a swaggering attitude like he knew it all, and seemed to resent being told what to do by officers half his age. Calmly, the younger men took the cigarette away from him and put it out, then handed him a life jacket and told him to put it on. Dean then brought out a thick pack and handed it to him, saying, "Here. Wear this, too."

"This looks like a parachute," the man said, looking perplexed.

"Yeah, it is," Dean replied, having found the old 'chute on board sometime earlier. "If you start smoking again, you'll be blown thirty thousand feet into the air, and you'll need this to get back down."

Dean's concerns were well founded. Donald R. Wellington, another merchant seaman, who worked on board the ammunition ship SS *Ames Victory* during the war, later wrote:

> The Port Chicago, California, ammunition loading facility had blown up in July 1944, and the Mukilteo (Washington) personnel handled their cargoes with "kid gloves." . . . We were warned that if the fuses and primers in No. 1 hold even tipped over, they could "blow" the entire ship. . . . In early March 1945, we (were) in the stormy Gulf of Alaska . . . I was at the log desk watching the inclinometer and noticed that she was rolling as much as 33 degrees. . . . The captain . . . sent the entire deck crew up into No. 1 hold to make sure those fuses and primers didn't tip over.[8]

The following morning, the SS *Brander Matthews* pulled out of San Pedro Harbor, took the channel out, and began its way across the Pacific Ocean. At sea they received an urgent message from the Navy, and were told to return to port. They had a special cargo of torpedoes that needed to be delivered to an Allied submarine base in Australia.

At a military dock in San Pedro, the Navy loaded five hundred new torpedoes onto the decks of the Liberty ship and on top of the number 1, number 2, and number 3 forward hatches, each one in a crate about 20 feet long and 4 feet square. They loaded for a couple of days and everything was strapped down securely. The boxes came up so high, around 20 feet, that the seamen had restricted visibility out through the three windows at the front of the wheelhouse. And even with the cargo holds already full, this did not technically overload the Liberty ship. With its flat bottom, the *Brander Matthews* could carry a lot of stuff; the ship would just displace more water—sink down lower—and go slower. This, of course, made it an easier, fatter target for enemy submarines.

For security purposes, Captain Nielsen was given a new route, with secret charts. The new instructions were necessary because two previous Liberty ships with torpedoes bound for Fremantle had disappeared, on routes that took them past Hawaii and the Philippines. They were never heard from again. So, instead of proceeding due west across the Pacific, the SS *Brander Matthews* was to head south past Peru and Chile, then turn west at the tail end of South America—at around 60 degrees south latitude, just before reaching Antarctica. They would sail across the southernmost reaches of the south Pacific Ocean. Then, south of New Zealand, they would set a northwesterly course, toward Fremantle on the western coast of Australia. This route was selected because Japanese submarine commanders would not expect Allied ships to be there, taking the long way around to Australia.

The crew of the *Brander Matthews* could only hope that the military planners were right, because the Japanese Imperial Navy had instituted a severe policy for their submarines: "Do not stop with the sinking of enemy ships and cargoes; at the same time you will carry out the complete destruction of the crews of the enemy's ship."[9]

NINE

THE RUSSIAN
GAUNTLET

*The sea is Death's garden, and he sows dead men
in the loam. . . .*

—FRANCIS MARION CRAWFORD

"THE SONG OF THE SIRENS"[1]

DEAN BEAUMONT WAS JUST ONE MERCHANT SEAMAN AMONG 215,000 WHO served the United States in the Second World War. These were civilians who volunteered for service. Some did it as an alternative to the draft, and because of that, the insulting term "draft-dodgers" was often used in reference to all seamen in the Merchant Marine. But name-calling has always been the lowest form of discourse, attempting to label a person or an entire group by fitting them into neat mostly negative categories—boxes from which they cannot escape.

The act of name-calling, so common in sandboxes and schoolyards does not require much thought. It is far more emotional than intellectual, and as such is inherently unfair. It is an attempt to dehumanize and reduce the stature of another person or organization, often for personal, self-serving reasons. Even if some merchant seamen were in fact eluding the draft, that did not detract from the fact that *they still served their country* by manning ships that aided the military effort.

Ships flying the Stars and Stripes of the United States.

It needs to be understood, as well, that some merchant seamen, such as Dean Beaumont, enlisted in the maritime service because they could not pass military physical examinations. Dean had always wanted to join the U.S. Navy, but medically was not able to do so. He did the best that he could, as a patriotic American. Still other men, in their middle years and older, were beyond draft age but wanted to give what they could to the country they loved. Captain Vincent F. Nielsen of the SS *Brander Matthews* was among them, a man who came out of retirement to command a Liberty ship.

Time magazine, in the December 21, 1942, issue, ran an uncomplimentary story on the men being recruited to replace merchant seamen who had been killed or seriously injured in the war. Up to that time, the Merchant Marine had been hit especially hard by enemy attacks, and the United States had not yet instituted adequate protective measures for the merchant ships—the armed guards and convoys that would eventually be in place. The story described recruits "who customarily greet each other as 'Slacker,' 'Draft-dodger' and 'Profiteer.'" In response, Captain Edward Macauley of the War Shipping Administration fired a heated telegram to the magazine, which read, in part,

> These "slackers" are training for a service which has suffered a higher percentage of casualties to date than have any of the armed services. . . . These "draft-dodgers" are volunteering for as tedious, as hazardous, and as essential a duty as there is in the whole war program. Those "profiteers" could make more money (on the United States mainland) than they will make on the long cold voyage to the arctic or running the gauntlet of "bomb alley."[2]

Captain Macauley's reference to "arctic" voyages concerned what came to be known as "the Murmansk Run," to two ice-free ports in the Soviet Union—the cities of Murmansk and Archangel. This route turned out to be the most hazardous of the entire war: more ships were sunk, and more seamen died, there than anywhere else. The journey was one of several rescue operations in which the U.S. Merchant Marine participated, transporting food, clothing, and military supplies to beleaguered notions in danger of falling to enemy forces. Among the beneficiaries were Russia, England, Australia, and the tiny but strategic island of Malta, in the Mediterranean Sea. The Merchant Marine even transported grain and other food to the starving people of Japan after the war.

Another rescue operation involved the British colony of Singapore. The U.S. Navy dispatched the American Mail Lines vessel SS *Collingsworth* to Singapore, under "special orders": to aid in the evacuation of American and British citizens while the colony was under attack by the empire of Japan. On this mission, the merchant seamen succeeded in rescuing eighty-two people. Captain Elmer J. Stull of the *Collingsworth* wrote this description in the ship's log:

> Ship anchored off Singapore during a bombing raid. Low clouds—and bombs dropped blindly . . . Raids increasing. Jap aim excellent. One big tanker goes up in smoke and flame. Much damage in city—twenty-six raids, most of them bombing, in five days. . . . AA (antiaircraft) guns barking. Shrapnel falling. Ship shivering as with bad malaria. . . . Ship ahead got two bad hits. . . . six bombs landed from one hundred feet to five hundred feet away. (Harbor) pilot arrives—shaky from having seen two pilots' launches near his get blasted with direct hits and all crews killed. Impossible (to) sail without tugs. All tugs fighting fires.[3]

During the centuries of seafaring, the weather has always been a deadly, unpredictable foe. The sea can be calm one moment, and a raging storm the next. In the arctic, mariners faced freezing-cold, powerful winds, and immense waves. Men were taxed to their limits, and so were their ships. Steel becomes brittle in extreme cold, as evidenced by problems with the hull of the *Titanic* when it went down in 1912, and by the welded-together Liberty ships that cracked and broke apart before their structural design problems were improved. If a man went into arctic waters, even wearing a life jacket, he would not survive for more than a few minutes. Sailors in open lifeboats either froze to death, or suffered frostbite and gangrene, forcing the amputation of hands, feet, arms, or legs.

Theodore Weller, one of the merchant seamen I interviewed, made the run on a ship with a Scotsman who had been on two Murmansk voyages earlier in his career, working in the engine rooms of Liberty ships. When a Liberty ship was fully loaded, it was only 15 feet from the deck to the water; whereas empty, it would be about twice that distance. This made it easy for submarine captains to distinguish full ships from those that were not, and to select their targets accordingly. It also caused a problem in high seas. The Scotsman recalled one incident when 30- to 40-foot waves washed over the entire ship and sent ocean water down the stacks, snuffing out fires in the boilers. It was eerie—the fires had gone out, one right after the other.* But weather was not the only foe on that most infamous of all runs.

One convoy, designated PQ-17 by the British Admiralty in charge, still stands as the biggest disaster of all. Winston Churchill referred to it as "one of the most melancholy episodes in the whole of the war."[4] It came to be known as "the Hell Convoy."

On June 22, 1941, the Germans invaded the Soviet Union, destroying or gaining control of much of their military production capacity, and inflicting severe losses upon the Russian Army. The

---

*Fortunately, these boilers did not explode. Other boilers exploded when cold water hit them—after their ships were torpedoed.

defenders needed to be resupplied with food, warm clothing, tanks, guns, planes, machinery, locomotive engines, and other important supplies.[5] The Soviets appealed to the United States for help, and in November received a lend-lease credit of one billion dollars from the Americans.[6]

The most efficient means of supplying the besieged nation was from Great Britain, using large, merchant-ship convoys. The shortest route to the Soviet Union involved going through the Denmark Strait, between Iceland and Greenland, then up around the northern coast of Norway to the ice-free port of Murmansk or the White Sea ports of Archangel and Molotov.[7] Unfortunately, ice floes sometimes narrowed the channel, forcing convoys to pass near large German military outposts on the coast, where there were air bases, submarines, and large warships. Thus the Nazis often had the benefit of a virtual shooting gallery along the Murmansk run, and took full advantage of it.[8]

Merchant seaman Peter Chelemedos was in a union hall in June of 1942, about to sign up for a ship taking part in Convoy PQ-17. Unknown to him, this voyage would become a complete disaster, sending hundreds of thousands of tons of ships and war goods to the bottom of the sea. While Chelemedos waited in the hiring room, he read about a Merchant Marine officers' school that was looking for candidates. On impulse, he signed up for it and became a Chief Mate—a decision that probably saved his life.

Perhaps this had been a premonition. Howard J. ("Howie") Hansen related a similar event to me. As a teenager—only thirteen years old—he had signed on to a merchant ship in Seattle, after claiming he was older.* He carried his seabag on board, went down a passageway and left the bag outside the quarters for the deck crew, where he had been assigned. It was around six-thirty or seven

---

*Mr. Hansen was the youngest known American merchant seaman to serve in World War Two. Other boys in the service were only a little older. Many of those under the legal age were seventeen years old, such as the mess boy from the SS *Jean Nicolet*, William M. Musser, who was murdered by the Japanese (see chapter 5, "War Crimes," page 61). Walter Silbersack (see chapter 14) enrolled at the Merchant Marine Academy at Kings Point when he was only fifteen or sixteen years old.

in the evening, in the middle of the war, and the ship was scheduled to depart in the morning, bound for the Far East.

Feeling nervous and apprehensive, Hansen wandered around the ship, looking around. Having grown up on the nearby Quileute Indian reservation, he had a strong sense of the spirit world, and he sensed something was not right here. The next thing he knew, he was back on the dock with his seabag over his shoulder, leaving. That ship would disappear out in the Pacific Ocean, never to be seen or heard from again.

On June 27, 1942, Convoy PQ-17 sailed from Rejkevik, Iceland, with thirty-four merchant vessels, including six new Liberty ships loaded with military supplies and equipment. Five previous convoys had been attacked and ships were sunk, so security was especially heavy this time around. The convoy was protected by an escort of four cruisers, two antiaircraft cruisers, nine destroyers, and two submarines, along with other vessels. In addition, one aircraft carrier, two battleships, three additional cruisers, and eight destroyers were nearby, in the North Sea.[9]

The following Wednesday, July 1, German torpedo bombers began attacking the convoy. I interviewed one of the merchant seamen who survived the PQ-17 debacle: Frank Medeiros of the SS *Gateway City*. His ship was an old World War One "Hog Islander"—named for the place it had been built, on the Delaware River. The smokestack of the *Gateway City* always belched black smoke.[10]*

Medeiros said that on July 3, "Lord Haw-Haw" (the German equivalent of "Tokyo Rose," whose real name was William Joyce) announced over the radio: "The Americans celebrate the Fourth of July tomorrow, and we shall provide the fireworks." Medeiros said they did exactly that—and they "almost cleaned us out," sinking three merchant ships in one day.

---

*The smoke made many merchant ships easier targets for enemy predators. Howard J. Hansen served as an able-bodied seaman on the SS *President Johnson*, an old silk liner that "belched black smoke all day and sparks all night." Liberty ships (such as the one Dean Beaumont was on) were also notorious for generating "billows of black smoke," making them even more susceptible to attack.[11]

That day, the American merchant ships were in radio contact with one another, and coordinated an act of remarkable bravery and defiance in the midst of the one-sided battle. To commemorate American Independence Day, the crews simultaneously raised large, new national flags, and sang "The Battle Hymn of the Republic."[12]

On the evening of July 4, the British Admiralty received a report from ULTRA reconnaissance planes that a German squadron had left port and was heading toward the convoy.[13] The attack force reportedly included the powerful German battleship *Tirpitz* (sister ship of the *Bismarck*), along with cruisers, pocket battleships, and destroyers. It was projected that this force would reach the British escort ships before the Allied escorts could move in and protect them. At nine o'clock that evening, the Admiralty notified the convoy that it was removing the naval escort, and gave the order for the merchant vessels to disperse.[14]

The decision to do this was not, as some have viewed it, an act of cowardice. Rather, it was a standard tactic in the *Merchant Navy Signal Book*, as a senior British naval officer explained:

> This was a pre-arranged manoeuvre, in which each ship had a course to steer differing from that of its neighbours. Thus, on the order to scatter, the convoy would open up like the petals of a symmetrical flower . . . the ships of the convoy would be steering away to every point of the compass, making it a lengthy business for the raider to round them up one by one and sink them.[15]

The men on the merchant ships were fearful, and some were upset at being abandoned in hostile waters. They were resentful, since they had embarked on this mission with the understanding that there would be strong military protection, and now that promise was being rescinded. Some of the men believed that the British sailors, like their American counterparts, considered merchant seamen beneath them, as second- or even third-class contributors to the Allied war effort.

That night, as the merchant ships fanned out in several directions, their uneasy crews did not sleep well. They wore their clothes, boots, and life jackets to bed.[16]

Over the next few days, the Germans used reconnaissance planes to locate merchant ships in these northern waters—a task made easier by the twenty-four hours of daylight at that time of year. The Germans never did send in the battleship *Tirpitz* or other surface warships. Instead they used Heinkel dive-bombers flying low over the water, and "Ice Devils"—U-boats that had been painted white.

The merchant vessels fired back with antiaircraft and machine guns, but to little avail. Ship after ship was sunk, their crews dying or cast into open boats on the choppy, frigid seas. One that made it through was the freighter SS *Bellingham*, hit by a torpedo that failed to explode. The next day, the ship's Navy Armed Guard shot down a Fock-Wulfe bomber, and the *Bellingham* finally made it to the city of Archangel.[17]

The losses to Convoy PQ-17 were catastrophic indeed. Twenty-three of the thirty-four merchant ships had been sunk, with a loss of more than one hundred thousand tons of cargo. This included 3,350 motor vehicles, 430 tanks, and 210 military aircraft—all desperately needed by the Soviet Union to fight off the invading German Army.[18]

When only a small percentage of Convoy PQ-17 made it to port, Russian authorities initially thought the Americans and British were lying to them, that they had not sent the promised supplies and equipment.* But as evidence accumulated, the Soviets soon learned what had really happened.

---

*After the war, David Milton, a merchant seaman who survived the Murmansk Run, described how desperate the Russians were for military equipment and supplies:

We finally got to Murmansk with these huge locomotives on the very top of the deck. The Russians unloaded them right onto the tracks. They brought up freight cars and attached them to the locomotives. We unloaded the tanks right onto these flatcars. They'd right away fire up the locomotives and shoot right out to the front. I mean, they weren't playing around.[19]

Subsequently another convoy was sent, and eight ships were sunk. This was an improvement, so to speak. But after that, the Admiralty decided it would be safer to send convoys at other times of the year, when northern lights would not provide round-the-clock visibility—even though the weather was worse, which had the benefit of making it more difficult for the Germans to attack them.

I asked Captain Frank Medeiros if he felt anger or any sense of betrayal toward the British Admiralty, and he gave me a surprising answer. Medeiros said he didn't blame them at all; that the Admiralty had had solid intelligence indicating their warships were in grave danger, and they needed to save them for another fight. Medeiros paused and added, in an emotion-filled voice, "We were expendable. The merchant seamen and their ships were expendable." [20]

No one could envy the plight of military officers who had to make tough decisions that sometimes cost the lives of merchant seamen. This also happened in 1943 when an Atlantic convoy sailed from Halifax to England. Thirteen ships were sunk by enemy submarines during the crossing. A naval commander in the escort group recalled going out to look for a U-boat and seeing the survivors of one of the sunken ships, on rafts and floating in the icy water in their life jackets; the escorts had decided to continue the pursuit of the enemy, and left them there. Upon searching for the men afterward, the escorts found no remaining survivors. Other crewmen in open rafts or in lifeboats were later rescued, but many of them died of exposure or had to have limbs amputated because of frostbite. [21]

One survivor said that many of the men had gangrene in their fingers and toes, and recounted the horrors of the hospital. "Unless you have personally smelled flesh rotting with gangrene, you could not imagine the stench." [22]

Even ships that made it through, often had serious problems. As David Milton recounted:

We were carrying tanks and locomotives. In the middle of the Atlantic, these tanks broke loose in a big storm. They were Sherman tanks, twenty, thirty tons. As the ship would roll, these tanks would just slide through the hole and bang up against the bulkhead. Then they'd roll the other way, just shaking the ship apart. So we pulled out of the convoy. We headed into the sea, while the deck seamen went down below to secure those tanks. They were riding them like cowboys, trying to hook cables through. Finally, they got the tanks lashed down. The convoy just steamed off and left us. They didn't even leave a destroyer with us. One ship wasn't worth it. They were trying to protect a hundred ships.[23]

Sitting in our comfortable homes, it is not always easy to visualize what it was like in those waters, The SS *Julia Ward Howe*—named after the author of "The Battle Hymn of the Republic"—sailed from New York City into the stormy waters of the North Atlantic. It was the middle of January 1942, and the ship carried sixty new Sherman tanks, four railroad cars, and other war cargo, bound for North Africa. The SS *Howe* joined a convoy, but the vessel's steering gear broke down and a fire broke out in one of the cargo holds.

In order to take care of these problems, the *Julia Ward Howe* had to depart the convoy. Cadet-Midshipman James J. Fitzpatrick later recalled the lonely, disheartening scene: "One by one the other ships of the convoy vanished over the horizon." He and his shipmates were left all alone in the North Atlantic, and a short time afterward they were hit by two torpedoes from a German submarine. Fitzpatrick, though knocked off his feet in the first explosion, survived. Others, including the captain and the chief engineer, were not so fortunate.[24]

Success in life is about priorities—about setting goals and pursuing them to completion. This becomes most apparent during the emergency conditions of war, when military planners and political leaders must make decisions for the benefit of nations and millions of people, at the expense of individual lives and equipment. Assets committed to a war effort are always at risk, and a certain percentage is always considered expendable.

Such was the fate of many of the valiant American merchant seamen, and the ships they sailed.

TEN

THE SUBMARINE

PARADE

	NO. SERVING	BATTLE DEATHS	% DEATHS
MERCHANT MARINE	215,000	8,380	3.898%
MARINE CORPS	669,100	19,733	2.949%
ARMY	11,260,000	234,874	2.086%
NAVY	4,183,466	36,950	0.883%
COAST GUARD	241,093	574	0.238%

—U.S. WORLD WAR TWO SERVICE DEATHS, RANKED BY
PERCENTAGE OF FATALITIES. (1 OF EVERY 26 AMERICAN
MERCHANT SEAMEN TO SERVE IN THE WAR DIED, AND EVEN
MORE WERE SEVERELY INJURED)[1]

THE CLANDESTINE MISSION OF THE SS *BRANDER MATTHEWS* WAS EXTREMELY important to the Allied cause. Two earlier attempts to deliver torpedoes to the submarine base in Australia had failed, with the disappearance of the ships and their crews. Now, as the *Brander Matthews* proceeded south along their secret route, Captain Nielsen quipped to Dean Beaumont, "I hope the third time is the charm." But the old man's voice was edgy, uncertain. On the decks of the Liberty ship, crewmen were more vigilant than ever, training their binoculars on the horizon, watching for any sign of the enemy.

They encountered very high seas along the way, particularly as they turned west around the southernmost tip of South America. When it was really rough, crewmen working on the decks (who always wore life jackets) were supposed to clip lifelines to railings or other solid immobile connections, to prevent them from falling overboard. As the ship approached Antarctica, the weather grew bitterly cold, with fierce, biting winds.

The urgency of the military situation had been caused by faulty torpedoes firing at the wrong times, or circling around and striking the very Allied ships that had fired them. The British had suffered heavy damage to two of their cruisers—the HMS *Trinidad* and the HMS *Edinburgh*—when their own torpedoes boomeranged and struck them, without actually sinking the ships. The Admiralty determined that severely cold temperatures had caused oil in the torpedo engines to solidify, jamming up the controls.[2]

American submarines were encountering similar severe, maddening problems. At the Newport, Rhode Island, torpedo firing-range, warheads behaved much differently than they did across the world's oceans. This was due to the fact that Earth's magnetic fields vary significantly around the globe. The torpedoes, designed to sense magnetism in the steel hull of an enemy ship, sometimes ran too deep or detonated too early in the Far East, since the magnetic fields there are stronger than on the eastern seaboard of the United States. U.S. destroyers used torpedoes designed to self-destruct if they went into a circular or "boomerang" pattern—but American *submarine* torpedoes did not have this feature. Also, in war games, American submarine commanders were taught to fire on sonar bearings at long range, which enabled targeted ships to see the white streams of exhaust bubbles and elude them.[3]

By the fall of 1943, the Allies had upgraded their torpedoes and were getting the new weapons into the fight, with improved results. The new design by the Westinghouse Company, called the Mark 18, was copied from that of a German electric torpedo, and closed the gap of technological superiority, which the Axis forces had held, to their advantage, up until that time.[4]

In 1944, however, serious problems surfaced. On March 30, 1944, the submarine USS *Tullibee* fired a Mark 18 torpedo at a target west of the Philippines. The torpedo circled around and hit the sub itself, sinking it.[5] This bewildering situation was brought to a head several months later, when a second U.S. submarine sank itself. That incident involved the USS *Tang*, the most successful American sub in World War Two. Its ace commander, Richard H. O'Kane, was credited with sinking a total of 31 enemy ships and 227,800 tons of shipping.[6]

On October 25, 1944, the USS *Tang* attacked a Japanese convoy off the coast of China, and, after a ferocious battle with enemy escort ships, was left with two torpedoes. It fired the first one at a damaged transport vessel. Moments later, the *Tang* fired at another ship, but the torpedo malfunctioned and traveled in a big circle, never reaching its target. Captain O'Kane saw it coming back toward the sub, and turned hard to port, trying to get out of the way at emergency speed.

The first torpedo hit the targeted transport ship dead center, causing it to burst into flames. But the errant second torpedo—filled with 565 pounds of Torpex explosive—hit the stern of the *Tang* and exploded. Only eight members of the crew and Captain O'Kane survived, out of the eighty-seven men aboard.[7]

Subsequently, the Westinghouse Company improved the Mark 18. There were suspicious that the rudders were jamming, and that the gyroscopic steering mechanisms weren't working properly. But the primary culprit turned out to be weak tail-vanes on the torpedoes, which were strengthened accordingly.[8]

Because of the types of problems that had been occurring, the U.S. Navy wanted to make certain that its submarines could use the redesigned torpedoes, such as those carried to Australia by the SS *Brander Matthews*. Unfortunately, the cargo ship had to take the long, slow route—all the way around South America—to make certain they got there at all.

Dean Beaumont, on board the vessel, thought about the new German acoustic torpedo he'd heard of—a concept stolen from his own father's design—and he wondered if the Japanese had any of them in their arsenal. Would the enemy ironically, sink his own Liberty ship with one of them? (Even if they didn't have that particular type of torpedo, the Japanese were said to have the best, most fail-safe torpedoes in the world at the time.)

The SS *Brander Matthews* had no escort for the long voyage, and only one 3-inch gun forward, four 20-millimeter guns on each side of the ship, and a single 5-inch gun on the stern. With its full cargo holds and packed decks, the vessel rode low in the water and plodded through the mountainous waves at only 8 or 9 knots an hour, making it an easy target for any predator that might happen to spot it.

But luck was with them. The trip to Australia took thirty-four days, and Dean saw nothing but water on the way—no ships, no Japanese, no icebergs. As the Liberty ship made its way northwest, toward the southwestern coast of Australia, the temperature warmed considerably and Dean found it too hot and stuffy to sleep below decks.

Forward of the wheelhouse, the torpedo boxes were piled twenty feet up, crates stacked five high and five across, strapped down to the deck. The military trucks were on each side of the deck, and Dean and other crewmen removed canvas truck covers from boxes inside the vehicles. They nailed wood braces onto the tops of the wooden torpedo crates and stretched canvas over them, then put cots and blankets under the coverings. This gave them a pleasant sea breeze in the evening, and protected them from frequent rain squalls. The men slept on top of the torpedoes, which were stored above the ten thousand tons of bombs in the cargo holds.

On hot evenings aboard merchant ships, crewmen often went outside and slept on top of hatch covers, not knowing how dangerous this was. If their ships were torpedoed, the hatch covers could fly into the air, the sleeping men along with them. When the freighter SS *Steel Traveler* was torpedoed on December 18, 1944, the Chief Mate was standing on top of a hatch cover at midships. Hurled into the air with the cover, the unfortunate man landed on a shattered piece of debris, which impaled him, a mortal wound.[9]

The crew of the SS *Brander Matthews* finally tied up at the dock in Fremantle, and found U.S. Navy personnel awaiting them. The Navy had big cranes and trucks, and unloaded the five hundred torpedoes quickly, then rushed them to the sprawling submarine base only a short distance away. Twenty torpedoes were loaded onto each submarine, in a special way. Since each torpedo was so long, it had to be loaded in at an angle, letting it down below the other decks and then, with a carrying mechanism, moving it into the torpedo room.

The following day, a parade of six submarines went slowly sailing by the Liberty ship, their torpedo rooms full. The naval crews stood out on the decks saluting the men of the *Brander Matthews*, in appreciation of the critical delivery. As he remembered that day in early 1945, Dean said to me, "It was quite exciting seeing them salute us. Afterward they went out and inflicted a lot of damage on the Japanese fleet with those torpedoes . . . so we helped win the war."

It did not escape his notice that the torpedoes would also be used against the merchant ships of the Japanese. One night as Dean went to sleep he thought of this, and felt compassion for the civilian crews of those vessels—much as submariners are known to empathize with their counterparts fighting on the other side of the war.

But such thoughts only lasted for a few seconds, as Dean remembered Pearl Harbor.

ELEVEN

THE HELPING
HANDS

Every man in the Allied command is quick to
express his admiration for the loyalty, courage,
and fortitude of the officers and men of the Merchant
Marine. We count upon their efficiency and their
utter devotion to duty as we do our own; they have
never failed us yet, and in all the struggles yet to
come, we know that they will never be deterred by any
danger, hardship, or privation. When final victory
is ours, there is no organization that will share its
credit more deservedly than the Merchant Marine.

—GENERAL DWIGHT D. EISENHOWER,

SUPREME COMMANDER OF ALLIED FORCES[1]

SINCE THE INCEPTION OF THIS NATION, THE PRIVATE OWNERS OF OCEANGOING
vessels have been accustomed to aiding the armed forces, providing
them with the essentials they need to conduct military operations. It
has not been merely a matter of law; the owners, and the merchant
seamen who worked for them, have considered it their patriotic duty.

By law, private ships become naval auxiliary vessels during wartime, available to transport war matériel and troops. In World War
Two merchant ships were under the direction of the U.S. Maritime

Commission, through the War Shipping Administration. President Franklin Delano Roosevelt referred to the United States Merchant Marine as "the fourth arm of defense"—in addition to the Army (with the U.S. Army Air Corps), the Navy (with the U.S. Coast Guard), and the marines.[2]

The cargoes carried by United States merchant ships during the war show clearly how much the Allied nations and armed forces depended upon these ships. Just a partial list of the essential cargoes hauled, included: tanks, LCTs (landing-craft tanks), field artillery pieces, munitions, jeeps, military trucks, ambulances, tires, fighter planes, airplane parts, PT boats, landing craft, locomotives, flatcars, boxcars, bombs, ammunition, TNT, dynamite, gunpowder, torpedoes, various other high explosives, poison gas (including mustard gas), gasoline, aviation gas (avgas), fuel, diesel oil, crude oil, kerosene, various other refined petroleum products, lumber and other building materials, steel, heavy mechanized equipment, bulldozers, tractors, telegraph poles, tools, ball bearings, medical and first-aid supplies, acid containers, chrome ore, asbestos, bauxite (the ore used to make aluminum for warplanes), bulk ammonia water, foodstuffs (including millions of cans of Spam and K rations), cigarettes, chewing gum, candy bars, soap, books, and U.S. mail. The merchant ships even carried homing pigeons for the Army Signal Corps, and war brides. Sometimes the cargoes were so secret and essential to the war effort that they were kept in sealed containers, under twenty-four-hour guard.[3]

After the war, one merchant seaman recalled what it was like on his Liberty ship:

> It took three, four weeks to load it. You'd see all these huge crates coming on board, labeled U.S.S.R: tanks, TNT, shells. Loaded to the gunnels. On the top decks, they put locomotives.[4]

A number of the trips were quite long and challenging. Just before the war, an 85-foot tugboat towed a 135-foot barge from the

West Coast of the United States to Midway Island in the Pacific. The barge had a crane on it for heavy lifting, and equipment to cut reefs, in order to provide safe harbor for Navy vessels. Another tugboat— either a "miki," with one engine, or a two-engine "miki-miki," according to the merchant seaman who told me about it—towed a military dry dock from the United States around Africa's Cape of Good Hope and up to the Persian Gulf, a journey of almost 14,000 nautical miles.

Merchant vessels also transported millions of American troops to war zones in the Pacific theater and across the Atlantic. In 1942 the Liberty ship SS *Joseph Holt* carried thousands of U.S. Army soldiers to Port Moresby in the Australian trusteeship of New Guinea on an emergency rescue mission. William C. Crozier, a third Assistant Engineer on the voyage, told me that the Japanese had been driving forward in New Guinea, routing Australian forces and threatening to invade the Australian continent to the south. The American soldiers were jungle fighters, trained in Panama, among the toughest men in the entire war. Even the cooks could handle rifles expertly. These forces pounded the Japanese into submission, driving them back across the Owen Stanley mountain range of New Guinea.

As described in chapter 9, "The Russian Gauntlet" (see page 92), the U.S. Merchant Marine was sent on a number of highly successful rescue missions—some involving the fates of entire countries, such as England and Russia. Australia was one of the largest trophies for the merchant seamen of the United States, yet another little-known fact in the history of these forgotten heroes.

The Merchant Marine carried enemy prisoners, too. The Liberty ship SS *Benjamin Contee* was transporting eighteen hundred Italian prisoners of war in August 1943, when it was attacked by a German torpedo plane, off the coast of Algeria. A torpedo hit between two holds full of Italians, causing them to panic and break past their guards in an effort to launch the lifeboats. There were only thirty-three British and American security personnel responsible for all those men. Fortunately, no merchant crew or Allied men were killed, but 264 of the prisoners died in the attack and ensuing melee.[5]

During the war, every U.S. Merchant Marine ship carried confidential military codes for communicating with military authorities and other merchant craft, documents the officers were instructed to destroy if the vessel were imperiled. Some merchant ships, such as the freighter SS *Malama*, also carried "ultrasecret" cargoes. Threatened by Japanese aircraft on January 1, 1942, the crew of the *Malama* scuttled their own ship, to keep the enemy from discovering the important military secret they carried.[6]

The United States government placed merchant seamen in harm's way as a part of the normal course of business during World War Two. Merchant ships, under the direction of the War Shipping Administration, were even insured by that organization against war risks. Despite the fact that the U.S. Navy did not succeed in making the Merchant Marine an official part of their service, the American armed forces, including the Navy, still held de facto control over the movement of merchant ships and what they carried in their cargo holds.

In comparison with seamen who served in the U.S. Navy, civilian merchant seamen faced a much higher risk of being killed or injured. This was due to the highly valuable nature of merchant-ship cargoes, combined with a lack of onboard armaments adequate to protect the ships. History is replete with examples of military forces attacking the weakest points in an enemy line—and that is exactly what the cargo ships represented. The sluggish merchant vessels were easy targets for aggressive submarines and surface raiders. The men aboard American merchant vessels, like the ships themselves, were considered expendable by Allied war planners, a necessary cost of waging war.

On board the SS *Brander Matthews*, Dean Beaumont, only twenty years old, was the ship's purser holding the primary responsibility of making certain that the travel documents of the crew were kept up-to-date and in order. He also kept track of finances, payroll, and foreign currency; and clerical duties, many of which involved typing, filing, and other typical office tasks. Dean worked closely with Captain Nielsen, helping to write up reports about activities such as disciplinary measures taken against crew members on the ship. In addition, the young ensign managed supplies in the ship's store, keeping track of what had been used and what needed to be reordered.

On top of all that, Dean was the only person aboard with medical experience, so Captain Nielsen made him "doctor and pharmacist," diagnosing maladies and prescribing medicines from the antibiotics and other basic supplies in the clinic on the ship. Dean's background in this area was not extensive, limited to his first-aid training with the Boy Scouts, and volunteer duties he'd performed for the California State Naval Guard. Still, he did his best.

Some of the mental conditions suffered by the crew were quite severe, compounded by the pressures of wartime, and involved severe psychological conditions, including schizophrenia. Depression was commonplace, and on a number of occasions Dean counseled men who were threatening to commit suicide. As young as he was, there were others aboard who were even younger—boys of sixteen, seventeen, and eighteen years of age. Some of them, having been under fire in the Saipan battle and in the aftermath, were nervous about the dangers of further submarine attacks.

Mail service was always erratic for merchant seamen, and at times nonexistent. But some letters and cards did get through. To a large degree Dean was strengthened emotionally by the strongly religious messages he received from his mother as he traveled around the world. He had always found inspiration from her, and did now more than ever, as she recommended biblical passages that were helpful in dealing with his own troubles. Whenever the ship pulled into port, Dean picked up letters from home and posted his own.

In one of her cards to him, his mother wrote, "May God bless you and keep you in the center of His Will for your life." Invariably his father would add a note to her message, wishing him good fortune on his voyage and a safe return home.

A devout Christian himself, Dean counseled his shipmates with the Word of God, saying, "Hey, there's a guy upstairs who can help you, and His Son is really going to help you." But Dean did not believe in shoving his religion down another person's throat; he used Christian principles, but never pulled out the Bible to quote verses, and never told anyone they would go to Hell if they didn't accept Jesus as their Lord and Savior.

Despite his inexperience, Dean was perfect for his job. Outgoing and personable, he was well liked on the ship. "I've never been afraid to talk to anybody," he said to me.

Dean Beaumont's willingness to help others was typical of the U.S. Merchant Marine itself—a fact that makes the unfair manner in which its servicemen were treated during and after the war, particularly upsetting to me and to those same seamen who served so valiantly. They deserve more from their government and from the citizens of the United States. Most of them were not fighting men in the traditional sense—except when some of them fired the guns — but that does not mean that they did not engage in "active duty" for the Allied cause. Every time they boarded a merchant ship carrying a military cargo and ventured into dangerous waters, these civilian seamen were in fact fighting for America and its Allies.

Immediately after World War Two, they should have received a full veterans' package, including medical benefits, education loans, home loans, and the like. But that never happened, and nothing can really be done to make up for it. So many of the merchant seamen who survived the war have died since then. They are but hazy memories to the current representatives in our government. But to the families of those men, and to their surviving wartime companions, they remain bright lights in memories—and will always be, for those who care to pursue the truth of the matter . . . who care to learn the forgotten history—the history that should be included in the schoolbooks of every child growing up in the United States.

How many American citizens know even a fraction of the true history of our Merchant Marine?

Unarmed, and lightly armed, merchant ships were placed in

war zones, by the U.S. government. This was like ordering an unprotected man to run across a battlefield carrying an important package while enemy soldiers fired big guns at him. The fact that he does not wear the uniform of the United States Navy, Army, or Marines, does not detract from his contribution. The essential package is delivered. In the Merchant Marine during World War Two, men died in the process.

As noted earlier (see "Introduction," page 15), the transport ship SS *Cynthia Olson*, was arguably the first casualty of World War Two, the victim of a Japanese torpedo launched moments before the attack on the Pearl Harbor. Those pivotal events occurred in the Pacific theater of war. Historian Ernest E. Barker says that a Merchant Marine vessel—the SS *Robert Moore*—was also the first American ship sunk in the Atlantic theater of war, torpedoed by a German U-boat.[7]

Merchant seamen were also hit by "friendly fire" from Allied armed forces. This occurred at Bari, Italy, on December 2, 1943, during a German air raid on merchant shipping vessels in the harbor. Seamen on those boats were killed when Allied shore batteries misdirected their fire and hit ships and men instead of the attacking aircraft.[8]

In addition to the merchant seamen who died in the war, more than six-hundred were taken prisoner by the Axis powers, and subjected to torture and forced labor. Conditions in the Japanese camps were particularly atrocious, since they never signed the Geneva Convention, which specified humane guidelines under which prisoners were to be treated during wartime.

When American merchant seaman Joe Vernick was imprisoned by the Japanese in the Philippines, he was kept first at the Santo Tomás camp and later at Los Baños. In three and a half years he nearly starved, as his weight dropped from 180 pounds to only 107. Recalling the difficult conditions, he said he only ate "banana-tree roots, morning-glory flowers, whatever we could find. . . . I remember a grain of rice slipping through the floorboards, and I'd spend hours digging at it with a toothpick until I got it."

Toward the end of the war, the Japanese decided to execute all the prisoners in the Los Banos camp, and lined them up in front of a large trench. "But at the last minute," Vernick said, "we were saved by the Eleventh Airborne. Someone had gotten word to [General Douglas] MacArthur, and nine C-47s flew over, dropping troops near the perimeter of the camp. . . . There was a lot of shooting and they rescued us."[9]

When prisoners were transported by the Japanese, they were often packed like sardines into the cargo holds of tramp steamers or into railroad cars that still had manure in them from cattle. In hot, confined quarters without water, adequate food, or medical attention, many men died before they ever reached the internment camps. Among the more horrible deaths were those suffered by the unfortunate prisoners on Japanese ships that were sunk by the Allies. Most of them had no chance for escape, and no life preservers, rafts, or lifeboats available to them.

Such was the case on board the *Junyo Maru*—"an old tramp steamer (that) did not look to have one more voyage in her," in the words of American merchant seaman Frank Patocka. An able seaman on the cargo ship *American Leader*, Patocka was taken prisoner by the Japanese after his ship was torpedoed. Patocka and other men were packed into cargo holds by the Japanese, who prodded them with long bamboo poles. He had to sit in a confined space beneath an improvised orlop deck, with only four feet of headroom.

During the voyage, Patocka was moved onto a crowded outside deck where he stood shoulder-to-shoulder with thousands of other men, with hardly any place to sit down. Just before sunset on September 28, 1944, the *Junyo Maru*, was torpedoed by the British Royal Navy submarine HMS *Trade Wind*, and broke in half. It sank quickly, but Patocka saw a life belt lying on the deck and jumped overboard with it. In the water, he was unable to put the life belt on, so he clung to it.

In one of the greatest sea disasters of all time, more than six thousand persons perished all around him—prisoners, laborers, and Japanese. Patocka saw desperate prisoners trying to board a small dinghy, and Japanese men in the dinghy fending them off with hatchets before being swamped themselves. Even prisoners who were taken on board Japanese gunboats, later drowned in the surf as the Japanese ordered them to jump off near shore and swim to a beach. Those who made it to dry land were packed into crowded Sumatran jails, where they slept on cement floors or platforms without any bedding.

The horrors were many. Years later, Patocka wrote:

> All through the night I kept clear of large groups in which many were drowning and grabbing at anything to stay afloat. I managed to get hold of a large plank that gave me support, but with this help I still could not get the life belt on. Early in the morning two English R.A.F. men floated by on a wooden ladder and asked me to join them. They were having trouble with the ladder and it was obvious that the problem was their uneven weight distribution. The three of us straddled the ladder and by keeping at proper distance we rode it all day. By afternoon we could clearly see palm trees and the beach but the joy of seeing land was soon nullified when we saw natives in their canoes spearing people in the water. They would spear a person, then drag them into the canoe, take off what clothing they had, then toss them back into the sea. The currents that took us close to shore took us back out again. At times we drifted (past) large groups of drowned (people). . . .

The following evening, Patocka and his companions were taken aboard a Japanese gunboat. He spent the next year in eight different Japanese POW camps, where he worked on various railroad-building projects. Toward the end of his imprisonment, Patocka was deathly ill from malaria, beriberi, pellagra, and dysentery. When the war ended, he was a miracle survivor, but weighed only 67½ pounds.[10]

Merchant seamen from American ships were put to work by the Japanese, building docks, roads, airfields, and bridges, and toiling in coal mines. They even helped construct the railroad bridge for the Japanese that was depicted in the movie *The Bridge on the River Kwai*.[11] It was so bad in the wartime slave-labor camps, that a bill was recently introduced in the U.S. Congress to allow survivors and their families to file lawsuits against the Japanese and German companies that operated the camps.[12]

The public perception is that only armed-forces veterans were victims of those infamous camps, but in fact that was not the case. All Americans in war zones were at risk, including the men of the Merchant Marine. On November 2, 1944, the American tanker SS *Fort Lee* was torpedoed and sunk by a German submarine in the Indian Ocean. Three men from the ship survived a 2,850-mile voyage in the number 4 lifeboat, over almost two and a half months. One of them died shortly after landing in Indonesia, while the other two were taken prisoner by the Japanese. Toward the end of the war, Japanese officers and soldiers went berserk in camps in that area, and attacked prisoners, killing and mutilating them. A war-crimes investigation determined that the two men from the SS *Fort Lee* were probably executed around this time, perhaps as late as September 1945—a month following the surrender of the Japanese.[13]

It is clear that merchant seamen not only worked in war zones under the direction of U.S. military authorities, but they were also treated like members of the armed forces when they were captured by the enemy.

In addition, there were numerous instances of merchant seamen coming to the aid of military personnel. On March 11, 1944, the crew of the SS *Marion Crawford* saved the lives of U.S. Army soldiers being transported on the ship, after an enemy artillery shell struck a hatch covering a hold containing ammunition. An explosion and fire ensued, and more explosions would be likely if the fire reached the rest of the ammunition. Faced with extreme danger, the merchant crew manned their fire stations and put out the blaze, enabling the soldiers to escape with their lives. For this, the seamen received a letter of commendation from the 382nd Port Battalion of the Army.[14]

Alan H. Knox related a story to me that occurred when he was working as second mate on the MS *Cape Henry*. Flying B-24 Liberators, the Royal Air Force had bombed German-controlled oil fields near the coast of Turkey. The bombers had to go in low for the mission, so a number of them were shot down by antiaircraft fire. The crew of the *Cape Henry* rescued fifty or sixty British Royal Air Force flyers from life rafts in the Mediterranean and took them to the port of Famagusta on the neutral island of Cyprus.

For the 1945 invasion of Okinawa by Allied forces, the SS *Sharon Victory* brought in C rations for the soldiers, and was in the process of unloading the containers when air-raid sirens went off. Civilian seaman Marvin Ettinger ran to the machine gun on the flying bridge of the ship, where he was a loader. Japanese kamikaze planes were attacking, and at precisely the wrong moment a U.S. Navy gunner "started to cry and he laid down at the bottom of the gun turret, moaning, 'This is nothing but awful.'" Remembering this, years later, Ettinger added, "You just don't know how anyone will react in the heat of the battle." The merchant seaman manned the gun himself, and survived to tell the story.[15]

In another battle near the Philippine island of Leyte, the freighter SS *Alcoa Pioneer* was hit by a kamikaze plane. Eleven men were killed in the nighttime attack, including five members of the Navy Armed Guard. One merchant seaman who survived the episode, Carl E. Nelson, recalled the horrific aftermath:

> Among the twisted metal and debris of every kind, including body parts of some of my shipmates, I searched, hoping to offer emergency aid to those who may have survived. One fellow, a good friend of mine, was lying on the deck groaning in pain, endeavoring to push part of his stomach back inside his abdomen, one of his severed legs laying on the deck beside him. He died in my arms in just a few minutes. Only two men

who had been on that flying bridge survived, both of them seriously wounded.[16]

On March 1, 1945, the SS *Columbia Victory** was approaching one of the western beaches of the island of Iwo Jima, to deliver ammunition to the U.S. Marine Corps headquarters there. As the cargo vessel neared the shore, however, two Japanese batteries opened fire, wounding a man on the aft deck—the fantail. Thousands of United States Marines were at the base and could have been killed in a huge explosion of the ammo carrier. Thinking quickly, the captain of the ship changed course and moved out of range.[17]

That merchant ship was one of the new "Victory" class, with powerful turbine engines and greater speed capabilities than Liberty ships. One wonders if a much slower Liberty ship could have survived the incident—a question that begs to ask: Why weren't Liberty ships made faster in the first place, to better protect their crews and cargoes?

At the very least, the answer points to the way Allied military planners gave precedence to warships instead of merchant vessels. Liberty-ship designers were not only told to keep the craft simple, but to design it in such a way that it could be built without conflicting with the wartime production of naval vessels. This had a direct bearing on the engine design selected for the Liberties. Allied military leaders wanted the manufacturers of turbines, diesels, and electric engines, to focus their construction efforts on power plants for new Navy warships. Thus the Liberty ships were designed with basic, reciprocating steam engines—power systems that could not move the heavily laden cargo vessels through the water very rapidly.[18]

At the onset of the war, the U.S. Navy also enlisted five thousand Merchant Marine masters and officers into the Navy, experienced men who had been trained for civilian service.[19] Because of

---

*Many of the Victory ships were named after colleges, while the C-type cargo vessels were frequently named after capes on the East Coast, and Liberty ships were often named after patriots and important black Americans.

this drain of valuable personnel, the operators of new merchant ships, which were being built at a record pace, had to obtain officers wherever they could find them. Men in their seventies were brought out of retirement to command ships—such as happened with Captain Vincent F. Nielsen of the SS *Brander Matthews*. Youngsters with no sea experience, like Dean Beaumont, were fast-tracked and made into officers.

Captain Nielsen and men like him were thrust into the war at an age when many of them were past the prime of their abilities, at a time when a greater number of crewmen would depend upon their decisions than ever before in their careers. Despite the obstacles presented by their advancing years, these men met the challenge admirably. So did the green, younger officers such as Dean Beaumont. But the whole situation was another example—like the inferior engines that went into merchant ships—where the Navy took the best of the resources first. The U.S. Merchant Marine was left to scavenge from the Navy's leavings, whether for manpower assets or ships and equipment.

This is not to denigrate the military or political leaders who made such decisions. Faced with the emergencies of war, priorities had to be set, and it was only natural that the armed forces would come first, to defend this nation and advance its efforts on all battlefronts. But it is one thing to make those tough decisions, and yet another to subsequently abandon the Merchant Marine when it came to granting benefits to the seamen.

As one justification for this, it has been said that merchant seamen in the war were "drunks" and "slackers," and no doubt there were some of both types in the Merchant Marine. But the drunks soon dried out on the ships, since they were not permitted to drink aboard most vessels, and even the slackers had to perform their duties or face the anger and disapproval of their shipmates and officers. The bottom line is that the ships passed through dangerous waters with critical war supplies and troops—and that could only occur if the vast majority of merchant seamen did their jobs and did them well.

Liberty ships, the "ugly ducklings," became beautiful swans in the heat of battle—delivering their precious cargoes over and over, no matter what the obstacles. Old men dug deeply and rediscovered their youthful abilities. Teenagers became men. Many of them were heroes.

For political forces to later deny military benefits to the entire U.S. Merchant Marine was like "throwing the baby out with the bathwater." It was not only foolish and a disgrace; it was not fair and not in the tradition of a great nation.

There are many, many stories of civilian seamen going to the aid of men in uniform. When the SS *Timothy Pickering* was bombed near Sicily in 1943, one of the merchant seamen, Second Mate George W. Alther, was killed when he helped a wounded naval gunnery officer.[20] When the crew of the SS *Jean Nicolet* were subject to torture by a crazed Japanese submarine captain in 1944 (see chapter 5, "War Crimes," page 62), seamen Harold R. Lee saved the life of a Navy Armed Guard sailor.[21] No rational person could ever claim that Alther and Lee were "cowards," "draft-dodgers," or anything other than great American heroes. But during and after the war, that is exactly how the men of the Merchant Marine were portrayed.

Even when merchant seamen did not have a well thought-out plan of battle, they demonstrated great courage and bravado. This happened early in the war when unarmed merchant ships went out with telephone poles set up on the fore and aft decks, rigged to look like guns, as the MS *Cape Henry* had done. The First Assistant Engineer aboard the Liberty ship SS *Knute Nelsen* talked about ramming an enemy submarine if they ever got the opportunity to do so; in addition, he recommended that officers carry sidearms, so they could leap from a lifeboat onto a surfaced submarine, gain entrance to the conning tower, and kill the commander.[22]

How many "slackers" and "drunks" were aboard the SS *Cedar Mills* when it answered the distress call of a French destroyer in the Atlantic Ocean? It was December 1943, and a ferocious storm had left the Allied warship in a perilous situation, short of fuel and listing at a 45-degree angle. The endangered French ship would have sunk, with all hands lost, if the SS *Cedar Mills* had not towed her a long way to safety, five days through bad weather and mountainous seas.[23]

Admittedly, there were heavy drinkers enlisted into the ranks of the Merchant Marine, and persons who did not wish to salute officers or demonstrate the traditional methods of showing respect and discipline. They completed their jobs, and did so efficiently, requiring far fewer men to operate a Liberty ship than the U.S. Navy needed in order to perform the same work.[24]

John C. Burley told me the U.S. Navy needed 220 men to operate a Liberty ship that the Merchant Marine could run with only 45, but the Navy—using Liberty ships as "attack transports"*—also had landing craft aboard. Burley said he was a fireman and water tender, one man performing both jobs; in the Navy, two men were required to do what Burley did alone. Similarly, Howard J. Hansen told me that the Merchant Marine had only twelve men on the deck of a Liberty ship during the war, their efficiency increased by using winches to pull in mooring lines. He said the Navy used manpower instead, and needed "twenty or thirty guys" to haul in the lines.

Of course, the U.S. Navy can dispute such numbers. An example of one ship, or a few ships, does not make a universe of all. The Navy might assert that they ran their Liberty ships better, or that they had operational responsibility for military gear on board that needed more men to handle. One retired sailor told me that the Navy-operated ships "more safety" with all of those men, without realizing what he was saying to me. The flip side of his argument shows how much danger the merchant seamen were in: They did their best with the small number of men they were allotted, and this inevitably resulted in safety hazards that caused work-related deaths and very serious, often disfiguring injuries on board.

The odyssey of Dean Beaumont on the SS *Brander Matthews*

---

*The U.S. Navy also used Victory ships as attack transports, which were larger and faster than the Liberty-ship versions.

was just one of more than two hundred thousand stories of American civilian seamen during World War Two. Their collective effort on behalf of the Allied cause was enormous.

In chapter 19, "They Earned Our Respect" (see page 180), I will show that merchant seaman were not actually paid *more* than members of the armed forces—one of many lies and distortions spread by detractors of the U.S. Merchant Marine. But it is also clear that American merchant seamen were grossly *underpaid*. They operated ships with skeleton crews, performing the work of at least half a million men, and were sent into battle with only the equivalent of peashooters to defend their decks.

TWELVE

THE LEAKY
LIFEBOAT

U.S. MERCHANT MARINE:	1775
U.S. ARMY:	1775
U.S. MARINE CORPS:	1784
U.S. COAST GUARD:	1790
U.S. NAVY:	1798
U.S. AIR FORCE:	1947

—FOUNDING DATES (FROM A SIGN AT A MERCHANT MARINE

CHAPTER OFFICE)

CONSIDERING STORIES LIKE THAT OF THE SS *CEDAR MILLS* RESCUING AN ALLIED
warship, and the captain of the SS *Columbia Victory*, who saved
thousands of U.S. Marines at Iwo Jima, we are presented with a difficult question: What have the armed forces done to show respect or
gratitude to the Merchant Marine?

The example of Convoy PQ-17 must be considered, and, to be
fair, it should be examined from all angles. Faced with annihilation
by German battleships and cruisers, the British Admiralty decided
to abandon the convoy in order to save their warships, keeping them
available for another fight. The result was one of the greatest maritime disasters in history, in which twenty-three of thirty-four mer-

chant ships were sunk. This demonstrates the priorities set by Allied military leaders: Armed forces and their equipment received precedence, while Merchant Marine ships and crews were secondary.

This attitude was in line with the allocation of officers before the war, when thousands of the best Merchant Marine officers were enlisted into the Navy. It held true for equipment, too, when the War Department decided to install inferior engines in new Liberty ships—making them sitting ducks as they plodded slowly through war zones—so that the factories producing turbines and other, more advanced engines would be sure to first provide whatever the Navy needed for its new warships. This competition over engines was only part of a larger picture, in which various shipbuilders scrambled for resources as well, including steel and other materials.

In the final analysis, the U.S. Armed Forces got the best equipment, and sometimes even superior manpower, and the merchant seamen got the worst of it—a situation that political and military leaders justified with the emergency priorities of wartime.

But the underlying atmosphere of antipathy toward the Merchant Marine remains troublesome, especially the fact that it did not change after the war. Because of the widely held belief that communists had infiltrated the ranks of seamen and their unions; that civilian seamen were disorderly, insubordinate, and overpaid; and that they were basically bums, the government and the armed forces only tolerated the men of the Merchant Marine, without embracing them.

The American war effort was a tense, complex relationship, involving the U.S. government, the military services, the Merchant Marine, and the American public. One government leader, President Franklin D. Roosevelt, tried to aid merchant seamen, but with his death in 1945, the Merchant Marine would lose its most powerful supporter and all hopes for a G.I. Bill–type program for the seamen would be dashed. Congress would put a stripped-down package of benefits, the Seamen's Bill of Rights, through the motions after the war, but the bill died in committee.

Some military leaders (such as General Dwight D. Eisenhower, Admiral Chester W. Nimitz and General Douglas MacArthur) made laudatory public statements about the Merchant Marine and the valor of its seamen, but in the end those comments would not result in anything tangible. There is an axiom that "Actions speak louder than words," and the military would turn against American merchant seamen after the war, lobbying in opposition to seamen's benefits. In effect, the military abandoned their comrades: the civilian seamen who had helped them win the war.

Early in the global conflict, when the Navy attempted to gain control of the U.S. Merchant Marine, the Navy did so knowing the military importance of the merchant ships, and that they had already been declared auxiliary naval vessels. The fact that the Navy's attempt to absorb merchant seamen into its ranks was unsuccessful, did not alter the basic fact that the men of the Merchant Marine performed the equivalent of military duties—in auxiliary naval vessels that traveled to war zones—and should have been entitled to full military benefits.

Sometimes when I write about the plight of the U.S. Merchant Marine, I feel like I'm standing on a soapbox, shouting at the top of my lungs in the hopes that someone will hear me. I feel powerful emotions, down through my fingertips, as I type. I think of all the merchant seamen who went down with their ships for the Allied cause.

I think of Joe Squires and Hal Whitney of the SS *Maiden Creek*. Squires, an able-bodied seaman, and Whitney, a deck engineer, stayed aboard the torpedoed ship to handle the lifeboat lines, allowing their mates to abandon ship in stormy, thirty-foot seas. Both men went down with the ship, but everyone else survived.[1]

I think of Oscar G. Chappel, of the SS *Dixie Arrow*. When the old oil tanker was hit by German torpedoes off the coast of North Carolina, the ship exploded and burst into flames. There were evacuation problems, and most of the crewmen found themselves trapped on the bow deck, unable to reach lifeboats. To protect his comrades, Chappel remained at the wheel and turned the ship into the wind, thus keeping the flames away from them. In doing this, the flames enveloped his own wheelhouse, and he died, as valiantly as any man in uniform.[2]

And I think of Chief Engineer Donald F. Haviland of the torpedoed Liberty ship SS *Henry Bacon*. He had a spot in the only lifeboat, but looked up and saw a young seaman, Robert Tatosky, still on the ship, at the railing. Haviland climbed out of the boat and said to Tatosky, "Here, you take my place. You are young and it does not matter so much if I get back." The chief engineer, with more concern for others than for his own safety, went down with his ship in the icy Arctic Ocean.[3]

There are so many more stories that could be told here—that *should* be told. But space does not allow for that, so I will just mention one more: the saga of Third Mate Edward J. Connor of the Liberty ship SS *John C. Calhoun*. His vessel carried a full load of high octane fuel. While it was moored at Finschhafin, New Guinea, a fire broke out on board, and the ship was in danger of exploding. To make matters worse, an ammunition ship was moored beside it, only a few feet away. Most of the crew abandoned ship, but Connor refused to join them. Instead, he rallied the chief engineer and the rest of the engine-room crew to fight the fire. While keeping the fire pumps going all night and eventually extinguishing the flames, Connor arranged for medical assistance for injured men, and managed to cut the lines that tied the *John C. Calhoun* to the adjacent ammunition ship, thus keeping the ships apart. Unlike other heroes who perished in the face of such dangers, he and the five men who stayed with him survived the war.[4]

After World War Two, American military authorities and their political lobbyists would fail to show respect or gratitude to the surviving men of the U.S. Merchant Marine.

Far from home, young Dean Beaumont had already seen battle, and he would soon face additional perils. He would learn, to his complete shock and dismay, that the nation he loved was about to abandon him.

THIRTEEN

PASSAGE TO
INDIA

With the Navy was always the Merchant Marine, in
which Americans have served with a devotion to
duty and a disregard for danger and hardship that
defies any attempt to describe.

—GENERAL DWIGHT D. EISENHOWER
SUPREME COMMANDER OF ALLIED FORCES[1]

EARLY IN 1945, THE SS *BRANDER MATTHEWS* DEPARTED FREMANTLE FOR A LONG
journey across the treacherous Indian Ocean, with ten thousand
tons of bombs in the five large holds of the ship. Even after the
crated torpedoes had been unloaded in Australia, the vessel was
still so heavily laden that it could make only 9 knots per hour, thus
keeping it very vulnerable to enemy submarines.

Aboard the ship, Dean Beaumont still bore the marks of the
injuries he had suffered in the fighting at Saipan. His knees had gotten banged up pretty badly, forcing him to hobble around and wince
with pain, especially when the seas were rough. He had pain in one
elbow, too. In addition, the deep scrape on his forehead had not
healed well. There had been no infection and the scab had fallen
away, but the area remained reddish purple.

But Dean was not a man to worry about such things, or to

complain. Almost overshadowing his new injuries, he was pleased that his chronic asthma had improved dramatically in the fresh, salty ocean air. He seemed to be breathing better than he ever had in his life.

A dedicated Christian, Dean came to believe more than ever that God was watching out for him, and that the good Lord would always bring him through even the worst of difficulties. The young officer had no fear of death or serious injury. Unafraid that an attack might occur in the middle of the night, Dean didn't sleep fully clothed with his shoes on, like some of the other men did: some even slept in their life jackets, as uncomfortable as that sounds. Instead, he tried to put his life completely in the hands of God.

Dean put it to me this way: "I never had any qualms about dying in the war. I knew I had done the very best I could, and that the guy upstairs was going to help me. That was all I needed to know."

But Dean was not without worries. Some of the younger men, hearing the war stories told by older seamen—and from their own limited battle experiences—had great fears for their own safety, and suffered a lot of anxiety over this. Dean, himself not much older than they were, counseled them, as much as he could, and they looked up to him. But he felt inadequate for the task, and empathized with the troubles they revealed to him. He was trying to allay their fears and depression, but felt depression himself.

In the Indian Ocean, a big storm hit the SS *Brander Matthews*, and the ship and its crew were knocked around quite a bit. As the "doctor and pharmacist" for the crew, Dean treated a number of minor injuries, including a broken hand. The storm subsided a little, but only down to gale force, and the water remained rough.

Dean noticed a young seaman standing on the stern of the ship, looking down over the edge. The man wore yellow rain gear with a hood, but the jacket was open at the front, flapping in the breeze. Dean hurried out to talk with him.

The young man said he came from a poor neighborhood, and he had a lot of troubles and regrets. He wished he had never volunteered for the Merchant Marine, and wanted to end everything. He was going to leap into the sea.

"You're going to jump?" Dean asked.

The man nodded. He had "peach fuzz" on his face, and kept staring down at the roiling water around the ship.

"Well, that's going to foul us up," Dean said, "because it means a whole lot of paperwork for me to complete. You do know that if you jump off in the middle of a storm, we can't come back and get you?"

"Yeah, I know."

"Do you know what's underneath the water out there?"

"Huh?" The seaman looked at Dean inquisitively.

"We're in an area where there are a lot of sharks—tigers, white-tips, great whites—and they are *huge*. You're swimming and you reach out, and all of a sudden you lose an arm. You're kicking, and all of a sudden you lose a leg."

The young man gripped the railing tightly. He appeared to be affected by the comments, and finally said, "I don't want to lose a leg."

Dean led him back inside and gave him a sedative, then watched over him closely for weeks, until he got better. In remembering the incident, Dean said to me, "He was going to kill himself, but didn't want to get bitten before he died, didn't want to lose an arm or a leg." Somehow, the young purser knew exactly what to say to avoid a tragedy.

But Dean didn't know what to say to himself, didn't have anyone to counsel *him*. Waves of despondency would hit him like storms, and then he would go through periods in which he felt a little better. His moods changed like the weather. Through it all, Dean noticed that it seemed to help his state of mind if he rendered assistance to others, because it took his thoughts off himself. He liked to feel he was making a difference.

But that was not always easy. In war zones, there were a lot of tensions on the ship. Sometimes merchant seamen couldn't take the pressures, and had to be sent to mental hospitals at the first oppor-tunity. The jobs on board ship were not easy, and the men working below decks, where they could not see what was going on, often had it the worst.[2]

The American merchant seamen who served in World War Two were not perfect, and I make no attempt to present them as such. There were drinking problems in the merchant service, and some officers permitted those activities—but, for the most part, only on shore. Of course, there were instances in which booze was smuggled aboard ships by seamen, or where alcohol was distilled on board from a mixture of fermented bread and vanilla extract, as well as the brewing of beer, but these were not widespread infractions. There were even stories of merchant ships carrying a lot more 100-proof alcohol than they actually needed to top off the compass.[3]

But members of the armed forces also had their own drinking problems; though, admittedly, their activities were better corralled by the military police and other authorities. The Merchant Marine did not have a comparable police force.

It must be kept in mind that the merchant service was—almost by definition—a far more casual operation. The men were permitted to behave as independent, sometimes grumpy sorts if they wanted to do so. Still, like their military counterparts, the merchant seamen got their jobs done. They just completed them in a different manner.

It is an observable fact of human nature that we tend to distrust and dislike persons who are unlike us, who think differently than us, who do things in ways that we do not understand or condone. I believe this was a factor in the attitude that certain Navy officers and other armed-forces personnel exhibited toward the Merchant Marine. But those critics, so judgmental and narrow-minded, overlooked a much bigger picture which should have been obvious to them all: The armed forces could not have succeeded without the fine work of the U.S. Merchant Marine.

Dean Beaumont witnessed the effects of heavy drinking by members of his own crew. He disapproved of the wild activities of some of his crew members whenever the SS *Brander Matthews* pulled into port. To make matters worse, some of the older crew-men took their younger counterparts in tow, and led them ashore in search of booze and loose women. Even though the alcoholics on the ship had been forced to dry out by the prohibition against drink-ing on board (which Captain Nielsen strictly enforced), they still remained binge drinkers when on shore leave. And, since there were no guards posted at the gangway, they were sometimes able to sneak women aboard to spend the night, or the occasional bottle of whiskey or rum. When the ship was ready to leave, however, things began to straighten out. The men went back to work, the women returned to the brothels and bars, and the Liberty ship sailed.

Whenever Dean went ashore himself, he often sought out places of historical or cultural interest—forts, museums, famous battle-fields, ancient religious sites. He didn't chase women, and he didn't drink. Some of his crewmates seemed emotionally lost to him, in a spiritual vacuum. He was one of the few Christians on the ship, one of the few men of any religious persuasion at all.

Added to the pressures of the war, Dean found this environment deeply troubling, and increasingly oppressive. The men were in effect self-medicating, using alcohol to forget their troubles. The sea has always been a dangerous place for sailors, and there have been drinking mariners for as long as there have been ships. But tensions were much higher in the wartime atmosphere, with every-one constantly on edge, looking for submarines and raiders. When the men reached port, they went off like pressure valves releasing steam.

There were those on the *Brander Matthews* who did not carouse or drink heavily, and Dean felt closest to them, including Bill Hower, a teenager who had signed on as radio officer for this voyage. Others who didn't drink to excess were Captain Nielsen, the chief engineer, and the Chief Mate, who Dean played bridge with. Also, the experienced Second Mate Victor Bash and Al Susala, an able seaman, practiced moderation. They were among the hardest-working men on the vessel.

There was no on-board entertainment, only books to read,

including a big trunkload of paperbacks brought aboard by the Navy Armed Guard. The crew had no movies, or even comics. Sometimes Dean found his father's sea-battle paintings in month-old newspapers from the United States that showed up in various ports—and they always thrilled the young man. He remembered going out on naval vessels with his father years before, and looked forward to the time when the war would be over and they could do that again, together.

Neither were there any musical instruments aboard, with the exception of a harmonica and a Jew's harp—a metal device held between the jaws and plucked, making, in Dean's words, "*boing-boing, whang!*" sounds. The seamen had a lot of time on their hands when their work was finished, but they didn't organize much of anything except card games. They talked and listened to the radio, including programs from the Armed Forces Network and from the Japanese propagandist "Tokyo Rose," a woman they ridiculed.

As usual, they would exchange sea stories, in the age-old tradition of seagoing men. Second Mate Bash, a ruddy fellow in his forties, told about Liberty ships lost on their maiden voyages. When Dean Beaumont related that to me years later, he could not recall the names of the ships, but Bash may have been referring to the SS *Richard D. Spaight* or the SS *John A. Treutlen* torpedoed by U-boats in 1943 and 1944, respectively. Another was the *Alexander Macomb*, torpedoed by a German submarine off the coast of New England. That ship, like the *Brander Matthews*, had carried a dangerous cargo, including ammunition and other explosives. When the torpedo hit the aft holds, they blew up and burst into flames, killing ten men.[4]

Another maiden-voyage loss was the tanker SS *Gulfamerica*, torpedoed by a German submarine in 1942. Moments later, the U-boat also shelled the ship, causing seamen to jump overboard. A number of them drowned due to trouble with their cork lifejackets, which rode too high up on their necks, forcing their heads underwater.[5]

Hearing such stories, and reading about them in English-language newspapers from various ports, some of the crewmen wondered if their luck would continue to hold, or if it would run out. The SS *Brander Matthews* had gone a long way around the world on two voyages now, and the longer time they spent in war zones, plodding along so slowly, the higher the odds that they would be discovered by an enemy submarine or surface ship. In just a few violent moments, things could change dramatically. And while the crew probably didn't realize it, their ship design—even though it had been produced for only a couple of years now—was already obsolete. The faster Victory ships were in production now, vessels that were much better suited for long runs across the Pacific Ocean and around the world.

To exacerbate the situation, the SS *Brander Matthews* was carrying a highly explosive cargo of aircraft bombs, making the ship susceptible to a terrible explosion if attacked. Similar merchant vessels had been known to disappear from the face of the earth after cataclysmic blasts.

A number of ships were sunk in nighttime attacks during the war, while men slept in their bunks. In 1942, the unarmed freighter SS *Caribsea* was torpedoed at two in the morning, and sank in three minutes, before lifeboats could be launched. The freighter SS *Losmar* was also torpedoed at two A.M. that same year, and sank in two minutes. The tanker SS *Gulfstate* was torpedoed at three-fifteen A.M., and sank in three minutes. In those three attacks, on dark, lonely nights in the middle of the ocean, a total of seventy-five merchant seamen and nine members of the Navy Armed Guard were killed.[6]

Finally, the SS *Brander Matthews* arrived at the mouth of the Ganges River. The gray-haired captain, Vincent F. Nielsen, stood vigilantly on the bridge of the ship, issuing terse commands. The ship proceeded carefully up one of the main channels, the Hooghly River, for an eighty-mile journey to the sprawling city of Calcutta. Due to extreme tidal changes, dangerous shoals, and shifting sandbars, the Hooghly required constant dredging and other engineering measures.

As the SS *Brander Matthews* made its way upriver, the captain had to be wary of such problems, and also of the numerous small boats, barges, and other vessels using the crowded, meandering waterway. Clumps of thick vegetation lined either side, along with ramshackle settlements. It was a hot, humid day, causing the crewmen to work with their shirts off.

The Ganges, along with its tributaries and channels, is considered the sacred river of the Hindus, since it is said to be the personification of the mythological goddess Ganga Mata, or "Mother Ganges." As the large gray ship pulled into its dock at Calcutta, Dean saw Hindu men bathing in the muddy river to cleanse them of their sins, drinking the holy water, and praying along the shore, dressed in simple white clothes and turbans.

The Liberty ship remained in port for several days, where damage from the storm was repaired and the vessel was repainted, from the masts down. The lifeboats had been bumped around in the storm and required special attention, along with the masts, booms, and riggings of the ship. While repair work commenced, bombs were unloaded from the holds into large trucks that would take them to a train bound for an Allied airfield to the north.

The Japanese had attacked the coastal cities of China, including Shanghai and Hong Kong, but had not been able to defeat Chinese forces in the western interior. Using the Burma Road, the Allies had been supplying those forces, which were under the command of General Chiang Kai-shek. In 1942, however, the Japanese conquered Burma, and their next step was obvious. They were attempting to isolate China and overrun it. The Allies countered this strategy by initiating an ambitious airlift program for China, flying cargo planes from bases in India over the rugged section of the

Himalayas known as "the Burma Hump." The 500-pound bombs from the SS *Brander Matthews* would be loaded onto B-24s for bombing missions against Japanese forces that were in China.[7]

The following morning, Dean and several of his shipmates were standing on the stern of the Liberty ship, watching activity around a vessel behind them that was unloading wheat. Some grain was spilling onto the dock in the process, right next to a railroad track. Back in 1945, as today, nothing was wasted in India. Children scurried about with bent pieces of cardboard and large tin cans with makeshift handles. They used the cardboard to scoop up grain and dump it into the cans. The kids then hurried off with their pickings.

Curious about where they were going, Dean and one of his friends followed a small boy and girl as they climbed a steep, rugged hillside with huts clinging to it. The children wore torn, dirty clothes, and were barefoot. Their black hair was long and raggedly trimmed. Dean always was interested in local cultures, and thought this might be interesting, and educational. So the pair of seamen, undetected since the streets were so crowded, watched as the youngsters reached the top of the hill and entered a lean-to. It was a simple tin structure adjacent to an old earthen wall, and had a little doorway. Soon the mother and father could be seen bustling about inside, excited about the arrival of the food.

The children were sent back out with empty buckets, and went back down the hillside. They went back down to the Hooghly River, to a place where people were bathing and washing their clothes, pounding them on rocks along the shore. Garbage floated in the river, and not far upstream the ashes of human bodies were being scattered on the water, floating in this direction. The boy and girl scooped up buckets of the dirty water and hauled them home, struggling to carry the heavy weights up the hillside.

Back at their hut, the mother and father were plastering brown muck on the outside of their little hovel, using pieces of wood as tools. Then the family disappeared inside and nothing more happened. It was getting very hot, well over a hundred degrees Fahrenheit. Finally, the curious Westerners gave up and returned to their ship.

From talking with other seamen, they soon learned what was going on. The people were drying cow dung in the sun, which hardened in a couple of hours, shriveled up, and dropped to the ground. They used it instead of firewood, which was very difficult to find in the crowded settlement. (Cows, on the other hand, were abundant; they are considered sacred by the Hindus.) In the little shelter, the mother of the two children would start a cookfire, boil the water to rid it of unhealthy bacteria, and then use it to cook the wheat.

The next day, Dean saw a cow walk into a food market and bump around inside, knocking things over and breaking glass. The shop's owner did not disturb it, but did rush ahead of the beast, trying to save his merchandise from destruction. Presently the sacred cow emerged onto the cobblestone street and dropped a load of excrement. Three women rushed forward with shingles of wood, scooped up the remains, and hurried off.

Now, Dean understood.

A couple of days later, the SS *Brander Matthews* took on water ballast and headed back down the Hooghly River and out into the Indian Ocean. The ship made its way southwest, bound for the city of Colombo on the island of Ceylon (present-day Sri Lanka), off the southern tip of the Indian subcontinent. It would be a journey of thirteen hundred nautical miles, from the mouth of the Ganges.

Relieved to have made it across the treacherous waters where storms and Japanese submarines lurked, the crewmen went ashore in Colombo and looked around. It was the middle of the day, and extremely hot. White buildings along the shore sparkled in bright sunshine.

Some of the crew caught local pedal-taxis and ventured out into the verdant countryside, unaware of the fact that there are more cobras per person in Ceylon than anywhere else in the world. But the luck of the *Brander Matthews* seamen still held, and no mishaps befell them—for the time being.

FOURTEEN

INVASION
FORCES

They brought us our lifeblood and they paid for it
with their own. . . . When it was humanly possible,
when their ships were not blown out from under
them by bombs or torpedoes, they delivered their
cargoes to us who needed them so badly.

—GENERAL DOUGLAS MACARTHUR[1]

MANY OF THE MEMBERS OF DEAN BEAUMONT'S CLASS AT THE MILITARY ACAD-
emy lost their lives during World War Two, including Jimmy Clune
and Erich von Stroheim Jr. All except two had enlisted in the U.S.
Army; Jimmy Carroll went into the U.S. Navy, and Dean joined the
U.S. Merchant Marine. The fighting men died on the islands of the
Pacific Ocean and on the beaches of Normandy. They were killed in
North Africa and in the landings at Anzio, and in the campaign to
free Rome from the viselike grip of the Axis.

In every one of those military operations, and more, the U.S.
Merchant Marine played an essential supporting role. The major
Allied invasions were made possible only because troop ships, many
of them merchant vessels, had transported millions of soldiers overseas. Approximately two-thirds of the military personnel were

taken to war zones across the Atlantic Ocean, and the rest went to the Pacific theater.[2]

When General Douglas MacArthur led U.S. forces in the liberation of the Philippines in 1944, he was supported by military supplies and personnel that had been transported by the U.S. Merchant Marine. In the battle of the Philippine Sea—which Peter Chelemedos heard about just before he was torpedoed—and in the battle of Leyte Gulf, the Merchant Marine was there, making victory possible. The Merchant Marine contributed mightily to the successful American invasions of Iwo Jima and Okinawa as well, only a few months later. Each American fighter in the Pacific theater of war needed around fifteen tons of supplies per year, even more than in the European theater.[3]

William C. Crozier served as an assistant engineer on three merchant ships during the war. One of them—a Liberty—transported water-purification equipment from Guadalcanal to Okinawa in 1945. It seems that the Japanese, before being forced out of Okinawa, had poisoned the water systems, in addition to other booby traps they left behind.

On another voyage, Crozier's ship carried TNT and construction materials needed to build the Burma Road. Another time, his ship had P-38 fighter planes on board, six of them lashed to cradles welded to the decks. The merchant crew took them—and the Chinese aviators who were going to fly them—to Karachi, India.

Hearing such stories, it is clear that the entire Allied war effort was a huge puzzle, with billions and billions of pieces, large and small, that had to be fitted together. Allied military planners worked on a massive scale, directing the movement of pieces all over the globe. Water-purification equipment was needed here, road-building materials over there, P-38s on the other side of the world . . . The U.S. Merchant Marine carried every type of cargo imaginable, and, when the picture puzzle was complete, victory would be achieved.

Generals MacArthur and Eisenhower were always highly complimentary of the contribution of merchant seamen, and so was President Roosevelt. They knew what it would take to put the final victory together. But that contribution would come at an extremely high price.

Some of the worst Merchant Marine losses involved the Allied invasion of North Africa, against German and Italian forces. On New Year's Day of 1943, the SS *Arthur Middleton* was torpedoed by a German submarine off the coast of Algeria, shortly after delivering the first LCTs (landing-craft tanks) to the Allied forces in Africa. With a cargo of munitions still on board, the ship blew up and broke in half at sea, killing seventy-eight out of eighty-one men aboard. Only three members of the Navy Armed Guard survived.[4]

In a Mediterranean convoy bound for North Africa, the Liberty ship SS *Paul Hamilton* was carrying high-caliber explosives and 504 U.S. Army Air Force personnel, in addition to a crew of forty-seven merchant seamen and twenty-nine from the Navy Armed Guard. On April 20, 1944, German torpedo planes attacked off the coast of Algeria, obliterating the vessel and everyone aboard. The destroyer *Lansdale* also was sunk in the battle.[5]

The Germans, with their scientists working on advanced military technology, had other surprises in store for the Allies. A friend of mine told me that his father—Walter Silbersack—had been an officer in the United States Merchant Marine during the war. During the "Battle of the Bulge," in late 1944 and early 1945, Silbersack's ship was docked at a pier in Brussels Harbor. The crew was unloading their cargo when a V-2 rocket struck, like those the Germans fired at the center of London during "the Blitz." The rocket came down on top of the merchant ship, penetrated the decks and hull, and exploded underwater, lifting the craft out of the water. Since they were in shallow water and rescue services arrived quickly, most of the crew survived, including Silbersack.

Similarly, in 1943, the British troop carrier *Rohna* was sunk by a German rocket, killing a total of 1,015 U.S. soldiers. In that same incident, however, a Luftwäffe bomber flew in close and dropped what looked like a small airplane. In reality it was an Hs 293 rocket-powered bomb, radio-controlled by a bombardier operating a joystick from inside the bomber.[6]

One of the most legendary episodes in the history of the U.S. Merchant Marine occurred during "Operation Pedestal," the code name of a convoy sent to rescue the strategic Mediterranean island of Malta.[7] The Allies needed to maintain control of this tiny island nation, serving as an "unsinkable aircraft carrier" for Allied attacks against German general Erwin Rommel's Afrika Korps and other Axis forces in the deserts of North Africa.[8]

Understanding the Allies' strategy, the Germans put the island under siege and conducted air raids on it. By August 1942, things looked bleak for Malta when the Allies ran out of aviation gas, preventing their planes from taking off for their missions. But in the nick of time, the American tanker SS *Ohio*, previously disabled by German attacks, was lashed between two destroyers and guided into the Maltese port of Valletta. The merchant seamen were greeted by a boisterous, cheering crowd on the shores, and subsequently were credited with saving the island. The rescue occurred on August 15, the feast day of the patron saint of Malta.[9]

The credit accorded this merchant vessel was rare indeed. Over the entire course of the Second World War and throughout the ensuing years, the U.S. Merchant Marine received few accolades. Typically, these seamen were treated like water boys who delivered sustenance to fighting men, hardly given a second glance or a kind word. For the most part, they didn't receive headlines, acclaim, or expressions of gratitude. There were no merchant seamen featured in heroic poses on the covers of *Life* or *Time* magazine.

Among the most famous merchant ships aiding Allied invasion forces in World War Two was the SS *Samuel Parker*. Dean Beaumont would later serve on that Liberty ship—after the war. Under executive orders from President Roosevelt, it was the first civilian vessel to be honored with the Gallant Ship Award by the War Shipping Administration, on April 9, 1945. Dean said that the award—which was half as big as a door—was mounted in the ship's wardroom.

He described one wartime incident, in which the *Samuel Parker* was bound for North Africa, carrying a thousand British soldiers and their invasion equipment. Off the coast of Africa, the German Luftwäffe attacked. The British were on deck with their weapons, including machine guns, which amounted to more than a thousand guns, in addition to the Navy Armed Guard for the ship. Several German planes were shot down, and the attackers finally gave up the effort.

The Gallant Ship Award citation said that the crew of the ship—working in the Mediterranean, transporting troops and war supplies—had aided not only the North African campaign but also the subsequent invasion of Sicily. During the summer of 1943, the *Samuel Parker* was repeatedly attacked off the coast of Sicily, but fought back and survived. One merchant seaman, Fred Aubry Anderson, saved the vessel from explosion.

The *Samuel Parker* was so battered in the attacks—though it stayed afloat—that Captain Elmer J. Stull reported to the vessel's owners at American Mail Lines, "Guess you'd better take another ship down off the shelf. I've just about used this one up."[10]

Other merchant vessels were not so fortunate. The tanker SS *Gulf Prince* and the Liberty ship SS *Mathew Maury* were sunk near Sicily by U-boats. Another Liberty ship, the SS *Timothy Pickering*, went down in those waters, too, when it was attacked by aircraft and blew up. The vessel had been carrying bombs, TNT, and other explosives, along with 126 British soldiers, one hundred of whom lost their lives. Also killed were eight members of the Navy Armed Guard and twenty-two merchant seamen. Some ships in that region were also sunk by skilled Italian frogmen who attached mines to the hulls of vessels in port or while at anchor.[11]

I interviewed one of the merchant seamen involved in the Allied invasion of Sicily. Teenager Jack Faulkner served as a wiper in the engine room of the SS *Frank B. Kellogg*, a Liberty ship that left Portland, Oregon, in the late spring of 1943. With a secret military cargo in the cargo holds (and bound for an undisclosed destination), the vessel crossed the Pacific Ocean to Sydney, Australia, for five days of repairs. It then proceeded across the Indian Ocean and into the Red Sea. At Massawa, Eritea, in northeast Africa, they took on an additional cargo of medical equipment and supplies from a temporary British hospital.

The *Frank B. Kellogg* proceeded north through the Red Sea to the Egyptian city of Suez, where the medical cargo was unloaded. A little farther north, at the port of Ismailia, they anchored and took on sand ballast and railroad ties. Still farther north, in Port Said, they unloaded the secret military cargo to the British Army there. The ship then proceeded to Beirut, Lebanon, where the sand ballast was adjusted, with railroad ties placed over it to make a floor. They then took on a new cargo of tanks, trucks, artillery guns, and ammunition.

In Alexandria, Egypt, landing barges were loaded on top of the forward holds. British soldiers also boarded the ship with all of their gear and stayed in the aft hold, where bunks and other facilities had been set up for them. When the Liberty ship got outside the Alexandria breakwater, young Faulkner saw a vast convoy of merchant ships and naval escorts, as far as the eye could see. A few hours later, just as the land dropped over the horizon behind them, the soldiers were given booklets entitled, *A Soldier's Guide to Sicily*, which they read during the seven-day passage. Now the soldiers—and the crew—knew where they were going.

The invasion of Sicily ("Operation Husky") commenced on July 10, 1943, when an overwhelming force of 467,000 Allied soldiers attacked a German defensive force of only 60,000 men, driving them out.[12] At four A.M. on July 11, Faulkner and his crewmen saw the bright red flashes of gunfire and explosions on the beaches of Sicily as their ship drew near.

At seven A.M., the SS *Frank B. Kellogg* anchored on the Syracuse side of Sicily and the ship was quickly unloaded. They completed it in the nick of time, since German dive-bombers attacked at dusk, when the twilight made it especially difficult to see planes overhead. Faulkner's merchant ship was in a group of five, and—while bombs came close to them—the attackers were thwarted by Armed Guard fire. None of these vessels were damaged, but

Faulkner learned that cargo vessels on the other side of Sicily were hit and sunk.

In September 1943, the British Eighth Army crossed the Strait of Messina from Sicily and invaded Italy.[13] Allied forces gathered in the south of the country, and prepared to push farther north. They soon took control of the seaside town of Bari in southern Italy, which had a large harbor and was the site of anti-Mussolini Italians. Allied cargo ships began to arrive there, filled with supplies needed for the campaign reaching into the rest of the country.

But the Germans had other ideas, and made a surprise night-time air raid with thirty Stuka dive-bombers on December 2, 1943, when the Bari harbor was filled with ships waiting to be unloaded. The lesson of Pearl Harbor had been forgotten too quickly, as the ships were packed closely together. This oversight would produce disastrous results.[14]

The attacking planes made high-pitched whistling noises, coming from devices attached to the wings—"Trumpets of Jericho"— that were designed to induce terror.[15] The second vessel that the Germans hit, the ammunition ship SS *John L. Motley*, erupted in a huge explosion, sending a giant ball of flames into the air and a tidal wave through the harbor, which was already saturated with dunnage and fuel oil dumped by ships during recent weeks. More explosions occurred, and the sky lit up like a fireworks display.[16]

One of the first ships to explode was the SS *John Harvey*, which carried a cargo of ammunition in addition to a top-secret cargo of mustard-gas bombs, which the Allies were keeping handy in case the Germans decided to employ gas against them first. President Roosevelt himself had authorized the shipment, a cargo so hazardous and potentially unstable, that it had its own safety crew of men to make sure it was handled correctly.[17] The memories of World War One gas warfare had not dimmed entirely, and there were reports and rumors that desperate Axis forces might resort to using it again.

The *John Harvey* disintegrated in the harbor, killing everyone aboard and spreading deadly gas through the air. One witness described a 3,000-foot-high "fountain of flame" rising above the ship. Soon the entire harbor was a wall of fire, keeping seamen from escaping, and hindering rescue efforts.[18]

Before the horror was over, seventeen ships had been sunk, and a thousand people killed, including hundreds of merchant seamen. The bodies of the men were covered with terrible burns and blisters, and their skin was yellow.[19] The presence of mustard gas on the *John Harvey*, and on another merchant vessel in the harbor, the SS *Samuel L. Tilden*, was so politically sensitive that the United States government attempted to cover it up.[20]

One bright spot in the disaster was the story of the Liberty ship SS *Lyman Abbott*, loaded with munitions and high-power explosives. After the *John Harvey* exploded, the *Lyman Abbott* almost capsized from the tremendous force of the blast. Fragments of disintegrating ships rained from the sky, tearing through the *Lyman Abbott*'s lifeboats and decks, and starting fires. While Captain Carl P. Dahlstrom was directing firefighting efforts, another merchant ship was cut loose from its moorings and bore down on them, on fire and out of control. The captain ordered his men to abandon ship in damaged lifeboats kept afloat only by their air tanks. Two of his men died in the oily, burning water.

When the two ships did not collide, the captain called for volunteers, saying he wanted to reboard the *Lyman Abbott* and take her out of the harbor. He and a group of brave men, all of whom were wounded and burned, went back on board their own crippled ship. They got it clear of the harbor and put the fires out, saving their valuable cargo.*

The disaster at Bari set back the Allied land offensive in Italy for

---

*For their courage and contribution to the war effort, the injured crewmembers of the SS *Lyman Abbott* received Purple Hearts—one of the few times that American merchant seamen received military awards. It represented concrete proof that these men—and others like them—were on a par with American armed forces, and deserved all of the benefits of military veterans. Many other American merchant seamen did not receive any medals at all, and none of them received the benefits of the G.I. Bill after the war.[21]

months. On January 22, 1944, an Allied force landed at Anzio, on the western shore of Italy, a Normandy-type assault that was supported by merchant ships playing a critical supply-line role. In that invasion, the merchant ships were the prime targets of a huge railroad gun called "Anzio Annie," which could fire a 500-pound shell over a range of thirty-eight miles. It was no picnic.[22] Allied forces coming from the west and from the south would finally march into Rome in the spring of 1944.

The D-Day invasion across the English Channel was originally supposed to have occurred in 1942, but was delayed for two years. One of the reasons for this was the need for additional troops and war matériel to be shipped to the embarkation point, and the Allies did not have enough ships to do it.[23] As the Liberty-ship construction program took hold during the war and the Americans were able to build far more of the boats than the enemy could sink, the plan for a cross-channel attack finally began to take shape.

Early in the war, President Roosevelt had vowed to build a "bridge of ships" from America to England—merchant-ship convoys filled with supplies. In the months before the D-Day invasion in 1944, the president saw his pledge come to fruition. At any one time, a bridge of a thousand merchant ships with civilian crews plied the stormy North Atlantic, carrying soldiers and military cargoes to Europe.[24] Roosevelt was winning the tonnage war against Germany. He was sending far more ships across the ocean than the enemy could sink, and at the same time was sinking more U-boats than the Germans could replace.

Many of those Allied merchant ships supplied the D-Day invasion on June 6, 1944, and even the craft that were beyond their prime contributed to the effort. Our military leaders had what were called "mulberries and gooseberries," concrete-and-steel barges sunk off the coast of Normandy to form breakwaters so that operations could be conducted more easily. But there were not enough of them, so a number of old merchant ships were also sunk intentionally, including the SS *Courageous* and the SS *Illinoian*.[25]

There are only two functioning Liberty ships in the United States today. One of them, the SS *Jeremiah O'Brien*, is based in San Francisco and operated as a floating museum by retired merchant seamen. It was involved in the D-Day invasion, making eleven trips to transport men and matériel to that theater of war. In 1994 the vessel was taken back to Normandy for a fiftieth-anniversary celebration, which included honoring our American merchant seamen with speeches.

Concerning D-Day, Senator John Breaux of Louisiana said, "Everybody that day was a hero. There were the people who walked on the beach, who lay on the beach, who died on the beach, and there was also the people who got them to the beach."[26]

One of the merchant seamen involved in D-Day, Hercules Esibill, said, "We not only carried the troops; we carried their equipment as well. We carried their landing craft on deck. On the day of the invasion, on D-Day, we'd go in, we'd put their landing craft over, and then have scramble nets over the side. The troops would go down the side, get in the landing craft, and go ashore. We'd also have their support units. Quite often we would have artillery units aboard, we'd have tanks, aircraft, up on the decks, deck cargo. And we'd have their provisions on board as well."[27]

Chief Mate Frank F. Farrar of the Liberty ship *Cyrus J. K. Curtis* had this recollection of Normandy:

> We hooked on to the big (amphibious troop carrier) right abreast of the hatch. Up she swung, with fifteen or more men in her, all loaded down with rifles, grenades, machine guns, draped all over with belts of ammo. . . . (It) splashed into the water and away she went. Troops pushed the next one down the deck, and the whole process was repeated till the forward deck was cleared. The same thing was taking place on the after deck.[28]

The SS *Oliver Wolcott*, one of the merchant ships that supplied the invasion of Omaha Beach on that fateful day in June, transported an Army artillery regiment of 450 men over there, along with ammunition, military vehicles, and artillery guns. Upon their arrival, they started unloading the ship immediately, and the operation continued throughout the night. In the darkness German planes attacked, but the seamen were ordered to keep working, to remain at their posts and keep unloading even as planes strafed them. Richard A. Freed, one of the seamen, later recalled, "I heard the shells *ping*ing around me." Off their starboard bow, the Liberty ship SS *Charles Morgan* exploded from an aerial bomb dropped into one of its holds, with more than two hundred troops aboard.[29]

It is clear that the men of the United States Merchant Marine were as much a part of every Allied invasion force as the soldiers themselves, who ran ashore with rifles. Every soldier who fought in the European and Pacific theaters was dependent in some degree upon the Merchant Marine for food, clothing, weapons, ammunition, and even for the small things that no one thought much about, but were still important for their recreational value: reading material, cigarettes, radios, and playing cards.

Unfortunately, any small amount of favorable publicity received by the Merchant Marine has always been overshadowed by the acclaim accorded the Allied armed forces. The American public may have heard about Liberty ships, or about convoys of merchant vessels in the Atlantic, but they did not hear very many stories of individual heroism.

They never learned what really happened.

FIFTEEN

HURRICANE
AT SEA

Dear God! My boat is so very small, and
Thy sea so very wide. Have mercy!

—BRETON FISHERMAN'S PRAYER[1]

IN CEYLON, CAPTAIN NIELSEN OF THE SS *BRANDER MATTHEWS* RECEIVED AN order from the War Shipping Administration to proceed to Portuguese East Africa (also known as Mozambique) to pick up a load of coal. It was early 1945, with the war still on, and the Allies badly needed coal in Italy.

Proceeding southwest over a distance of twenty-six hundred nautical miles, they passed through the dangerous Mozambique Channel between Madagascar and Africa. This was a particularly treacherous area, where Axis submarines prowled. In that favored hunting ground the German submarine *U-862* sank four merchant vessels, including an ammunition ship.[2]

But there were other perils. In the channel, the SS *Brander Matthews* was caught in a huge storm, a cyclonic hurricane that caused the Liberty ship to creak and pop, and to list—up to 41 degrees at times. In the ferocious winds and mountainous waves, lifeboats came out of their cradles and were damaged. Balsa-wood life rafts went overboard.

Endangering the entire ship, the jumbo boom and block broke loose just forward of the bridge. The cargo-hoisting block, weighing a ton with its large hook, was swinging back and forth, slamming into either side of the vessel. To young Dean Beaumont, his ship seemed very small and isolated when confronted by such powerful natural elements. They were all by themselves out there, and could not even send out an S.O.S. since the radio antenna had been damaged.

To make matters worse, Captain Nielsen did not like where the block was hitting the sides of the ship, right where "Rosie the Riveter" might not have welded it very well. He said the heavy weight could weaken the hull and cause the ship to split in half—the fate of many other Liberties.

That was when Dean came up with an idea. He wondered if it might be possible for the crew to make lariats and use them to lasso the block, and get it under control. The captain thought this might just work. He called for volunteers, and two men stepped forward, the teenage radio officer Bill Hower and the able seaman, Al Susala. They didn't have much experience with western-style rodeo roping, but wanted to give it a try. The pair went down to the bosun's locker and each of them got a length of line, which they tied into lariats, with knots.

The wind let up, but huge waves were still crashing over the top of the ship, all the way to the bridge. Water came underneath doors and swept down the decks. *Crash!* The block slammed into the ship. Moments later it hit again, with a rattling *thud*, on the other side.

After the water went down, Dean opened a wheelhouse door that faced forward and the men scurried out onto the drenched deck with their lariats. Dean slammed the door behind them. The men missed the first time, and had to run back inside when they saw another wave coming, and the heavy block still swinging wildly. Moments later, Dean opened the door again, and they ran outside once more.

While all this was going on, a young seaman went up on the bridge, to the wheelhouse where the officers were. He was only sixteen years old, and very frightened, just a pimply-faced kid.

"Mr. Beaumont, are we sinking?" he asked.

Dean fixed him with a hard stare. "I won't lie to you. There's a good chance that we won't make it." He scanned forward through the windows, saw lifeboats on the port side, full of water, and lifeboats on the starboard side smashed up against the wheelhouse. Crewmen were working to secure the boats.

The teenager was deeply disturbed. "How can I be sure that I'll go to Heaven? I've never been to church so I don't know much, but some of the guys say you know all about it."

"It might be too late for you," Dean said. "We could sink any minute now."

"But there must be some way!"

"All right. If you pray real hard to God, and if God believes you, He will try to help you."

Unsuccessful in their efforts to lasso the block, Bill Hower and Al Susala rushed back inside the wheelhouse and waited for the next wave to pass, which it did with a thunderous sound that shook the ship. Bravely, the pair of "cowboys" then ran back outside.

While they were out there, Dean quoted the Lord's Prayer to the young seaman. Tears ran down the boy's face as he tried to find some comfort. Dean put an arm around his shoulders.

On the third attempt, Bill Hower was successful in getting a lasso around the hook, and his companion got a line around it afterward. They quickly tied the hook down to bitts on the deck. Dean said it reminded him of the Lilliputians tying Gulliver down in Jonathan Swift's novel. The ship was badly beat up, and several of the lifeboats did not look seaworthy.

Bill Hower and Al Susala still had work to do, however. Captain Nielsen asked the men if they would climb up the foremast to string up an emergency radio antenna, so that they could transmit the ship's position. The eye of the storm passed directly over the vessel, and the wind let up. The men nodded. Wearing only shorts and T-shirts they climbed the mast, with Hower going first, carrying a heaving line and another radio antenna wire. Spindrift was blowing and it was cold and wet up there. The waves were still formidable, and the ship pitched this way and that. The men didn't wear lifelines.

With no cargo, the ship was light, so the helmsman could not maintain the bow into the weather. The propeller kept coming out of the water as the vessel pitched, and then the screw would dip into the water for a few turns. Thus the Liberty ship—which vibrated badly when the propeller was in the air—only had power through the water for a few seconds at a time.

High over the deck, Hower climbed out on the crosstree of the foremast, inching along on his belly. It was a flat surface, eighteen inches wide, and he was able to maintain a good grip. Susala was just below him, helping with the heaving line and antenna wire. They finally got the antenna rigged up, making sure it was clear of metal contact. Then, cold and trembling, they went back down.

Bill Hower dried off and sent a message to GMBH—the call sign for London—with their position. It was not an S.O.S., but Captain Nielsen wanted to report in, just in case they got into more trouble when the wind picked up again.

The crew of the SS *Brander Matthews* survived this ordeal. I told Bill Hower that he had performed two heroic acts, under extremely difficult conditions. He said he didn't consider himself a hero, that the ship needed to be kept in operable condition, including the jumbo boom and the radio. "At sea, you depend on your shipmates," he said, "and the ship is your only survival vehicle."

Many radio operators were called "Sparks," a nickname that Hower adopted himself. While he did not consider himself heroic, his actions speak for themselves. He was one of many brave Merchant Marine radio operators in World War Two.

When the SS *Carrabulle* was shelled and torpedoed by a U-boat in 1942, the last person off the ship was the radioman, who sent out distress calls that resulted in the rescue of eighteen men.[3] That same year, the unarmed tanker SS *China Arrow* was torpedoed by a U-boat, setting off explosions and an intense fire. The captain and radio officer remained aboard until the last possible moment. They rigged up an emergency radio antenna and sent out an S.O.S.,* which resulted in the rescue of thirty-seven merchant seamen—the entire crew.[4]

Such acts were especially noteworthy, since Axis submarines invariably tried to shell or machine-gun the radio shack and antenna in order to keep messages from going out that would provide the ship's location, and information on where the submarine was operating.[5] This happened to the tanker SS *Gulfamerica,* torpedoed by a German submarine in 1942. The attackers shelled the superstructure of the ship, trying to take out the mainmast and the radio antenna.[6] On the SS *Stephen Hopkins* (see chapter 7, "Valor at Sea," page 75), radio operator Hudson A. Hewey lost his life while continuing to transmit, even though he knew enemy gunners were targeting him.[7]

Returning to his cabin after the hurricane, Dean Beaumont noticed a fresh crack along a weld on the hull, letting in splashes of seawater and drenching the floor. He contacted the captain, and was moved to other quarters until repairs could be completed.

Back in Calcutta the ship had been repainted gray, including the masts. But now the *Brander Matthews* looked peculiar, a different color on each side. In the storm they had taken the brunt of the intense weather on the port side, and the gray paint had been blasted off, revealing red lead paint beneath. The starboard side of the Liberty ship was still gray.

While this had been the biggest storm the SS *Brander Matthews* had survived so far, it was not the first on this voyage. The vessel was taking a beating from the weather, and more repairs would be needed. Still, for a Liberty ship that had been designed to be expendable after one voyage, this one was holding up pretty well.

Some of the men didn't think much of it, though. They called it their "Kaiser coffin."

---

*In addition to "S.O.S.," two of the other radio distress messages that were typically sent were "KDHP" ("I have been torpedoed") and "S.S.S." or "555" ("Attacked by submarine").

At the port of Lourenço Marques in Portuguese East Africa, regional military officers and police officials came on board, aware of the arrangements the U.S. War Shipping Administration had made, to purchase coal in the country. The Portuguese inspected the ship and provided information about how to get repairs completed locally.

While repair work commenced, Captain Nielsen supervised the loading operations. The SS *Brander Matthews* was docked next to a railroad track, and the Portuguese brought in a train of coal cars. Then, one car at a time, they lifted the coal up to the ship on a big conveyor and dumped it down a chute into one of the holds. After dumping two or three cars this way, the coal was mounded up above the top of the hatch.

At that point about twenty Africans were sent aboard, teenagers from a nearby compound, housing a couple hundred of them for this type of work. All boys, some as young as fourteen, they carried buckets and little baskets. They climbed down beneath the mast to the tween decks and into the hatch, where they crawled over the sharp coal and loaded their containers. Then they crawled to the outside edges of the pile and redistributed the material, and continued this process until the hatch was ready for more coal. At night the teenagers were virtual prisoners, locked up in the housing compound by local coal merchants, who held them there under tribal labor arrangements.

As always, curious about cultures and customs, Dean learned that the young men were paid the equivalent of ten U.S. cents a day. After two years one young man had around seventy dollars saved up, and finally obtained his release. He went a few miles up the Limpopo River to a village and spoke with the chieftain, telling him he wanted to purchase a cow. The animal cost him the equivalent of fifty dollars, which he handed over. Then he went to another village where there were lots of girls, and selected a pretty fifteen-year-old for his wife, swapping the cow for her. As part of the bargain, he also obtained a machete, fishing line, and fishhooks.

The chieftain of that village conducted the wedding ceremony, and the young couple set off back down the Limpopo River. At a sandy place on the riverbank, the industrious husband chopped down palm trees and made a lean-to type of dwelling. Every day he sat on rocks and caught fish, which his young bride cooked for dinner. At that point the couple seemed to be living an idyllic life in their African hideaway, except that the husband had been breathing in coal dust for years, down in the holds of merchant ships. That young man, and others like him, was likely to come down with "black lung" disease and die within a few years.

A few miles north, Alan H. Knox and his mates on the *MS Cape Henry* made their way up another river, heading for the port of Beira in Portuguese East Africa. On the way in, they spotted a German "picket" or "spotter" boat, which was around 85 or 90 feet long and had a high aerial. This boat kept track of Allied shipping that was coming and going, and radioed information to U-boats waiting to torpedo them out in the Mozambique Channel.

Since this was a neutral country, neither vessel fired on the other, but the crews watched each other warily. That evening, Knox and his comrades went to a nightclub in Beira, where they struck up a conversation with several husky German men, who spoke some English. It turned out they were the same Germans who had been spying on the Americans earlier in the day. By the end of the evening, after a few beers, the men on both sides were on friendly terms. "We were buddies for a while," Knox recalled, "but all of us knew we would have to go back to our jobs the next day."*

The MS *Cape Henry* picked up a load of ammunition and then made its way north toward the Suez Canal, using its superior 15-

---

*This is reminiscent of the famous Christmas truce that occurred on the front lines between German and British soldiers in World War One—men setting aside their differences for a short time and then resuming the battle the following day.

knot speed and a zigzag course to avoid being torpedoed. The C-1 cargo ship made the trip safely, but Dean Beaumont's Liberty ship was far more vulnerable.

The crew of the SS *Brander Matthews* had time to take an excursion up the Limpopo River recommended to them by one of the men in town. It was an area that would suffer severe flooding decades later in 1999, killing thousands of people and washing entire villages away. When Dean was there in 1945, though, the Limpopo was serene and beautiful, with a little train that ran alongside the water, connecting settlements on the the coast with the interior of Africa. Dean and twenty of his shipmates rode for a couple of hours, and got off at a station that had an elegant dining room that had catered to tourists before the war.

Everything was set up for the crew in advance, at a long table with white linens. There were seven big plates arrayed in front of each person, with oversized napkins, three knives, three forks, three spoons, and an assortment of wineglasses. African waiters in white jackets served leopard steaks to them, along with other native delicacies.

Afterward, the crew went aboard a 50-foot fishing boat, up a tributary of the river where immense green plants and jungle vines hung low over the water, right above the boat. Most of the passengers lined up along the rail, while Dean found a place to sit with a glass partition between him and the river. They rounded a bend in the river, and big trees were just overhead. A huge African rock python could be seen crawling along one of the branches hanging over the water, and the big snake appeared capable of dropping onto the deck of the boat. The men quickly moved out of the way, then returned to the railing when the boat was clear of the danger.

They rounded another bend, and through the glass Dean saw a herd of hippopotamuses in the water. A large dominant male, threatened by the approaching boat, shooed his herd back to the shore, and opened his mouth toward the boat to bellow at it, revealing decayed brown teeth. Suddenly the hippo went after the boat and smashed his head into the hull. Then he turned around and moved away a little distance. His head sank down in the water and his hind end came up, and he went, *Bmmmph . . . Splat!*—leaving a big spray of yellow dung. The mess got all over the seamen on the railing, but not on Dean, since he was sitting behind the glass partition.

By the time the crew returned to the *Brander Matthews* the coal had been loaded, along with an additional deck cargo needed by the British for mine-detection operations: barges made of wood and bronze, with very little steel.

The ship headed northeast toward the Red Sea and the Suez Canal, ultimately bound for Malta and then southern Italy, through waters where many American merchant vessels had already been sunk.

SIXTEEN

THE DARKEST
DAYS

*Despite heavy losses the U.S. Merchant Marine and
the Navy Armed Guard never, never gave up.*

—MIKE SACCO,
PRESIDENT, SEAFARERS UNION OF NORTH AMERICA[1]

IN APRIL 1945, THE SS *BRANDER MATTHEWS* MADE ITS WAY NORTHEAST AROUND
the bulge of Africa. The ship dropped anchor off Yemen, where the
elderly Captain Nielsen and his crew received permission to proceed northwest, into the Red Sea. Ahead of them, in Europe, things
were moving to a rapid conclusion. In a short while Benito Mussolini
would be captured and executed while trying to flee, and Adolf
Hitler would commit suicide. But, for now, the war still raged on.

There were a lot of jellyfish in the Red Sea as the Liberty ship
made its way through, heading toward the Suez Canal. At the canal
they received clearance, and passed through it, on a one-ship-at-a-
time basis. In several places they passed wider spots where ships
were anchored off to the side, awaiting instructions. The *Brander
Matthews* finally docked in Port Said, Egypt, at the northern end of
the canal, where the crew was allowed to go ashore.

Some of the seamen were getting quite wild, due to the long
time away from home. On shore leave they drank more heavily than

ever, and a few of them took drugs. Captain Nielsen had to take disciplinary action against some of them, which he didn't like to do. The men were ordered not to bring women aboard, and this time no one did.

Nine or ten Egyptian salesmen did sneak onto the ship, though, and concealed themselves around the vessel. They slept in lifeboats and behind partitions; and, when the seamen woke up in the morning, the salesmen were all over the decks and crew rooms, hawking baskets full of watches, fake artifacts, and trinkets. The salesmen also stole whatever they could get their hands on, including food, money, and the personal effects of the crew.

In short order the salesmen were evicted, and the *Brander Matthews* left port. The ship hugged the northern coast of Egypt and stopped at Alexandria, where they took on food supplies. Following the unfortunate events in Port Said, many of the crewmen did not have much money to spend ashore, or were not feeling very well. Most of them remained on the vessel.

Typically, merchant seamen didn't ship out with a lot of money in their pockets, and whatever they earned en route, they spent on shore leave. In World War Two there was good reason for this. As one veteran said, "I never went to sea with more than two dollars . . . the Germans were blowing up tankers galore . . . I figured I didn't want to have any money in my pockets when I went over the side."[2]

Even though convoys of merchant ships with escorts of Allied warships, were common at this stage of the war, the SS *Brander Matthews* was always sent out alone. So far, the ship had passed through war zones in the Pacific and Indian Oceans—but now it was about to test its luck in the region where fighting was more concentrated than anywhere else in the world: the Mediterranean Sea.

Only lightly armed, with its small deckguns, the Liberty ship set out in a westerly direction across the Mediterranean, bound for southern Italy. On the way, Dean Beaumont and his shipmates went through yet another bad storm, with high winds and towering waves that crashed over the decks. After surviving the hurricane in the

Mozambique Channel, however, the men were more confident this time. Younger crewmen shouted to one another that this one wasn't so bad. One of the barges on deck did break loose and bang around, but the men were able to secure it, with only minimal damage.

Coming out of the storm into an orange-splashed sunset, the lookout spotted a new danger: a squadron of planes heading toward them from the south, off the port side of the ship. On the bridge, Captain Nielsen barked commands. The Navy Armed Guard manned their guns and watched with binoculars. All over the ship, men ran to their stations.

"They're Jerries!" the lookout shouted, as he saw swastikas on the aircraft. "Two bombers and six fighter planes!"

Captain Nielsen ordered more speed, but held to a westerly course. Moments later the aircraft flew directly overhead, and the men of the SS *Brander Matthews* braced for attack.

But the planes never broke formation. They kept going north and didn't turn back to attack the Liberty ship. Captain Nielsen said they had to be on a mission, or returning to base after completing one, too low on fuel or munitions to attack.

It went without saying that the planes might return—or send others to attack—now that the Liberty ship had been spotted.

With tensions high among the crew, Captain Nielsen headed for the Allied-controlled island of Malta, just south of Sicily. Reaching Malta, they unloaded the barges on the deck, then made their way north to Syracuse, on the southeast side of the island of Sicily, only a few hours away.

Dean Beaumont was intrigued by the history of Sicily, which once had been a famous Greek metropolis and the home of Archimedes, whose military inventions were successful in delaying a Roman conquest in the Second Punic War. Later, the city was ruled by the Byzantines and by the Moors, and ultimately fell to Norman conquerors. Dean went ashore and visited an old fortress that had been used by "knights in shining armor" as a stepping-off point for their Crusades against the Moors in the Holy Land.

After taking on a supply of food in Syracuse and unloading half of their coal there, the SS *Brander Matthews* received orders to proceed to other cities in Italy that needed fuel—first to the city of Taranto, in the "arch" of Italy's "boot." Even though the Allies had taken Rome and Florence the year before, their forces were just then reaching the Po Valley in the north, and fighting continued against Fascist and Nazi forces. In regard to southern Italy, the surprise German air raid on Bari in 1943 had proved the danger of this region. Bari was only forty miles from Taranto by air, and German bombers were still active in the entire area.

During this time, the crew of the cargo ship was nervous and upset. The vessel had been ordered to proceed north to other cities in Italy, and the crew faced an increasing danger of attack by enemy planes. The men would do their duties, but the circumstances were taking a toll on their emotions. The merchant seamen had already been through quite a lot—and Dean Beaumont, despite his youth, had seen as much as most of them, or more, especially taking into consideration his earlier voyage to Saipan.

When the ship left Syracuse, Dean changed cabins and took a smaller room, since the "stack gas" from the engines was bothering his asthma. In addition, he had been isolating himself from the crew in recent weeks. For months Dean had not even been opening the letters and cards from his mother. Instead of finding her religious quotations comforting, he had been increasingly troubled by them: they made him feel guilty, that he wasn't doing enough. In his position as the ship's purser and "doctor," Dean had tried to counsel some of the younger crewmen, but didn't feel his message had gotten through to most of them. Among the younger crewmen and officers, only his friend Bill Hower seemed to understand, or even care about, what he was saying. Things seemed out of control all around Dean—storms, the war, the crew—and he felt frustrated.

Life was wearing him down.

The *Brander Matthews* docked at the port in Taranto, and Dean Beaumont already knew some of the city's history. In ancient times this had been a Greek trading post and a Roman harbor. In

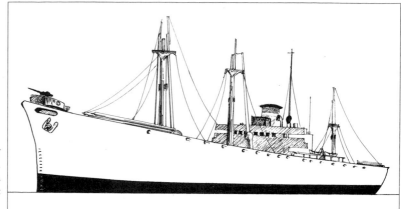

Liberty Ship, by
James P. Morrison.
*With the permission
of the artist*

Liberty Ship, by Buck Braden. *With the permission of the artist*

Balloons Tangle Nazi Planes Attacking Convoy

A German airplane attack on British shipping in the English Channel, when for the first time balloon barrages were used to protect British ships in a convoy, is graphically depicted in this drawing by Arthur Beaumont, famous artist. Balloons floating from cables attached to the ship's decks keep the Nazi planes high enough in the air to spoil their bombing aim and the cables make dive bombing too dangerous.

Arthur Beaumont's thrilling battle reenactments appeared in
American papers during the war.
With the permission of Dean Beaumont

Dean Beaumont on
the upper bridge of the
SS *Brander Matthews*,
off Saipan, 1944.
*With the permission
of Dean Beaumont*

Dean Beaumont in his
Lieutenant JG uniform, 1945.
With the permission of Dean Beaumont

The type of freighter that Dean sailed on
with American President Lines.
With the permission of Dean Beaumont

Postage stamp designs by Arthur Beaumont, 1944. Since the artist was still alive during the war, a legal technicality prevented postal authorities from using these paintings. *With the permission of Dean Beaumont*

Survivors of the torpedoed SS *John A. Johnson*, 1944. U.S. Navy photo courtesy of Peter Chelemedos, who was Chief Mate on the ill-fated voyage.

Lieutenant Peter Chelemedos, 1944.
Courtesy of Peter Chelemedos

MS Cape Henry. The crew of this C-1 cargo ship rescued British Royal Air Force fliers from life rafts in the Mediterranean during the war. *Courtesy of Puget Sound Maritime Historical Society*

Military tanks as deck cargo on the way to Murmansk, USSR. *With the permission of Ian A. Millar*

Troops aboard a Liberty Ship going to war. *With the permission of Ian A. Millar*

Military aircraft on
deck of merchant ship.
*With the permission
of Ian A. Millar*

Moment of impact. A merchant ship takes a torpedo.
With the permission of Ian A. Millar

SS *Martin Van Buren*, torpedoed off the coast of Nova Scotia. Here she rests
after drifting ashore. *U.S. Navy Photo*

Liberty Ship off-loading military vehicles at Normandy.
With the permission of Ian A. Millar

SS *Samuel Parker*, winner of one of the few Gallant Ship Awards,
by Arthur Beaumont. Dean Beaumont sailed on this ship after the war.
With the permission of Dean Beaumont

SS *Elk Basin*. Dean sailed on this ship after the war.
With the permission of Dean Beaumont

Cargo ship off-loading in the Pacific, by Arthur Beaumont.
With the permission of Dean Beaumont

Arthur Beaumont, Artist Laureate of the United States Navy.
With the permission of Dean Beaumont

Dean Beaumont in his familiar U.S. Merchant Marine cap, 2001.
With the permission of Dean Beaumont

November 1940, the British had staged a surprise air raid on the Italian navy base there, and sank several warships in shallow waters—a major blow to the Italian fleet, which had set them back for the remainder of the war. The British had used an aircraft carrier as their base of operations, and had sent Swordfish biplanes on missions in the middle of the night, firing shallow-water torpedoes. Afterward, Admiral Isoroku Yamamato of Japan had obtained intelligence on the mission, and used it as a blueprint for his sneak attack on Pearl Harbor, which occurred a year later.[3]

In Taranto, at least a dozen crewmen went on drinking binges, and two of them took the opportunity to jump ship. They simply disappeared—the legal equivalent of soldiers going AWOL, since merchant seamen worked on civilian ships in lieu of military duty. Some of the men who came back to the ship had women on their arms and tried to sneak them aboard. One of the older sailors came to Dean and asked for a couple of vials of penicillin to treat a venereal disease. Dean duly provided the medicine.

Early one evening, when some of the crew were out drinking and carousing, Dean felt a deep despondency. He was confused. He felt so tired, but it was more emotional than physical. For months he had been dealing with the mental and physical problems of the crew, in addition to feeling his own stresses during wartime. As a youth, Dean had dreamed of joining the U.S. Navy, of going off to war on one of the great capital ships he had visited with his father. Instead of that glorious vision, he had ended up here, in a dark hole.

It didn't help that there was no entertainment to speak of on the ship, and not much else to do except read, play cards, and tell tall tales. Most of the time, the vessel was at sea. Dean and his mates just sailed on and on, woke up each day, went out on deck and looked at the changes in the sky and the water. Many days were miserably cold, and foggy, and the crew was looking for submarines all the time. Every seaman knew that torpedoes usually struck suddenly, without warning. At any time the men could be only moments from death, seconds away from going up in a huge explosion and fireball. The *Brander Matthews* was only lightly armed, and was repeatedly sent into harm's way, with the equivalent of BB guns to protect it. Everyone was on edge, not getting enough sleep, and the young purser was feeling worse than ever.

Dean Beaumont's nerves were shattered.

On another Liberty ship—the SS *Joseph T. Robinson*—one crewman could no longer stand the steady stream of air raids in the Mediterranean as they sailed toward Malta and Sicily. He ran across a catwalk that had been rigged over tanks and planes on the deck, and tried to take charge of the bridge. The officers wrestled him down and locked him in a cabin, where he screamed for weeks, with no real medical attention available.[4] Some men simply disappeared at sea, jumping overboard—or shot themselves—or killed themselves in other ways. To protect the families from additional grief, the crewmates of suicide victims tried to conceal what really happened.

Dean went into his cabin and tried to relax on his bunk, but thoughts churned away in his mind. They were not good thoughts, and he was ashamed of them. As a Christian, he knew he shouldn't be thinking this way, but he couldn't avoid it. Barely twenty-one years old, he didn't want to live anymore.

One of Dean's responsibilities was to keep track of the ship's stores. In his shorts and T-shirt, Dean went to the bosun's locker and got a length of line, much like the one Bill Hower and Al Susala had used during the hurricane in the Mozambique Channel to lasso the wildly swinging jumbo block.

Almost in a trance, as if he were sleepwalking, Dean made his way through the ship's corridors with the line in his hands, passing a couple of seamen heading out for a night of drinking. They hardly gave him a second look, and he barely noticed them.

Dean went into a large storeroom and locked the door from the inside. He took the line and draped it over a steel ceiling pipe, then tied a noose and flipped off the lights. Feeling his way around in the darkness, he climbed up on top of a shelf and sat there, then pulled the noose toward him, put his head through the loop, and tightened it around his neck.

Now he just had to jump off the shelf, into the black void.

For several moments Dean hesitated. On the Liberty ship he had counseled his shipmates—had even saved one teenager from jumping off the stern during a storm. In recent days another sea-man had tried to kill himself by drinking caustic soda, and the young purser had arranged to send him to a British hospital. Many of the crewmen respected Dean, despite his age. Others had resisted his efforts, and some had even ridiculed him for his efforts to keep them from going to bars and carousing with loose women. Dean had tried to use Christian principles to help his fel-low crewmen, and now no one was there to help him. Or so he thought.

The line around his neck was made of hemp—what would be called a "rope" if used on shore. He felt its rough, prickly edges on the skin of his neck, and didn't like the sensation. It jolted Dean to awareness.

"I can't do this," he said to himself.

In the pitch-blackness of the storeroom he removed the deadly loop from his neck, then tried to untie the knot. He heard men in the corridor outside, shouting his name and pounding on the door. He had been seen with the length of line, and his friends knew he was in low spirits. He recognized the voice of Bill Hower out there, and that of Second Mate Victor Bash. They had been searching for him.

Dean continued to fumble with the knot, but couldn't get it untied.

Suddenly the door burst open and the room was filled with light and men. His friends saw the hangman's noose, and Dean sitting on top of the shelf, glassy-eyed. His neck was abraded, which made it look as though he had jumped into the noose, slipped out, and then climbed back up onto the shelf. He had not actually jumped, how-ever, but had tightened the line around his neck before changing his mind.

Captain Nielsen was contacted, and he sent a radio message to

British forces in Taranto, asking for help. They promptly dispatched an ambulance.

Bill Hower walked Dean off the ship and then accompanied him to the hospital. Dean seemed dazed. He hardly said anything at all.

SEVENTEEN

THE CIGARETTE

SALESMAN

The sea is my ground and origin;
I have no other point of departure.

—LINCOLN COLCORD[1]

AT THE END OF APRIL, 1945, ENSIGN DEAN BEAUMONT WAS DRIVEN BY AMBU-
lance to the British-run Twenty-sixth General Army Hospital at
Bari—north of Taranto, on the back of Italy's "boot heel." It was a
large, well-run facility, but overcrowded with wounded men, so
Dean was put in an underground section and given a clean bed and
medicines.

Some of the bathroom facilities down there were quite primi-
tive. To reach them, Dean had to enter a tunnel and descend stairs
to a subterranean stream, then climb stone steps that had indenta-
tions where people had been walking for centuries. There were
well-worn rocks on the edge of the water, where a person stood to
do his business. Dean thought about how this area must have been
used for the same purpose two thousand years ago, at the time of
Julius Caesar.

The doctors at Bari conducted tests on Dean. He had suffered a
nervous breakdown—called "battle fatigue" at the time, and what
might well be called "post-traumatic stress disorder" today. He was

mentally worn-out and tense from all the months at sea . . . all the times he had watched the water for submarines, and the sky for enemy planes. The situation with the crew had tipped the scales for him, and almost sent him into the abyss.

Dean was kept under observation at the hospital. Through the windows on the upper levels, where he went for some of his treatments, he saw the results of the terrible disaster that had befallen Bari a year and a half earlier, when the merchant ships full of ammunition and mustard gas had blown up. Dean would later compare what he'd seen in Bari to the effect of an atomic blast. The attack had leveled much of the town. A number of structures had been repaired or rebuilt in the intervening time, but evidence of the disaster remained: damaged buildings and fields of rubble.

After a week, the British took Dean and other patients to the airport, since they were closing down some of their operations in Bari. Patients were flown out of there on military airplanes, moved to the U.S. Army's Nineteenth General Hospital in Naples. The hospital was in a beautiful old palace on a hill overlooking the harbor, part of the stone-and-marble structure dating back to Roman times. The grounds featured a spectacular view of the temperamental Mount Vesuvius (with steam erupting out of it), and of the elegant Italian ships anchored in the Bay of Naples.

It was quite the setting, but Dean wasn't feeling much better. He remembered an old saying: "See Naples and die." But he tried to put that troubling thought out of his mind.

A couple of days after Dean arrived in Naples, the war in Europe ended and people were celebrating in the streets, great cheers rising with the sounds of music and partying. It was "Victory in Europe" day—V-E Day—May 8, 1945.

Buoyed by the unexpected good news, Dean's spirits were lifted. In recent days there had been intense fighting at nearby Anzio Beach, and suddenly it was over. He thought of home in California, thinking of his family and of returning to college there. He still had all those unopened messages from his parents, and began to read them. The biblical passages from his mother helped. He had not opened his personal Bible for months, but now began leafing through the pages again, reading the verses and applying them to his own situation.

After a couple of weeks of treatment, Dean was feeling better and the doctors said he could be released. He packed up his belongings and was taken to the local airfield by one of the hospital workers, where he awaited his flight. Dressed in a light-gray Merchant Marine officer's uniform, Dean boarded a military plane along with soldiers and sailors. After stowing his gear, he took a seat with them on a long bench, and struck up a conversation with an Army sergeant who was next to him.

Suddenly, a man with a clipboard came aboard and looked around. He went up to Dean and informed him that he would have to give up his place; he had been bumped by a Navy commander. Dean was embarrassed and disappointed, but said nothing. He collected his things and trudged back to the waiting room of the airfield, where he remained for two more days, sleeping on a wooden bench and eating at a café.

Dean was bumped from flights five more times: twice by Army officers, but three times by enlisted men—soldiers who were not even officers matching his own rank.

It felt like a slap in the face, and Dean didn't know what to do. The European war had just ended, and space on the military transport planes was at a premium. He didn't know when he would be able to get out, and didn't have enough money to pay for a commercial flight home. Since he was off the ship and his position had been filled by someone else, Dean's pay was stopped. It was that way on all the Merchant Marine ships, in an industry that provided no financial cushion for its seamen. Dean telephoned the hospital and explained the problem. They said he could have a bed there until a flight became available for him.

But he would spend two more months at the U.S. Army hospital, waiting. Most of the patients in the facility were military, with a few Merchant Marine. The hospital arranged for military officers who were not ready to be released to go on excursions to Mount Vesuvius and the romantic island of Capri, but Merchant Marine officers were not invited.

Another slap in the face—and there would be many more. Dean felt humiliated, and increasingly bitter.

There were other merchant seamen in the hospital under similar circumstances, and Dean befriended three or four of them. While they waited for a way to get back to America, they felt the financial pinch. Their ships were gone.

But there was a way to get money. It just took a little ingenuity. The Red Cross gave each man in the hospital cartons of American cigarettes on a regular basis. Dean was about to give them away, but a friend—a Merchant Marine lieutenant—told him to keep them, and that he would show him what to do with them later. Intrigued, Dean began saving cartons.

One day his friend said, "Put your cigarettes in a bag and let's go into town."

Dean didn't see how they could do that. The hospital kept the patients' clothing, and issued institutional garb to them. He scratched his head and asked, "How can we go anywhere? We're wearing pajamas, slippers, and bathrobes."

"Come with me and I'll show you," the lieutenant said.

Carrying a bag of cigarettes, Dean followed him down a flight of stairs into the shadowy catacombs under the hospital. They walked through an ancient corridor for a hundred yards or so, then climbed a ladder. At the top, the lieutenant opened a trap door, and they entered a large, brightly illuminated room, filled with around a hundred nuns who were ironing men's clothing—uniform trousers, jackets, and shirts. It was a big operation, something Dean hadn't imagined could be there.

The nuns were very cute and smiling, with the olive-toned skin common to Mediterraneans of the region. One came over to speak with Dean's friend, and he gave her a carton of cigarettes. She led the men to another room, where the ironed clothes were on hangers and piled neatly on shelves, then left them alone. The pair got out of their hospital clothes and donned Army officers' uniforms, including hats, ties, shoes, and socks. A few minutes later, they walked out the front door and caught a bus that pulled up in front.

The bus took them past buildings that had been damaged by British bombing raids, and structures that were no more than piles of rubble now. In downtown Naples, they got off and walked through a maze of alleys. The lieutenant, of Italian-American heritage, spoke Italian to a man in a small shop, and struck a deal to sell the cigarettes for the equivalent of thirty dollars a carton, an astounding price at that time.

Now they had Italian money, and Dean's friend said they should go and get a good meal, since the food in the hospital was so wretched. With their newly acquired liras the lieutenant purchased a bottle of red wine and then led the way to an old residential apartment building, where they climbed stairs to the fifth floor. He knocked on a door, and a matronly Italian woman opened it. Smiles and hugs ensued, and conversation in Italian, which Dean didn't understand.

The woman invited them inside, and Dean was introduced to her husband and her daughter, an attractive girl of around eighteen. Apparently the family had given Dean's friend an open invitation for a meal, but, due to hardships, they didn't have much food on hand. The woman rummaged around in her small kitchen but found only potatoes, fresh tomatoes, and olive oil.

The lieutenant suggested that they make french fries. So all of them, including Dean, started peeling and slicing potatoes, which then were cooked in the olive oil with the tomatoes. It was surprisingly delicious, especially with the wine. Dean had a little wine himself, a few sips. Then the two of them left the family with some money, which they desperately needed.

That evening the men caught a bus back to the laundry next door to the hospital, and returned the uniforms to the nuns. They put their pajamas, robes, and slippers back on, went through the trap door and returned to the Army hospital.

During the months he spent there, Dean took a lot of cold showers, since they didn't have any hot water. But at least he now had a way of making up for his lost salary, and it began to pile up, in Italian liras. He saved quite a bit of money. He exchanged it for U.S. dollars and then purchased war bonds, which he sent back to his mother in the United States.

It was quite an enterprising operation and might almost seem amusing, until you consider the fact that United States Merchant Marine seamen—who had served their nation so well during the war crisis—had been abandoned overseas and were forced to scrounge up money by selling cigarettes.

EIGHTEEN

NOT COVERED!

War is like a giant pack rat. It takes something from you, and it leaves something behind in its stead. It burned me out in some ways. . . . It made me grow up too fast.

AUDIE MURPHY,

MOST-DECORATED AMERICAN SOLDIER IN WORLD WAR TWO[1]

AFTER TWO AND A HALF MONTHS IN NAPLES, ARRANGEMENTS FINALLY WERE made for Dean Beaumont and other wounded Americans to return to the United States, on a Red Cross hospital ship. The men were taken to the vessel by ambulance, and set sail for Charleston, South Carolina. Dean's injuries were troublesome, but not nearly as severe as those of some men on board the ship, who were very badly wounded—including Merchant Marine seamen with severe burns and lost limbs.

When they reached Charleston, the war against Japan was still going on, as the Americans had not yet dropped the atomic bombs on Hiroshima and Nagasaki. Those cataclysmic events were a few weeks away. In Charleston, the men were put on a Red Cross train—with crosses on top of the cars—and taken to Lexington, Kentucky, where they were picked up by ambulances and taken to a military hospital. The checkups, however, were not extensive, and even today Dean still has physical injuries from the war—to his forehead and knee—that were never treated. But such concerns were not foremost in his mind at the time.

Dean just wanted to get home and put the trauma of the war behind him.

Dean and two other merchant seamen boarded a bus and rode it to Long Beach, California. Within five minutes of arriving—even before going to see their families—they caught a taxicab and took it to the Long Beach Naval Hospital. Carrying suitcases, they walked inside. The men had varying maladies, and at the very least needed tetanus shots, because of the danger of infection from all of the lines and wires that were handled on a ship, along with other exposures. Basically they wanted to obtain complete physical examinations, including blood-pressure readings and the like, and to begin any needed medical treatments or rehabilitation programs.

In recent weeks Dean and his companions had received some medical attention from military hospitals, although it was by no means comprehensive. Seriously injured merchant seamen were given more assistance than he had received, and Dean assumed that he would get even more attention when he returned to his home-town, where there were extensive facilities. He had not discussed medical coverage with anyone aboard the ship. All of the men had just assumed that the private shipping companies they worked for, or the U.S. government, would take care of them.

When they had disembarked their last ships, they just signed off, took their clothes, and left. No one thought about medical-insurance specifics. The merchant seamen had been sent into war zones, after all; they had been through a lot—and somebody owed it to them.

But there is an old saying that came to haunt these men: "The devil is in the details."

At the Long Beach Naval Hospital, a nurse asked the trio of civilian seamen for their papers. A heavyset women with blonde hair, she spoke in a very officious tone.

"Well, I was a purser," Dean said, as he knelt down and rummaged through the contents of his suitcase. "I was responsible for keeping papers in order, so I should be able to give you anything you want." His companions brought out their own papers, and every document the men had was handed over.

The nurse frowned as she looked over the documents. Finally she asked them, "Are you Navy, marine corps, or what?"

"None of that," Dean said. "We're Merchant Marine."

It was all right there in front of her, but she was slow to comprehend. Then she said, "We don't take care of the Merchant Marine."

Stunned, Dean said, "What?"

"Just Navy, coast guard, marine corps, and Army, including the Army Air Corps. You don't qualify."

The men argued with the nurse for several minutes, pointing out that they already had received some treatment. The whole thing didn't make sense to them.

But the woman shook her head stubbornly and, with a terse, "I'm sorry, but . . ." she refused to help, and told them, further, that they would have to pay for their shots and medical tests.

Dean and his companions didn't have much money with them, but they paid for the services anyway. They were not pleased, and felt confused and betrayed.

As he left the hospital, Dean became angrier and angrier. The U.S. Merchant Marine had contributed thousands of ships and merchant crews to the war, providing critical services to the Allied cause, and that was worth *nothing*? He thought of his own missions transporting docks, barges, bombs, torpedoes, military trucks, and coal, and he did not understand. It seemed outrageous to him, and to his companions. One of them had escaped from a German prisoner-of-war camp, and the other had been the survivor of a torpedoed American merchant ship that carried tanks, jeeps, and fighter planes.

The three shocked seamen would soon learn that they also had no place in the G.I. Bill, which meant they would receive no preferential treatment in a number of important personal and business categories—benefits that every military veteran was entitled to after the war.

It was just like dumping these men off a ship out in the middle of a turbulent ocean after they had completed their work, with no lifeboats, water, or food supplies. How could they ever survive?

Many of them did not. They became derelicts on the streets of America, wandering from town to town without jobs. After the war, the United States Merchant Marine began a steep decline that has continued to this day—from hauling 45 percent of U.S. imports and exports, to only 3 percent.[2] By 1946, most of the Liberty ships and other merchant vessels were no longer needed by the United States, so the companies sold them off to other countries.

The U.S. Navy contributed to the decline by enlarging their own transport division, performing the same tasks previously done by merchant seamen. In this manner, the Navy finally got much of what it had tried and failed to obtain early in the war: control over the shipment of military personnel and matériel.

Most American seamen could not get jobs on commercial ships in postwar America, since there were so few seagoing positions available. In addition, they had to compete with returning armed-forces veterans for the available civilian jobs. If two men of equal ability applied for the same job and one of them was a veteran and the other a merchant seaman, the veteran was invariably selected. To make matters worse, the veterans received free education, low-interest home, business, and farm loans, medical and disability coverage, and other benefits under the G.I. Bill of Rights, while merchant seamen got none of that.

In the months following World War Two, many of the civilian seamen who lost their seafaring positions were still quite young or not highly educated, since they had dropped out of high school to enter the Merchant Marine and serve their country. On the SS *Brander Matthews* there had been seamen even younger than Dean Beaumont, and he learned this was a common occurrence throughout the service: "In the beginning they didn't even know what a rowboat was. Anyone could join the Merchant Marine. There were kids fifteen years old who said they were eighteen, and they would be accepted, and away they would go to sea and they would get sunk."

After the war many of those young men did not have the experience or financial means to pursue their own rights. They fell through the cracks of society. The World War Two merchant seamen who *did* succeed after 1945, had to work much harder than ex–military personnel to get employment, because of all the obstacles placed in their paths.

One of those who had to work extra hard after the war was another officer from the SS *Brander Matthews*. Before World War Two he had worked as a meat cutter for a large packing company on the West Coast, and had given up that job in order to serve in the U.S. Merchant Marine. Following the war, he went back to work for the company as a meat cutter in order to support his family. But this was a man of high intelligence and talent. Dean told me that if he had only been given access to the G.I. Bill, he might have been able to attend college and become a manager at the packing company. Unfortunately, like so many other merchant seamen, he was held back by financial constraints.

Another young man who had to struggle for success after the war was Bill Flury. A steward on the Liberty ship SS *Jean Nicolet*, he'd escaped atrocities committed by the psychotic Japanese submarine captain Ariizumii, in the shark-and barracuda-infested waters of the Indian Ocean. (See chapter 5, "war crimes" page 56.) At the conclusion of the war, Flury received no G.I. Bill or other benefits. "My two younger brothers went into the Navy at the latter end of the war," he said, "and neither one of them saw any action. But they came home, and one of them went on to college, and the other one bought him a nice home through the G.I. Bill."[3]

Years later, Dean Beaumont met a man who had joined the U.S. Army in July 1945, and never saw any enemy action at all. By the time he enlisted, the war in Europe was over, and the armed conflict against Japan would end in a matter of weeks. Even so, the uninitiated soldier received a victory medal, and a ribbon that went with it, to wear on his uniform. Dean also knew men in the Navy who had served for only a month or two and then suffered psychological problems and were given Section 8 dismissals. They still received generous disability payments, pensions, and all of the other benefits.

Of the millions of men and women who wore military uniforms for the Allied cause, many of them never engaged the enemy, or even entered a war zone. Only one out of eleven—less than 10 percent—engaged in actual combat.[4] But they still received the generous lifetime benefits of military service that were denied to merchant seamen who had faced great dangers at sea. Dean knew this, and couldn't help feeling anger about it, as well as dismay.

I make no claim that every member of the Merchant Marine served his country valiantly. But it is also true that all of the people who served in the U.S. Army and in the other armed forces were not like Audie Murphy, the fearless soldier who single-handedly killed or captured 240 heavily armed Germans.[5] There were varying degrees of service, varying degrees of dedication and accomplishment. The Merchant Marine had its own heroes of World War Two, men who risked their lives, or lost them, and received very little recognition in return.

Consider this, as well: As brave as Audie Murphy was, he could not have won twenty-eight medals—including the Congressional Medal of Honor and three Purple Hearts[6]—if he and other soldiers in the European theater had not been supplied by the merchant fleet of the United States of America. The typical Allied soldier in Europe needed seven to eight *tons* of military supplies a year in order to sustain his ability to fight, and 80 percent of that was provided by the Merchant Marine.[7] Much of it was hazardous cargo, since infantry and armored divisions required six to eight times as much gasoline as food.[8]

In the Army, the Army Air Corps, the Navy, and the marine corps, there were people who performed "Merchant Marine–type" supply operations during World War Two, and who were considered "armed-forces personnel" simply because they wore uniforms. They worked on board ships or in cargo planes, drove trucks, and fulfilled any number of warehousing, loading, and delivery functions on the ground, in the air, and on the sea, providing support for fighting men. And in all of the armed services there were countless other support staff, even legions of office workers who never stepped onto any field of combat but still received full military benefits. How were any of them more valuable than our neglected merchant seamen?

The maritime historian Ian A. Millar put it this way:

> It is time to realize that the failure to recognize the World War Two U.S. Merchant Marine as being on a par with the U.S. Armed Forces is a black spot in American history. I . . . grew up taking part in various sports. I never played (on) a team that won where all the players were not honored as equal partners. We never took two or three men and said they were not good enough to stand up for the trophy. The Merchant Marine was part of our winning team during World War Two and Americans are too good a people to see these brave men denied their true place in our remembrance.[9]

There is an old saying that stands as true today as it ever was: "The uniform does not make the man." This country was served at its time of greatest peril by seamen who dressed as they pleased and did not have to salute anyone. They were *individuals*—the very essence of America and everything for which it stands.

They were *patriots*, too. Who can ever forget the image of doomed merchant ships raising American flags in the midst of a German assault on their convoy? That occurred on our Independence Day—July 4, 1942—while the ships were en route to Russia on the deadly "Murmansk Run." As torpedoes and bullets sped toward them, the valiant, patriotic men on board sang "The Battle Hymn of the Republic"! (See chapter 9, "The Russian Gauntlet," page 96.)

Retired seaman John C. Burley wrote this touching passage, as he recalled the day when he sailed past the Statue of Liberty, on his way home after the war:

> We then returned to New York where I saw the prettiest lady I had ever seen and what that statue stood for, and said a prayer of thanks to our Lord for bringing me through these past years. And that I would never forget those who did not come home to be greeted by her.[10]

The men of the United States Merchant Marine were loyal to this country—and this country let them down.

After the war, some merchant seamen were rescued from life's stormy waters by loving friends or family, while others saved themselves, swimming to "shore" on their own. Still others—the less fortunate—drowned in the attempt.

NINETEEN

THEY EARNED OUR
RESPECT

*There is always inequity in life. Some men are killed
in a war, and some men are wounded, and some
men are stationed in the Antarctic and some are
stationed in San Francisco. It's very hard in military
or personal life to assure complete equality. Life is
unfair.*

—PRESIDENT JOHN F. KENNEDY[1]

IN 1944, PRESIDENT ROOSEVELT SIGNED THE G.I. BILL OF RIGHTS FOR MILITARY
veterans. Just before he died the following year, he asked Congress
to draft a Seamen's Bill of Rights that would provide education for
young seamen who had dropped out of school to join the Merchant
Marine, along with employment assistance and medical coverage for
wartime injuries. In comparison with the G.I. Bill, it was a much
more limited program.

Even so, it was actively opposed by military authorities, who
told a congressional committee that the Merchant Marine had
refused to merge with the U.S. Navy, and was paid high wages during the war. Without President Roosevelt, as its primary sponsor,
the bill died in committee in 1947.[2]

It was no wonder that merchant seamen deeply mourned Roosevelt's death, as shown by the banner headlines in their industry publications. He not only championed the Seamen's Bill of Rights; he was also instrumental in the creation of the Gallant Ship Award for the crews of Merchant Marine ships who performed heroic acts during the war. The first award, to the SS *Samuel Parker*, was issued on April 9, 1945. The president died just three days later, in Warm Springs, Georgia.

His successor, Harry Truman, had been a U.S. Army major at the conclusion of World War One, and was not nearly as supportive of the civilian merchant service as Roosevelt had been. Roosevelt's awareness of the Merchant Marine was a familiarity that went back to his position as Assistant Secretary of the Navy from 1913 to 1921.

The late president had fully understood and appreciated the connection between the civilian maritime service and the armed forces—the way they worked closely together during times of national emergency. It must be kept in mind as well that the U.S. Merchant Marine of World War Two was built to its wartime levels by Roosevelt himself, when he signed the Merchant Marine Act of 1936, which had launched a large-scale shipbuilding program. Like the love of a father for his children, Roosevelt felt real empathy for the thousands of merchant seamen who were hired to man those brand-new vessels.

There is the myth—used as a justification for not granting a "Bill of Rights" package to merchant seamen—that they were overpaid, that they were self-centered mercenaries working for high wages, that they were an organized force of war profiteers. None of that is true. It is important to realize that the shipping companies, and the Allied cause, received excellent value for what was actually paid. As shown in chapter 11, "The Helping Hands" (see page 120), American merchant ships were run with spartan crews, requiring fewer men than the U.S. Navy needed to operate comparable ships. That amounted to a substantial savings for labor costs.

The United States government profited from these savings, and then refused to provide fair treatment and military benefits for merchant mariners.

When Frank Medeiros was a young seaman—on the SS *Gateway City*, in the ill-fated Convoy PQ-17 making the Murmansk Run—he received $3,000 for thirteen months of dangerous work. This included an unpaid period of 172 days during which ships were laid up in Iceland while German scout planes watched them, and the actual running of the gauntlet to Murmansk through the most dangerous waters in the world. His ship, the SS *Gateway City*, was subjected to continual air raids. Over the entire time in which Medeiros had dedicated himself to the war cause, he earned $231 a month—hardly a king's ransom.

It may be useful to look at the respective wartime salaries of two comparable positions—chief petty officer in the U.S. Navy, and able-bodied seaman in the Merchant Marine. (Both examples are for a man with a wife and two children, and twenty years' experience at sea.) The chief petty officer earned $385.20 per month, including $251.10 basic pay plus $37.20 for hazardous duty, plus a total of $96.90 for his dependents. The able-bodied seaman earned $405 per month, including $110 basic pay plus a $110 war bonus, plus $60 (approximate) overtime and $125 if bombed.[3]

A point often overlooked is that U.S. Navy personnel received a long list of hidden benefits, all of which saved them substantial amounts of money:

- Members of the armed forces did not have to pay federal or state income taxes, while the Merchant Marine were taxed on theirs. Howard J. Hansen told me that he was even taxed on the value of the food he ate on board ship, and on the linens he used! "They treated us like dirt," he said. Even death provided no escape. After Norbert J. Schmitz of the SS *The Dalles* died at sea, taxes of 40.9 percent were deducted from the final paycheck due to his estate.[4]
- Enlisted men were able to purchase clothing, food, and

household items at discounted prices from post exchanges, facilities the Merchant Marine did not have.

- The Navy and other military services provided housing for their families back home, and paid their moving expenses, while the merchant seamen had to pay all of their own family living expenses. Howard J. Hansen said his basic pay was $110 per month as an able-bodied seaman,* with no additional payments for a wife or children. In comparison, a Navy man, performing similar work received a *clothing allowance*, and even had clothing allowances for his wife and children.

- Military personnel received generous hospital, medical, and dental insurance, along with disability compensation, pensions, and vocational rehabilitation—while the Merchant Marine didn't get anything like that.

- Howard J. Hansen said that he and other merchant seamen received no paid vacation, while Navy sailors got a month off every year, with pay. Under the Serviceman's Readjustment Act of 1944, more popularly known as the "G.I. Bill of Rights," military veterans also received education and training for jobs, generous loan provisions (for homes, farms, and businesses), mustering-out pay, and unemployment compensation. In contrast, merchant seamen received nothing but a worthless slip of paper—a discharge certificate.

When merchant seamen left their ships, their salaries and limited benefits (such as room and board) were terminated—*completely*. They had to pay all of their own expenses, and didn't even have workers' compensation or unemployment insurance.[5] Incredibly, this occurred even if the men had had their ships shot out from under them in a war zone, and even if they became prisoners of war.

One merchant seaman, Lincoln R. Masur of the SS *William*

---

*With his characteristic good humor, Mr. Hansen also said that able-bodied seamen were affectionately referred to as "deck apes" on merchant ships.

Dawes, wrote a letter after his ship was torpedoed, saying he'd had to spend $300 of his own funds for clothing and other personal possessions that were lost with his ship.[6] Wilson J. Taylor, another seaman whose ship was torpedoed, lost his clothing, and was paid only $150—not nearly enough to replace the items.

One thing is clear: The merchant seamen were treated inconsistently when it came to such payments, and invariably did not receive enough.

The same is true with respect to medals, as will be noted in chapters 20 (see page 194) and 23 (see page 228). Most of the merchant seamen from World War Two received no medals at all from the American government, but a few did, for reasons never explained by officials.

When all of this is added to the obstacles these men faced in obtaining jobs—at sea and on land—it shows why so many merchant seamen floundered and became destitute after the war—why they drank, took drugs, and contemplated suicide. It was just too difficult, and *too unfair*. These men knew what they had been through, and were frustrated by the lack of support from their government, and from their fellow citizens of the United States.

Captain Frank Medeiros expressed it poignantly, his voice filled with emotion: "All I wanted was the respect from my government because I gave everything I had. I was willing to give my life, and what else can you give?"[7]

In analyzing the compensation paid to servicemen versus merchant seamen, the value of benefits must be included. Each civilian seaman lost hundreds of thousands of dollars in benefits; and to this must be added all the hidden costs these seamen sustained—including stress-induced mental and physical illness they suffered because of the difficulties they faced during and following the war.

Again unfairly, they had to continue fighting—for their just deserts—even after the Allies had laid down their arms against the Axis powers. The men of the United States Merchant Marine are still engaged in that fight, and will be until the day the last World War Two merchant seaman dies. Most of all, beyond any monetary compensation, which they undoubtedly deserve, these men want respect; they want the recognition and acceptance of a grateful nation.

Even the passengers of taxicabs in the major cities of the United States have a "Bill of Rights" posted in the passenger compartment. This includes having the car's meter on, having access to air-conditioning, and the like. The Seamen's Bill of Rights that died in committee in 1947 would have provided only limited benefits— more restrictive than what military personnel received under the G.I. Bill of Rights—but the seamen were denied even that.

The United States has paid reparations to Japanese-Americans who were held in detention camps in World War Two, and to Native Americans whose lands were unfairly taken. America is a great nation, but in the course of its history it has committed misdeeds against certain segments of society, including the aforementioned groups.

The U.S. Merchant Marine is yet another segment of society damaged by the steamroller of American history—men who were forgotten and left behind. Those seamen are in their seventies and eighties now, and are dying off.

For more than four decades after the war, the Military Service Review Board of the U.S. Department of Defense consistently refused to grant active-duty status to World War Two merchant seamen, since the board did not consider their contributions "equivalent to active-duty service in the Armed Forces of the United States."[8] In 1988, though—in response to a 1986 lawsuit brought by three merchant seamen, and the AFL-CIO—the board reconsidered and granted veterans' status to American merchant seamen who had enlisted in the oceangoing service during the period of armed conflict: December 7, 1941, through August 15, 1945. Those men became eligible to receive DD-214 armed-forces discharge certificates. However, this did not include the men who had delivered war supplies just before the Second World War, nor the other Merchant Marine veterans, from World War One, the Korean War, and the Vietnam War.

The legal battle for World War Two Merchant Mariners' benefits actually goes back to 1980, when there were four merchant
seamen plaintiffs—Edward Schumacher, Stanley Willner, Lester
Reid, and Dennis Roland—against the Military Service Review
Board. Their dedicated attorney, Joan McAvoy of New York City,
battled on their behalf for eight years, and finally achieved some
degree of success.

The plaintiffs were strongly opposed all the way by military
groups, including the American Legion, the Veterans of Foreign
Wars, and the U.S. Air Force. The National Commander of the
American Legion, John Comer, said, "Clearly they are not veterans. . . . They did not take the oath for four years like members of
the armed forces did, and they did not wear uniforms."[9]

The U.S. Air Force, with a key role on the Military Service
Review Board, was involved in another legal battle in which they—
to their credit—were seeking to obtain veterans' benefits for civilian
women who had flown military planes in World War Two, delivering
them to air bases around the world. When the Air Force won that
right, the judge said they also needed to grant the same status to
Merchant Marine seamen and other deserving groups.

The granting of veterans' status to the U.S. Merchant Marine
would, however, prove to be too little, too late. By 1988—forty-
three years after the end of the war—fewer than half of the wartime merchant seamen were still alive.[10] Our government did not
see fit to honor these gallant volunteers when it really counted,
when they were in the prime of life. When the authorities on the
Review Board finally granted anything at all, they did so only
halfheartedly, in response to legal action, as if the men of the
Merchant Marine were no more than whining, second-class contributors.

In addition, the surviving families of deceased men did not
receive any compensation—much less recognition—at all, even
though the spouses and children of wartime merchant seamen suffered immensely themselves, from the loss of income, and a lack of
benefits and respect.

When merchant seamen became eligible for veterans' benefits in 1988, Dean Beaumont did not receive any notification. Perhaps it was because he had moved, and the Veterans Administration* and other groups did not have his current address. In 1993, he was living in Kailua-Kona, Hawaii, on a very limited income. He and his wife Carol were doing volunteer work for the University of the Nations, a Christian institution that operates hospital "mercy ships," providing doctors to help sick and injured people around the world. Always a generous man who was more concerned about others than himself, Dean had given away many of his father's paintings that had been left to him—paintings that, over the years, had substantially increased in value.

In the forty-eight years since the end of World War Two, Dean had grown disgusted with the lack of recognition and benefits for the men of the Merchant Marine. A number of his friends had suffered even more than he had, and one of them suggested that he write a letter to the president of the United States, Bill Clinton.

Dean thought it was a good idea, but sent the letter to former president George H. W. Bush instead. Knowing that George Herbert Walker Bush had been a young fighter pilot in World War Two, Dean said he had been a young Merchant Marine officer himself. Dean told Mr. Bush about his own experiences in World War Two: how he had been injured and was subsequently informed, upon his arrival home, by Long Beach Naval Hospital that he had no medical coverage, and was forced to pay for his own tetanus shots and blood tests. Dean also sent along a couple of lithograph prints of his father's paintings of U.S. Navy vessels. He had done this before, and found that it made his letters stand out, improving the chance of a response.

Three months later Dean received a letter from the head of the Veterans Administration, who told him that President Bush had

---

*The Veterans Administration is now known as the Department of Veterans Affairs. In this book, which deals primarily with Merchant Marine veterans of World War Two, I use the more common reference—the Veterans Administration—which is the governmental name these men still use in their conversations and correspondence.

asked him to answer the letter. The VA chief asked for information about the ships on which Dean had served, how involved they were in action against the enemy, and what kind of injuries Dean had sustained. With that information, they would see what they could do.

Dean sent in the information, and a short while afterward he received a notice that he qualified for 50 percent disability pay, which entitled him to $700 a month in compensation. He also learned that he was entitled to the provisions of the G.I. Bill of Rights, which included educational benefits. While still angry and hurt over all the years his Merchant Marine service had been scorned, Dean was now very excited, and willing to forgive.

He remembered how he had been forced to work his own way through college after the war, while military veterans got free education under the G.I. Bill. Seeing this as an opportunity to obtain what was long overdue, Dean hurried over to Captain Cook Junior. College on the island of Hawaii, about three miles from his home. He told the administration there that Merchant Marine veterans were now eligible under the G.I. Bill, and he wanted to sign up for free computer education. The school had no information relating to this, and sent him down to the Veterans Administration office in Kailua-Kona, where he discovered, again to his dismay, that the bill was only good for the ten years following the end of World War Two.

Benefits had ended in 1955!

"They gave it to us and took it away immediately," Dean told me, barely able to control the anger in his voice.

He also said that a woman at the VA office had told him that he might be entitled to receive more than his current $700 a month, if he would just write up his experiences and fill out an application. After Dean provided a great amount of further information, he was informed that only men who been shot or lost a limb could qualify for those benefits. He needed to formally cancel the first application and write another one, which had to be sent to a different department of the Veterans Administration—and everything had to be signed and notarized. Frustrated by this runaround, Dean decided to forget it; he would rather provide the information to me for this book—*The Forgotten Heroes*—and we could then send copies of it to representatives and senators in the United States Congress.

Since Dean Beaumont is himself an educated, capable man, it made us wonder how many Merchant Marine veterans of World War Two had even been notified of the benefits to which they were entitled, and whether they could subsequently negotiate the maze of bureaucratic paperwork required by the Veterans Administration. Such extensive paperwork can be especially burdensome for seamen in their retirement years.

As time passed, Dean spoke with a number of other aged merchant seamen who did not understand the veterans' benefits. When Dean told them about the paperwork requirements, some of them didn't take any action at all—instead assuming it would all be taken care of by the United States government. But Dean was very concerned about this. He thought the Veterans Administration needed to offer more assistance and counseling, so that deserving merchant seamen could obtain the limited benefits they were entitled to receive.

If Dean and others with his strength had not been such survivors, they might have ended up out in the streets, as so many of their comrades had.

Even though the U.S. Merchant Marine participated in the amphibious landings on D-Day in June 1944—and was given limited veterans' status in 1988—the seamen were recently denied any type of display at the National D-Day Museum.[11] They have also been denied membership in the VFW, the Veterans of Foreign Wars organization.

And while the U.S. Merchant Marine is beginning to participate in Veterans Day Parades and other events (as a result of the limited recognition they received in 1988), they are often treated like water boys for soldiers. In the July 4, 2002, ceremonies, held in Washington, D.C., the U.S. Merchant Marine Veterans of World War Two were mentioned, along with other veterans' groups. Each branch of the armed forces then marched out with their color guards, but the Merchant Marine—even though they have a fine color guard of their own—were not permitted to do so.

The proud men of the U.S. Merchant Marine keep sailing on anyway, never giving up the fight. In parades around the country on military holidays, merchant seamen display scale models of merchant ships, or old Liberty-ship lifeboats that they have fixed up and put on trailers. Some of those floats have even won first place in competitions, and the men themselves have received generous applause. But for more than forty years—from 1945 to 1988—there was no sign of the U.S. Merchant Marine at such events. Except for the men standing on the sidewalks, watching.

When I see those lifeboats, I can't help thinking of the stories of the gallant merchant seamen who drifted in them, for days and months after their ships were torpedoed—and I think of the men who never made it that far, who were machine-gunned and shelled in lifeboats and on rafts as they sought safe haven from their sinking ships.

Sadly, the organizers of some Veterans Day and Fourth of July celebrations still do not invite the Merchant Mariners of World War Two to participate. The stark truth is that such celebrations should not even be held without these men, since the Allied victory would not have been possible without them.

The whole experience has been extremely painful for American merchant seamen, and for their families. Maritime historian Ian A. Millar wrote about his father, Adrian E. Millar, who served in the British, Canadian, and American merchant navies:

> As a youth I remember well that my father was not regarded as a war veteran; he was never invited to take part in an Armistice Day parade. When he died he was not officially entitled to have his nation's flag over him. Did he need any veterans group to pronounce him a veteran? No, a German torpedo* accomplished that on a cold night off Greenland.[12]

---

*The British merchant ship SS *Gypsum Queen*, which sailed in the summer of 1941 as part of Convoy SC-42.

TWENTY

LAST MAN
TO STAND

*Basically the public never heard our story. We were
all volunteers and we delivered the ammunition, the
tanks, and the planes to our fighting men overseas.
With those supplies, our forces loaded up and went
out and defeated the Germans and the Japanese.
The Merchant Marine contributed a great deal to the
victory, but we never got the message out, and it hurt
us a lot.*

—LIEUTENANT DEAN BEAUMONT,

UNITED STATES MERCHANT MARINE

IN AUGUST 1945, DEAN BEAUMONT SIGNED ON AS PURSER ON A FREIGHTER SHIP
and sailed from San Pedro, California, to the Philippines with a load
of general cargo. The war against Japan was still on when he left
port, and there were some crewmen with him who'd had their ships
shot out from under them. One of the mates had been on two different merchant ships torpedoed in the battle for the Atlantic in convoys traveling between America and Great Britain. An engineer,
only in his mid-twenties, had suffered severe burns on his face, from
an attack on his ship by Japanese aircraft. But those men—and
Dean, too—were going back to war.

190

It was like that on other American merchant ships as well, for the entire duration of World War Two. There are countless stories of men who kept going back to sea, ignoring the danger. Jack Faulkner, who served on a number of Liberty ships during the war, told me that his crewmates on one voyage included three men who had previously been on freighters that were torpedoed and sunk in the Caribbean.

While Dean Beaumont's ship was at sea, Japan surrendered and V-J Day was declared, on August 15, 1945. Like V-E Day earlier that year ("Victory in Europe"), there were raucous celebrations, but not on Dean's ship. The crewmen were all pleased that hostilities had been concluded, but there were no wild parties—not even when they reached the Philippines—just a numb sense of acceptance. The same was true for merchant seamen from other ships and other theaters of war. Despite their monumental contributions they were not permitted to be anything more than spectators for the victory festivities, watching the members of the armed forces as they were honored with parades and marching bands.

Ironically, our merchant seamen were frequently treated better in other lands than they were in their own. Working as a Third Mate, Peter Chelemedos had to abandon his ship, the MS *Cape Decision*, after it was torpedoed in the middle of the Atlantic Ocean in January 1943. A harrowing nine-day journey in a lifeboat ensued, until finally he and forty other men in the boat reached Barbados in the West Indies—almost one thousand miles away. There, the inhabitants threw a big party in honor of these men who had endured so much, and even gave them free hotel rooms, food, and new clothes.[1]

Other nations who benefited directly from American merchant shipping operations have expressed strong appreciation, including Malta, Great Britain, and the Soviet Union. In 1991, the Soviet Union awarded medals to American merchant seamen and members of the U.S. Navy Armed Guard who served on American ships, for their service on the treacherous arctic convoy routes to Russian ports during World War Two. A big ceremony was held at the Soviet Embassy in Washington, D.C., attended by many of the American veterans who had served so valiantly almost half a century earlier.[2]

Some merchant seamen were able to pull themselves up by their own bootstraps after the war, despite the obstacles they faced. In addition to what he had endured already, Dean Beaumont experienced frustrations in business and personal matters in the postwar years, and suffered a stress-related condition that caused him to be hospitalized in Los Angeles. He and his family had to pay for the treatments themselves, since he received no benefits from the Merchant Marine. But Dean persevered and eventually overcame his difficulties. He made a decision to live, and to do something important with his life.

Dean resumed his studies at Occidental College, and eventually went on to UCLA, where he graduated. He had to work to pay his tuition since Merchant Marine seamen had no "Bill of Rights," but he did so quietly, without rancor. The money he had earned from selling cigarettes in Naples helped with the tuition, and also enabled him to purchase a nice 1941 Chevrolet convertible. During summer breaks he still served on merchant ships, and rose to the rank of lieutenant. Later, Dean operated a successful contracting business for a while, and eventually went to work for U.S. Steel, and then Westinghouse Electric Company, where he became one of their top salesmen in the early 1960s.

Following World War Two, the paintings of his celebrated father, Arthur Beaumont, increased in value, to the point where some of them were worth hundreds of thousands of dollars apiece. Today, the U.S. Navy owns around 10 percent of Arthur Beaumont's estimated four thousand works, including those Dean had donated to the U.S. naval MIDPAC headquarters building and to the USS *Arizona* memorial, both located at Pearl Harbor, Hawaii. He did this despite his feelings that the U.S. Navy had not treated the men of the Merchant Marine fairly during the war or afterward.

Dean sent me a remarkable letter concerning the postage-stamp designs his father had come up with during World War Two, the program that had been abandoned because of a bureaucratic problem in which the stamps could not be produced until ten years after the death of the artist. (See chapter 6, "The Battle of Saipan," page 65.) In his letter, Dean wrote,

> *Recently I ran across those stamp paintings and informa-tion on them. It has been more than twenty years since the artist Arthur Beaumont died. Since the time require-ment has been fulfilled, now would be a good time to bring out the U.S. Navy stamps. There are still many World War Two Navy men around—the stamps would bring back memories to them and would create new interest in the old Navy that contributed so much to vic-tory. I will gladly give up any interest I have in the paint-ings of the stamps—and hope they benefit our Navy.*
>
>

Sincerely,
Dean Beaumont

The letter impressed me because my friend had no interest in making any money on the project; he only wanted to help sailors who went through the war with him, even though they had already been treated better than Dean and the rest of his U.S. Merchant Marine comrades.

Dean always has been generous, and quick to forgive. But there is a difference between forgiving and forgetting.

In 1987, Admiral Ronald J. Hays—referring to Dean Beaumont as "an ambassador of the U.S. Navy"—gave him the Superior Public Service Award, similar to an honor the Navy had earlier bestowed upon his father. With characteristic good humor, Dean quipped, "My father got his for making the paintings, and I got mine for giving them away."

Other Arthur Beaumont paintings are displayed prominently in government buildings, museums, academies, war memorials, and palaces around the world. In 1982, Dean visited Buckingham Palace and presented Prince Philip with an original Beaumont painting of the American naval cruiser USS *England* (DLG-22). The prince, taken with the ship's name, and with the quality of the artistic rendition, also obtained the legal copyright and set up a program to sell prints of the painting in order to raise money for the salvaging of the *Mary Rose*, the sunken sixteenth-century flagship of King Henry VIII.

Dean told Prince Philip that the ship wasn't named for the prince's country. It was named after Ensign England, one of the many men killed in the Japanese raid on Pearl Harbor. The prince didn't care. He said it was the most beautiful picture of a ship he had ever seen, and sent Dean a letter of appreciation, written on the royal stationery. Former presidents Ronald Reagan and George Herbert Walker Bush also received prints that Dean Beaumont sent to them as gifts. The Beaumont family has donated prints to the Los Angeles Maritime Museum as well, and to other major museums around the world.

While Dean occupies himself today with his father's legacy, and with important humanitarian efforts, he has never been able to escape his feelings of anger and deep disappointment over the way he and his fellow merchant seamen have been treated. Everywhere he turns, there are still painful reminders.

After World War Two, the veterans of the U.S. Merchant Marine received little cardboard "medals," but they had to write in to the War Shipping Administration to get them.* Each one was the size of

---

*The War Shipping Administration policy under which medals were awarded has been woefully inconsistent. Captain William C. Crozier was a Third Assistant Engineer on the SS *Jack Carnes*, which was torpedoed and sunk in 1942. He was not injured in the attack but subsequently received a cloth "Presidential Citation" ribbon—the Merchant Marine Combat Bar with a star. The award specified that he had been involved in "direct enemy action." But so was Dean Beaumont, on the SS *Brander Matthews*, and Dean had actually been injured. His ship, however had not been sunk. (Also see chapters 19 and 23, pages 181 and 228, respectively, regarding such inconsistencies on the part of the government.)

a business card, with a color picture of a medal printed on it. Dean got four of them: the Merchant Marine Combat Bar, the Pacific War Zone Bar, the Atlantic War Zone Bar, and the Mediterranean–Middle East War Zone Bar.

Dean also received another little card that looked like the others, except it was called a "Victory Medal," and confirmed his "active service with the United States Merchant Marine or Maritime Service during World War Two." Again, it had a little color *picture* of a medal printed on it.

Holding his "Pacific War Zone Bar" over his chest, Dean winked at me and asked, with his characteristic good humor, "How am I supposed to wear a cardboard medal?"

In response, I have this question for the United States government: How tacky is *that*?

It was not until forty-three years after the end of the armed conflict that a decent medal was made available to the Merchant Marine, pursuant to House Resolution 1430, passed in October 1988. Even then, the medal was not *given* to them—the men had to pay around twenty dollars for each one.

The U.S. government cited budget difficulties, to justify this. Even so, thousands of medals were awarded to Desert Storm veterans, free of charge. Concerning this, Ian A. Millar, the son of World War Two seaman Adrian E. Millar—wrote, "So much for the heartfelt thanks of a grateful nation."[3]

In yet another piece, Mr. Millar put it this way:

> (Thousands of) war veterans of the Merchant Marine gave their lives for their freedom and ours during World War Two, and now we find that not one of those lives was worth a $20 medal. None of those brave men who died in the mustard gas at Bari, none of those who were beaten from pillar to post in the death camps of the Far East, and none of those who survived all that the enemy could throw at them are worth a $20 medal. How pathetically sad that for those who suffered (such a

large) percentage of combat casualties . . . America holds such contempt and insult.[4]

Dean Beaumont said to me, "I feel so hurt by this medal business. What a slam for the men who did so much in the war. We saved England and Russia with food and equipment. We supplied every battle the Allies fought. We spilled our blood."

It should be noted that, historically, military authorities in the United States have been parsimonious when it comes to awarding medals to civilians. During the Civil War, Dr. Mary Walker, a battlefield surgeon for the Union Army, was awarded the Congressional Medal of Honor for her heroism. This was a very controversial decision, and unprecedented in the history of the nation. In 1917, an Army review board revoked her medal, but Dr. Walker—quite elderly at the time—held on to it, in defiance. Mary Walker died two years later, in 1919 but in 1977 President Jimmy Carter took the courageous and long overdue step of reinstating her Medal of Honor.[5]

Veterans Day, November 11, 2001, fell on a Sunday. Dean Beaumont and his wife Carol attended church on the Kona coast of Hawaii, and the minister asked all war veterans in the congregation to stand, so that they could be honored. A number of men rose, from various wars, but Dean remained seated, still feeling anger and resentment.

He thought back to his boyhood, when he had dreamed of joining the United States Navy, and of the times when he had accompanied his father on trips to the USS *Arizona* and other important battleships that were subsequently sunk at Pearl Harbor. He remembered wearing his spit-and-polish military academy uniform, and a little sword in a scabbard, and feeling proud to be an American.

He recalled years after that, too, when he joined the U.S. Merchant Marine during the war, and how he initially had felt great pride to be part of a great Navy fleet, albeit in a supporting role. His

Liberty ship, anchored near an aircraft carrier in the Marshall Islands, was delivering important war supplies, and Dean was doing his part for the cause.

Since his youth Dean Beaumont had been a patriotic American, and he still felt this sentiment in his retirement years, but in a much different, more mature way. He still loved his country deeply, from the depths of his soul, but he did so now with an awareness of the flaws of our nation and its leadership. The naive luster of boyhood dreams was gone, and he felt deep pain, from wounds that had never healed and probably never would.

"Stand up, dear," his wife Carol urged him, in a low voice. "You're a veteran, too."

Reluctantly, Dean rose to his feet. He was the last man to stand.

TWENTY-ONE

THE QUEST
FOR JUSTICE

War changes you forever.

—COLONEL OLIVER NORTH[1]

THERE IS NO DOUBT THAT THE SEAMEN OF THE U.S. MERCHANT MARINE SHOULD have accepted Navy control during World War Two. Their refusal to do so, spurred on by shortsighted union leaders and shipping company executives who were in control of the affairs of the seamen, created enmity from all ranks of the U.S. Navy, with a rippling effect throughout the armed forces and the American public.

The widely publicized reports that the civilian crews of the SS *Nira Luckenbach* and the SS *Thomas Jefferson* were refusing to perform work because of bad attitudes were false. But those stories, once in circulation, were impossible to stamp out. No more than ugly, totally unsubstantiated rumors, they were accepted as fact.

Some of the bluejackets that I interviewed have expressed passionate disdain for the Merchant Marine. Navy personnel of various ranks have told me that wartime merchant seamen were "feather merchants" and "drunks," and—the most common complaint against them—that they were overpaid in comparison with military personnel. These and other baseless stories poisoned the atmosphere against the Merchant Marine like radioactive contamination, which takes a very long time to dissipate. One retired Navy veteran recently even made the incredible statement that merchant seamen were paid "ten times as much" as Navy sailors during the war! This sounds like a "fish story" in which the fish keep growing larger with each telling. (See chapter 19, "They Earned Our Respect," page 181, for actual salaries and benefits.)

The truth is, the U.S. Merchant Marine didn't get paid more; they just got *killed* more. And the "killing," in the form of character assassination, has not stopped to this day, with all the disinformation, innuendos, and outright lies that have been spread about these hardworking seamen.

During and after World War Two, the U.S. Merchant Marine could have used a good public-relations agency. In 1944, Dean Beaumont's Navy friends didn't know much about the civilian maritime service. Bill Flury, a survivor of the *Jean Nicolet* atrocity (see chapter 5, "War Crimes," page 61), said recently, "Half the people don't even know what the Merchant Marine [is]. Or if they know of the Merchant Marine it's something derogatory. . . . I think it's a shame."[2]

The all-pervasive disinformation campaign against the Merchant Marine stemmed to a large extent from the fact that the U.S. Navy had become a thwarted suitor and never forgave the rejection. Some naval officers saw it as a failure to play as a team, and as a hindrance to the war effort. This position on their part may very well have been true. But why should individual Merchant Marine *seamen* have suffered for the infraction? And, no matter how much responsibility those men had for the actions of their union leaders, they did not deserve what happened to them after the war, the way they were thrown out like used-up garbage.

The U.S. Navy had powerful allies—the other branches of the armed forces, the Veterans of Foreign Wars, and the American Legion—and in this particular confrontation they all played the political game better than the representatives of the Merchant Marine. It was a war with severe causalities: civilian seamen "torpedoed" by powerful military lobbyists who influenced congressmen and senators to either vote against Merchant Marine bills, or to let them die in committee.

The VFW—Veterans of Foreign Wars—has steadfastly blocked the Merchant Marine. At their national convention in 1998, they passed a resolution to deny VFW membership to "World War Two–Era Merchant Mariners." In the resolution they recognized "the important contribution the American merchant seamen made" during the war, but also stated: "Be it resolved, that based on documentation, World War Two merchant seamen do not qualify for VFW membership, simply because they were never part of our armed forces and therefore did not receive military campaign or service awards; and be it further resolved that no request be made to Congress to alter the VFW Congressional Charter to provide membership eligibility to any person who has not worn the uniform and served as a member of the Armed Forces of the United States."[3]

With the good humor characteristic of so many merchant seamen, Peter Chelemedos—who lost two ships to torpedoes—told me: "Those old vets are still mad at the Merchant Marine because we fed them Spam during the war." In contrast, another merchant seaman said to me, in an angry tone, "Guys in the VFW are still listening to what was said in barrooms sixty years ago. They never saw through the lies and half-truths."

I interviewed a number of family members of deceased World War Two merchant seamen, and some of the comments were surprising. Two sons told me that their fathers never wanted veterans' status. The historian Ian A. Millar put it this way, concerning his father Adrian E. Millar: "Dad was proud to be a civilian war veteran. He didn't want military status." In a letter to me, Jack Urstadt wrote, "My dad [John George Urstadt IV] did not want any recognition and expected no military honors or benefits. . . . He said there were many like him in the Merchant Marine, and they did it because they were patriots."

Men of great pride made these poignant comments to their families, men who learned how to cope in an atmosphere of hostility and rejection. They found ways to accept the sometimes cruel fate forced upon them by others, and to rise above it.

To their credit, the American Legion began to invite World War Two merchant seamen to join their organization, immediately after the seamen were granted their limited veterans' status in 1988. One of the men I interviewed for this book told me in a bitter voice that the American Legion had done that only because their membership numbers had fallen so low by that time. He said he'd felt like telling them to "shove it," but he knew men in the American Legion whom he liked and respected for their own contributions to the Allied victory. So, setting aside the past, setting aside the fact that the National Commander of the American Legion had once declared merchant seamen unworthy, this man swallowed his pride and joined. He set his old memories aside, but he did not forget them.

Recently, the American Legion honored a World War Two veteran of the U.S. Merchant Marine—eighty-five-year-old Arthur Olsen of Oregon—by bestowing upon him, along with twelve armed-forces veterans, the "Veterans of the Year" award. It was the first time in history a merchant seaman had received the award.[4]

Each man copes with the past in his own way. Some merchant seamen have carried bitterness and anger in their hearts for more than half a century. Others died, still having such feelings, without ever having resolved them. The false portrayals of these men should stir the outrage of every decent American. This should never have happened in our country. The lies cannot be left to stand unchallenged and unexposed. It is a national tragedy, and a national shame.

An able-bodied seaman who went around the world seven times on merchant ships, Howard J. Hansen, said to me, his voice edged with sarcasm: "We were the most loyal bunch of 'drunks' you ever saw, completely dedicated to the cause of the United States of America."

The U.S. Merchant Marine suffered more battle deaths per capita than any branch of the American armed forces. To draw direct parallels with the American service branches that operated ships, the United States Merchant Marine sustained losses that were *16.4 times greater* than those of the U.S. Coast Guard. (See epigraph for chapter 10, "The Submarine Parade," page 101.) Also, the U.S. Merchant Marine experienced losses that were *4.4 times greater* than those of the U.S. Navy. American naval forces operated in distant war zones alongside merchant ships, so this comparison is especially enlightening. Contrasting the heavily armed Navy vessels of World War Two with the unarmed or lightly armed Merchant Marine vessels of the same period, it is easy to see which service branch faced the most peril. The Merchant Marine went to war underarmed, but their ships kept going to sea, and their brave seamen kept manning the vessels.

Considering the facts, it is impossible to understand why a U.S. Navy or Coast Guard sailor received full military benefits after the war, including those provided by the G.I. Bill, while the U.S. Merchant Marine seaman got nothing. Every American merchant ship flew the Stars and Stripes going into battle, and the men on those vessels served this country as much as any military veteran.

Admiral Chester W. Nimitz admitted that the Merchant Marine did a good job, when he said to Emory S. Land of the U.S. Maritime Commission, "Never before has any comparable fighting force been supplied with the materials of offensive warfare over such vast ocean distances as those now being transported to the Fleet by the commercial ships operating under your jurisdiction."[5]

When the U.S. Navy attempted to gain control over the Merchant Marine in the early 1940s, the head of the National Maritime Union that represented seamen on the East Coast—Joseph Curran—fought back. In a union publication, he gave one reason for the Navy's efforts:

> [The] union had exposed to various government agencies many inefficiencies with respect to safety equipment, inadequate arming of ships, improper stowage of cargo etcetera. It was hoped that if a campaign were started to induct the Merchant Marine into the Navy, it would stop these protests, which were causing the American people to ask questions as to why better

safety equipment and patrols were not being given to the merchant service."[6]

Certainly most union officials had the best interests of their memberships at heart. To a large degree Mr. Curran was referring to the early months of the war, when many American merchant ships were torpedoed by U-boats off the East Coast of the United States and in the Caribbean, killing more than a thousand civilian seamen. Those ships were unarmed, for the most part, and effective convoy systems had not yet been instituted. Another important element contributed to those deaths, at least the ones off the East Coast: U-boats were easily able to see the ships, profiled at night against the lights of American coastal cities such as Miami and Atlantic City. For too many months, officials in those cities refused to impose black-outs at night, until forced to do so.

But the World War Two–era unions also wanted to maintain their own power base—which would erode if their membership fell under military control. In alliance with the unions, the shipping-company owners wanted to keep their lucrative shipping contracts. For their part, the U.S. Navy had their own power base to expand. In their defense, however, it must be admitted they were also motivated by patriotism, since they honestly felt that military control over civilian seamen and ships would enable the Allies to more efficiently prosecute the war.

It is possible to justify the stance of the unions, the shipping companies, and the Navy as they all jockeyed for position. In the midst of all the vitriol, however, it is clear that our brave merchant seamen were caught—and shredded—in the crossfire. Seafaring men, while suffering heavy losses at the hands of the Axis powers during World War Two—deaths and horrible injuries—were also the victims of another war, one that was not so easy to recognize or fight. It was a war that did not end with the declaration of V-E Day or V-J Day; a war that continues to this day, and will go on for as long as it takes—until justice is served.

Hindsight is invariably twenty-twenty, but it appears to me that another course of action might have been better. The unions and shipping companies could have negotiated to grant the Navy only temporary control during wartime, and to have the U.S. government pay reparations to the companies and unions for their financial losses.

Some merchant seamen were actually entitled to veterans' benefits under an old law of the U.S. Code (46 U.S.C. 225, dated May 28, 1896), which stated:

> Service During War—No master, mate, pilot or engineer of steam vessels licensed under Title L II (R.S. 4399–4500) of the Revised Statutes shall be liable to draft in time of war, except for the performance of duties such as required by his license; and while performing such duties in the service of the United States every such master, mate, pilot or engineer shall be entitled to the highest rate of wages paid in the Merchant Marine of the United States for similar services; and if killed or wounded while performing such duties under the United States, they or their heirs or legal representatives shall be entitled to all privileges accorded to soldiers and sailors serving in the Army or Navy under the pension laws of the United States.

However, Lewis B. Hershey, director of the Selective Service Administration, decided to suspend this statute during the war and supersede it with the provisions of the 1940 Selective Service Act. His critical decision, which went unchallenged by the U.S. Merchant Marine, was another blow to merchant seamen. A Merchant Marine veteran of the war who researched the matter, Captain Warren G. Leback, said that merchant seamen were "too busy fighting the war" when these political machinations occurred, and he went on to say:

> Unfortunately, we only go around once and we cannot change what was decreed in 1942; we only can, how-

ever, as seamen, add a few expletives when Lewis B. Hershey's name is spoken or he is written about.[7]

In the poisoned atmosphere at the conclusion of World War Two, anti–Merchant Marine lobbying intensified, even though the seamen had already suffered far too much. After all they had given to this country, and all their war-related injuries and deaths, their Seamen's Bill of Rights crashed on the rocks in 1947. (See chapter 19, "They Earned Our Respect," page 179.). Then they were forced to endure even more humiliation, when the old accusation that seamen's unions were run by communists resurfaced. Communists had been involved in the American labor movement of the 1930s, and this kernel of truth was distorted for a long time—a common tactic used by persons and organizations who wish to advance their own agendas through misinformation campaigns. By wartime, though, the influence of communists in the sea unions had proven insignificant.

But the House Un-American Activities Committee (HUAC) pressed the accusation for years, emphasizing the fact that many Merchant Marine radio operators belonged to the American Communications Association, which, the committee said, was "more predominantly communistic than any other union." Of course, this whole premise was proven absurd during the war, since radio officers were often among the most heroic of merchant seamen, staying on board their ships after enemy attacks in order to continue to transmit distress messages.[8] It was the same kind of drivel that William Randolph Hearst's "yellow journalists," Walter Winchell and Westbrook Pegler, had used—accusations without proof.

There is an old saying: "The only thing worse than being proven wrong, is to be proven wrong at the top of your voice." That happened to the bellicose Winchell in particular, since he was sued by the National Maritime Union for his absurd remarks and forced to pay a settlement. (See chapter 2, "All the Ships at Sea," page 28.)

By the early 1950s, the hysteria had built to such a level, that for several years—until "the Red Scare" subsided—merchant seamen were forced to undergo screening tests to determine their political affiliations and loyalties. Many of them failed the tests, but were not told why. Absolutely no details were provided.

One of the experienced seamen who was booted out of the industry was Bill Bailey, a leader in the firemen's union—the men who worked in the engine rooms of merchant ships. Concerning his own mistreatment, he said, "They took my seaman's papers away from me. . . . I couldn't sail. I couldn't ship. And here I am with a wife and a kid. What . . . am I gonna do?"[9]

Captain Frank Medeiros, the soft-spoken, thoughtful veteran of the dangerous and fateful Murmansk Run, was moved by emotion when he described the plight of his comrades. He told me that merchant seamen should have marched on Washington, D.C., to demand their rights, and cited the example of World War One armed-forces veterans who had done exactly that, in 1932. Eight years previous, Congress had voted to provide a bonus, or "adjusted compensation," to the veterans, but it was in the form of paid-up life-insurance policies that were not due to mature until 1945—still more than a decade away.[10]

In the midst of the Great Depression, the unemployed veterans of World War One needed their bonuses on an emergency basis, so fifteen to twenty thousand of them went to Washington, set up a shantytown in the shadow of the Capitol dome, and engaged in rallies and marches. Their strategy—while it also resulted in a violent confrontation with the U.S. Army—ultimately led to the servicemen receiving their bonuses in 1936.[11]

It took those military veterans four years to obtain their rights. More than fifty years after the end of World War Two, the veterans of the U.S. Merchant Marine still do not have theirs. As I discussed this with Dean Beaumont, one of the things I brought up was the need for the Veterans Administration to explain "veterans' benefits" to the merchant seamen who had qualified for medical payments under the 1988 extension, under which they were eligible if they had served on oceangoing vessels between December 7, 1941, and August 15, 1945.

In response to my suggestion, Dean said, "What benefits?"

It was more than a matter of semantics. His point was well taken. Under the G.I. Bill of Rights, the military veterans of the Second World War were given a broad range of benefits, only one of which was medical payments. But in Dean's view, the 1988 benefits package was *so* little and *so* late—with so many exclusions and limitations that only applied to the Merchant Marine—that it amounted to hardly anything at all.

Unfortunately, the Merchant Marine and military personnel are still at odds today, as they argue over how much recognition merchant seamen should receive for their role in World War Two. Recently, I spoke with a retired officer of the U.S. Marine Corps, and told him I was writing a book about the Merchant Marine. He smiled and said, "There's a big difference between the two, you know."

"But is there, really?" I asked him. "We've all heard stories of the Marine Corps' bravery, and we've seen the famous photograph of marines raising the American flag on Mount Suribachi at Iwo Jima. The corps received a huge amount of publicity for that photograph. But if there's 'a big difference' between the two services, as you say—in the way you mean it—why is it that the U.S. Merchant Marine suffered 32 percent more losses per capita in World War Two than the U.S. Marine Corps?"

He was stunned, and didn't believe the statistic until I showed it to him, and cited the references. (See epigraph for chapter 10, "The Submarine Parade," page 101.) I went on to tell him how dangerous it had been for the Merchant Marine during the war, and that they didn't get the publicity necessary to convey their story to the American public. Then I got off my soapbox. But only for a short time.

Any fair person, military or civilian, would have to admit that the fighting men of World War Two could not have been effective overseas without the support of the civilian seamen who delivered essential cargoes to them. The U.S. Merchant Marine was the third leg of a tripod that supported the Allied war effort: war-production operations in America, our armed forces overseas, and the Merchant Marine providing supply lines.

Unfortunately, the anti–Merchant Marine mantra has been repeated for so many years—for decades now—that it has been accepted as fact by millions of people, without question. It is negative publicity, and that's the hardest kind to overcome. But there are a lot of questions about that "supposed" truth. With the available evidence, the military position would not hold up in any court of law. The overwhelming evidence is on the side of the United States Merchant Marine.

TWENTY-TWO

MAN ON A
MISSION

*I signed up to be a purser because I wanted to be
topside where I could see what was going on. That
way I could jump overboard if I had to.*

—LIEUTENANT DEAN BEAUMONT,
UNITED STATED MERCHANT MARINE

TODAY, DEAN BEAUMONT WORKS ON HUMANITARIAN MISSIONS FOR THE "MERCY ships" of the University of the Nations. Calling themselves "the Christian peace corps," they have thousands of volunteers in more than three hundred locations around the world, helping people wherever there is a need. Dean and his wife Carol go on some of those missions themselves, and wherever he travels, Dean also talks about the artistic legacy of his father, Arthur Beaumont, and about the subject that is so close to his heart—the plight of World War Two merchant seamen. Until moving to Arizona recently, he was the Hawaii representative for the U.S. Merchant Marine Veterans of World War II—one of the national chapters.

A natural salesman, Dean will talk your ear off about any one of his pet subjects—the mercy ships, the paintings of his father, or the merchant seamen. But anyone leery of salesmen will quickly soften if they only give Dean the opportunity to speak with them for a few minutes. He believes passionately in what he is saying, and he speaks the truth. I met him on board an ocean liner—the *Queen Elizabeth II*—as it crossed the Pacific Ocean, and he told me the incredible story of his wartime service. As he spoke, he wore his ever-present dark blue Merchant Marine cap, with its gold insignia.

When I returned home, I began to do my own research, and I was astounded at what I discovered. I could not understand how such a monumental injustice could have gone on for so long after the end of the Second World War—for more than five decades.

Dean still has injuries from the Japanese air attack on his Liberty ship in 1944. When he fell, running toward the gun-tub, he skidded across the steel deck on his face, tearing off skin from his hairline to the bottom of his jaw. The wound is still visible, after all these years. It scabs over and peels off about once a month, to reveal what looks like a pink birthmark—sixty years later. "I got no treatment or hospitalization," he said, "only a big scab." But that wasn't the most significant of his injuries, considering the fact that he very nearly took his own life at the tail end of the war.

Despite all the hardships that Dean has seen and endured, he is cheerful and outgoing. Rising above his strong feelings that the U.S. Navy let him and his fellow merchant seamen down, he has many friends in high places in the Navy, including some of the top admirals. He and his family, as stated earlier, have donated many of his father's paintings to the Navy—and Dean grumbles only a little when the Navy makes him pay for prints of those works.

When he was much younger, Dean met a man who had a picture of a naval vessel on the wall behind his desk, the USS *Indianapolis* (CA-35). The man had served on that ship when it was torpedoed by a Japanese submarine, resulting in a terrible loss of life and many injuries to sailors. After the attack this man had survived in the water for three or four days in only a life jacket, and was horrified to see many of his shipmates devoured by sharks. Dean went home and located a print of one of his father's sketches: the *Indianapolis* at sunset. He had it framed and gave it to the Navy veteran.

One of the things to understand—and to admire—about Dean

Beaumont is that he does not look at most issues in black-and-white terms; he does not see people (or the institutions they represent) wearing black or white hats. He believes in the adage, "Do something for someone and something nice happens to you in return." He is not thinking of personal monetary gain when he says that, or even of receiving something from the person he has helped—other than a smile, perhaps, or a thank-you note.

After Dean delivered one of his many lectures about the Merchant Marine during World War Two, he was approached by an Englishman who appeared to be in his sixties. "I just want to thank you so much," the man said, shaking Dean's hand briskly. "I was a little boy in England during the war, and my family was starving before your ships started coming in. Some got through, but many were sunk. I want you to know how much we appreciated it."

Dean told him that he had not personally served in the Atlantic convoys, and the Brit said he understood, and that he appreciated all the seamen of the United States Merchant Marine. In his world travels, Dean had met other British people who expressed similar sentiments. Many of them came up to him after seeing his distinctive cap and asked about his own experiences.

On board the *Queen Elizabeth II*, I saw Dean approach a retired Japanese pilot and strike up a friendly conversation with him through an interpreter, despite the fact that Dean had almost died when Japanese planes attacked his ship shortly after the battle of Saipan. But Dean, with his ever-present, boyish curiosity, wanted to know what the man—who had only one arm—had been through during the war. Discovering through the translator that he had in fact flown missions at Saipan, Dean wondered if he could possibly have been one of the pilots who attacked his own ship, the SS *Brander Matthews*. (By the end of their conversation that point was not proven conclusively one way or another, but it remains a possibility.)

Sometimes Dean goes to elementary schools and tells war stories to the children. He has a flair for the spoken word, for resurrecting the fever pitch of long-ago battles, much as that wonderful

Englishman, Sir C. Aubrey Smith, did in the classic 1939 movie *The Four Feathers*.

Dean recently visited a school and told the story of the 1944 Japanese air raid on his Liberty ship at Saipan. Making battle sounds with his voice, he described emergency sirens going off, antiaircraft fire, and jumping out of his bunk in the middle of the night.

Then he asked the children, "What did I forget? Did I forget my pajamas? Did I forget my slippers?" After a pause, he said, "No, I forgot that I was on the top bunk!" The students enjoyed his animated, energetic war story, and were hanging on his every word.

Finally, Dean got to the point where the two-ton boom was falling toward his head, and he paused again—longer this time.

"What happened? What happened?" the children wanted to know, leaning forward at their little desks.

With a twinkle in his eye, Dean responded, "That's why I'm one foot shorter today."

To some extent, Dean Beaumont uses humor to mask his pain. Following the inauguration of President George W. Bush in January 2001, there was a big parade featuring the military forces of the United States. No mention was made of the U.S. Merchant Marine. "That's because we don't know how to march," Dean told me. "All we do is sail, and they don't want people weaving in and out of parade formation."

He smiled, but I saw the deep sadness in his brown eyes. Then he added, "After the war, the Merchant Marine wasn't considered one of the fighting forces. We only lost seven hundred ships and eight thousand men."

TWENTY-THREE

HEALING THE
WOUNDS

*The veterans of the World War Two Merchant
Marine, like the veterans of Vietnam, are due
much better treatment from their country. And, like
the Vietnam vets, they will never be swept under the
rug of forgetfulness as long as there are sons and
daughters and grandchildren of these men still
living in this country.*

—IAN A. MILLAR[1]

IN HIS ILLUSTRIOUS CAREER AS AN AUTHOR, MY FATHER, FRANK HERBERT, LIKED
to think of himself as an investigative reporter, turning over rocks to
see what scurried out. When I met Dean Beaumont on board the
ocean liner and heard what he had to say, I immediately recognized
it as an important story, one that needed to be told. For decades,
parts of the story—letters, pictures, and personal remembrances—
have been relegated to the pages of family scrapbooks and to industry publications with limited circulation. More people need to learn
what really happened.

The nation needs to learn, and to examine its very soul.

The first twenty-two chapters of *The Forgotten Heroes* consti-
tute a mountain of evidence against the United States government,

and could be used as the basis of a class-action lawsuit by Merchant Marine veterans and their families. If that were my intent, I might have titled chapter 23 differently—something like "Damages," "Reparations," or "Prayer for Relief."

In fact, rumors are swirling in the Merchant Marine community, of just such an impending lawsuit, in which seamen and their families would seek to recover lost college tuition, medical benefits, and other damages against the government. The evidence of A Great Wrong is there for all to see; the truth is filtering out.

Dean Beaumont and I are sending copies of this book to political leaders in the United States Congress, with the hope and expectation that they will step forward and do the right thing. This should be resolved quickly and fairly for all concerned, without dragging it through the courts for years, enriching a lot of lawyers.

If a lawsuit is still necessary, the basis of the complaint might be, in part, discrimination against the handicapped, the elderly, and children, even though, undoubtedly, during the 1940s the comprehensive laws to protect such people that we have today, were not in place. As I pointed out in chapter 4, "Reporting for Duty" (see page 48), some of the men who volunteered for the Merchant Marine had serious physical disabilities, such as asthma, malformed torsos, wooden legs, or only one arm. Still others were blind in one eye, or deaf.[2] These were men who did not qualify for military duty—or even for the draft—but chose to serve their country anyway.

Some men, such as Captain Vincent F. Nielsen of the SS *Brander Matthews*, were elderly, and came out of retirement to serve. Others, such as my own godfather, Howard J. Hansen, were but children. "Howie," as we have always called him in our family, was only thirteen years old when he first went to sea during World War Two. There are many stories of boys, fifteen, sixteen, and seventeen, who served—and *died*—on merchant ships during the armed conflict.

Whatever laws existed in those days to protect children were ignored by the government of the United States, which looked the other way in order to advance the cause of the Allied war effort. The government should have sent inspectors in adequate numbers to monitor hiring practices, but did not do so. It is a basic principle of our society that we enact laws to protect people who are too weak to protect themselves—and that those laws should be enforced.

In addition, as I will discuss later in this chapter, and in appendix 2, "Seamen of the American Revolution" (see page 241), there may have been some level of racial prejudice against American merchant seamen, because such a high percentage of them were minorities.

The handicapped, elderly, and children—and racial minorities—who served in the U.S. Merchant Marine were neglected not only during the war. They were also shunted aside afterward, when they—like every other American merchant seaman—were cast out onto the streets of this country.

Some Merchant Marine seamen have been plaintiffs in a class-action lawsuit, arising from the extensive use of asbestos in the construction of the ships on which they sailed during the Second World War. One man I spoke with had extensive scarring of his lung tissue from inhaling asbestos particles in the engine rooms of Liberty ships and had to have part of one lung surgically removed. He also said, however, that some of the proceeds had been misappropriated by a lawyer (since deceased), and that he had only received around $3,500 for his injury—only a fraction of what he should have been paid.

I investigated this further, and spoke with still other merchant seamen. Soon I had a thick pile of asbestos-litigation documents on my desk, and I found that it was a complex matter, involving thousands of lawsuits against a number of manufacturers, including the Fibreboard Corporation, Johns-Manville, Bethlehem Steel, Babcock & Wilcox, Lykes Brothers Steamship Company, Pittsburgh Corning, and other companies that were once among the largest firms in the United States. Many of them were forced into bankruptcy because of the flood of lawsuits.

The merchant seamen who were exposed to asbestos hazards during World War Two acquired lung cancer, mesothelioma, asbestos lung disease, and other deadly ailments. Seamen were also exposed to the carcinogen benzene, which can cause leukemia.

Benzene was in the gasoline and jet fuel hauled on merchant ships—military cargoes. It was also in many other products commonly found on board the vessels.

Many dedicated, honest lawyers were involved in the litigation, but the documents showed that one of them apparently misappropriated money from one of the trust funds, and then died. According to letters written by his former law partners who investigated the matter after his death, this lawyer underreported the amount of money that was received from one of the defendant companies and then kept the difference for himself.[3]

Will our government ever step in and rescue those World War Two merchant seamen who are still alive, as those men once rescued this nation? I can only hope that the people in authority will take action that is long overdue—and begin the healing process.

Some of the merchant seamen I interviewed had grudgingly accepted the lack of recognition, the lack of respect, the lack of fairness. Others were crusty, grouchy, even bitter. And they have every right to be.

Short of a huge class-action lawsuit, what can be done to rectify the injustice that was committed against more than two hundred thousand men and their families? This is one of the biggest questions of all, and I have devoted a lot of thought to it. In considering the potential courses of action, I find myself filled with melancholy, because of the thousands of seamen who died after World War Two, still feeling they had been abandoned by their nation.

I think of the old men who came out of retirement to serve as captains, of the green teenagers, and of the handicapped who were on board those ships, which our government sent into war zones. Those men—and their families—gave all that they had.

But it is not too late to do something. I see several things that can still be done.

•SEAMEN'S BILL OF RIGHTS

H.R. 1235, which granted limited veterans' benefit to World War Two merchant seamen in 1988, did not go nearly far enough, and in fact was so worthless that many Merchant Marine veterans did not even bother to send in the Veterans administration paperwork to apply for it.

A proper Seamen's Bill of Rights is desperately needed by the men of the U.S. Merchant Marine. The benefits should be as broad as those granted to armed-forces personnel, and should be customized to fit the needs of seamen. For example, education rights should not have expired in 1955 (only ten years after the conclusion of World War Two), as is the situation now under the G.I. Bill. This needs to be broadened so that aged seamen can take computer classes, or other classes that are of use to them. Even if that extension is granted, it will be only a pittance in comparison with what the men should have received. All of these men are elderly now, and most of them would utilize educational benefits on a much more limited basis than they might have done when they were younger.

Over the years, Dean Beaumont has been engaged in a letter-writing campaign with important political and military leaders, attempting to obtain decent benefits for veterans of the Merchant Marine. His relentless pursuit of justice for merchant seamen has advanced their cause considerably, but he is not the only one trying to do this, and certainly not the only person who deserves credit. It has been an uphill battle, against powerful opponents.

On July 20, 2000, Dean wrote to Patsy T. Mink, congressional representative for Hawaii's Second District. The following month the liberal congresswoman told him she supported H.R. 1893, which was introduced on May 20, 1999, and was still in committee at that time. The bill, if passed, would have granted broadened military benefits to merchant seamen who served in World War Two. Subsequently, Representative Mink reported to Mr. Beaumont that the bill was killed in committee. (Unfortunately, Representative Mink died in September 2002, a loss of another supporter of the Merchant Marine cause.)

Recently, two other Merchant Marine bills were being considered by the U.S. House of Representatives:

On June 25, 2001, Representative Tom Lantos (D–Calif.) (co-sponsored by Representatives Patsy T. Mink, Anna G. Eshoo, and Donald A. Manzullo) introduced H.R. 2302, to provide lump-sum payments of accrued retirement pay to merchant seamen who served in World War Two and in the Korean War.[4]

Dean Beaumont has also been in touch with U.S. Senator Daniel K. Akaka of Hawaii, who informed him that another bill, H.R. 2442, was introduced by Representative Felix J. Grucci Jr. (R–N.Y.) on July 10, 2001, to enable merchant seamen to receive veterans' benefits if they served for at least twelve months during a period of war.[5] This would pick up benefits for men who served on merchant ships in the Korean and Vietnam conflicts.

Earlier, Dean was also in contact with U.S. Senator Daniel K. Inouye of Hawaii, who served in the Japanese-American 442nd Regimental Combat Team during World War Two, and lost his right arm.[6] A supporter of the rights of merchant seamen, Inouye said he was on board a Merchant Marine ship in the Atlantic Ocean in the Second World War, when he saw another American merchant ship explode and sink after it was torpedoed by a German U-boat. In a letter to Dean, he wrote, "I have not forgotten their bravery and commitment to duty I witnessed firsthand. I salute the family and friends of the unsung heroes of World War Two—the merchant seamen."[7]

The AMMV (American Merchant Marine Veterans) has formed a "Just Compensation" committee, and has put together a proposal to ask both houses of the U.S. Congress for a lump-sum payment to merchant seamen who served in harm's way during World War Two. The committee made a comprehensive analysis of the limited benefits that were granted to Merchant Marine veterans in 1988, in comparison with what armed-forces veterans were receiving. In each example, armed-forces veterans received much broader coverage than merchant seamen:

- The medical benefit to merchant seamen was reduced by a co-payment requirement.
- Burial benefits to merchant seamen were less.

In addition, the AMMV pointed out that American Merchant Marine veterans who served in World War Two never received the following:

- disability payments*
- medical coverage for their families
- educational benefits, including tuition, books, supplies, and living expenses
- financial assistance in home-buying
- unemployment assistance
- assistance in obtaining jobs

The AMMV also noted that living merchant seamen from World War Two were now an average age of eighty-one, and that many of them had outlived their available funds. The AMMV decided to ask, quite appropriately, for "a fair cash value in place of the unpaid benefits of the G.I. Bill"—both for the forty-three years of no coverage, and for the very limited coverage that was granted after 1988.[8]

---

*(See chapter 19, "They Earned Our Respect," page 187.) There have been a few exceptions, under an inconsistent government policy that has not been applied equally to all Merchant Marine veterans. Dean Beaumont, for example, received 50 percent disability payments, but not until long after the end of World War Two when he was in retirement.

•LUMP-SUM PAYMENTS

This can be called retroactive pension money, retroactive medical or lump-sum payments, or anything else, but it should be granted to every living American merchant seaman who served in World War Two. The merchant seamen of Canada who served in the war were recently granted a lump-sum payment (in tax-free Canadian dollars) of $20,000 apiece if they served two years or more; $10,000 if they served six months to two years; or $5,000 for one to six months of service.[9]

As it is now, under the 1988 extension of veterans' status to merchant seamen (H.R. 1235), the men do not receive anything if they were not injured in the war. And, as Dean Beaumont discovered firsthand, the process of handling the required paperwork is cumbersome and confusing, especially for elderly people.

In determining the amount to be paid, it should be considered that the Merchant Marine veterans of World War Two paid their own medical expenses for decades after 1945, and they should have been paid by the U.S. government as part of a G.I. Bill–type package. From a legal standpoint, they suffered damages because of this. They also suffered extensive damages from the loss of educational benefits they should have received under the G.I. Bill—and from the loss of low-interest home, farm, and business loans. The list of damages can be broadened even further when you consider how much pain and suffering these men suffered at the hands of military personnel and the American public after the war, when they were called "riffraff," "bums," "draft-dodgers," "drunks," and a litany of other names.

If merchant seamen had their ships shot out from under them, and/or were taken as prisoners of war, their pay was stopped. Bill Flury, who survived the Japanese atrocity committed against the crew of the SS *Jean Nicolet* (see chapter 5, "War Crimes," page 61), was a prisoner of war during the time he was held on board the Japanese submarine. He suffered immeasurably, but received no hardship pay or "bonus" for this traumatic experience. After the war, the U.S. armed forces gave POW medals to military prisoners—but Merchant Marine POWs received nothing.

A few years ago, Wilson J. Taylor of Lake Oswego, Oregon, discovered that his friend Bill Flury of the SS *Jean Nicolet* had never received a POW medal, despite being held as a prisoner by the Japanese, who attempted to murder him. Taylor, a World War Two veteran himself, obtained a real POW medal on what he called "the black market," and had it presented to Flury at a Merchant Marine convention in Portland, Oregon. The story was publicized, and someone at the federal government heard about it. A short while later, the government awarded Bill Flury his own POW medal, and gave him monetary compensation for the suffering that he endured.

This is an example, among others, of the selective treatment our government has given to merchant seamen. A few men receive medals and benefits, but most do not. The squeaky wheel gets greased.

The men of the Merchant Marine never would have been treated in this manner if their government had not abandoned them. During and after the war, American Merchant Marine seamen lost the most productive years of their lives.

Some of the states did authorize bonuses to merchant seamen who resided in them at the time of their enlistment into the US Merchant Marine in World War Two, but such payments typically amounted to only $10 or $20 for each month they served in the war. The state of Louisiana offered a flat $250 bonus, but the deadline for applications expired on July 1, 1999.[10] They were nice gestures from the participating states, but merchant seamen didn't receive nearly enough, and there was no uniformity across the country.

The lump-sum payment needs to be made in tax-free dollars. These men have already paid their "taxes," many times over.

The AMMV's "Just Compensation" committee is seeking a lump-sum payment of $50,000 for each merchant seaman who served at least 90 days in harm's way during World War Two—which is even more restrictive than the eligibility requirement used for the branches of the armed forces, who received benefits no matter where they were stationed, or for how long. The "Just Compensation" group placed a value of at least $1,000,000 per man for forty-three years of lost benefits (from the end of the war in 1945 to 1988), but they decided to seek a lower, more attainable amount.

In their draft proposal, the AMMV pointed out that merchant seamen bore arms in defense of their country during World War Two, contrary to the stereotypical "draft-dodger" stories that were spread about them. Whenever a General Quarters alarm went off on board ship, the merchant crew was assigned to gun stations in order to assist the Armed Guard gunners. Some merchant seamen—such as Edwin J. O'Hara of the SS *Stephen Hopkins*—"fired the guns and inflicted serious damage on the enemy."[11]

Many merchant seamen were trained in military-style boot camps during World War Two. At the huge Sheepshead Bay Training Station in New York, which processed thousands of men, each trainee received thirty hours of gunnery instruction. That knowledge came into play more than once, out on the floating battlefields where merchant ships were sent by United States military authorities.[12]

Dean Beaumont served as a loader for an antiaircraft gun on the SS *Brander Matthews*—the equivalent of a gunner's mate in the U.S. Navy—and he was nearly killed in a kamikaze attack. Merchant seamen performed other tasks on the guns, as recalled by a Navy Armed Guard gunner on the ill-fated *John A. Johnson*. After the ship was torpedoed in the Pacific Ocean, he ran to his station.

> When I reached my 20-millimeter gun I didn't have a loader. I never saw that young man again and suspect he was killed by gunfire. I pulled off the gun cover, mounted a full magazine, and cranked one into the chamber. There I stood, strapped in and ready. I knew my gun was in good shape. A mess man (I'm not sure of his name) and I had recently cleaned the gun. I showed him how to load a magazine and also how to change a hot barrel.[13]

•EXTEND BENEFITS TO FAMILIES

In order to rectify an injustice that has been committed against the families of the merchant seamen of World War Two, the spouses and children of those seamen—whether those seamen are alive or deceased—should receive educational benefits, as well as loans for homes, farms, and businesses at preferred VA rates. This is a morally and legally correct position, since the families of seamen suffered financially by being forced to live at reduced standards of living.

The "Just Compensation" committee of the American Merchant Marine Veterans is seeking a lump-sum payment only for merchant seamen who are still alive at the time that the bill is passed into law.[14] But this does not address the suffering of the wives and children.

If the breadwinner of a family lost income because he could not get the education he deserved, or a home loan, or essential medical benefits, he was not the only one who suffered. The standard of living of the entire family was reduced substantially, and all of the members of his immediate family in the household deserve consideration.

This is just a matter of basic fairness, a concept that has not been used with respect to the U.S. Merchant Marine or their families.

•PUBLICITY

The Veterans Administration should publicize the U.S. Merchant Marine veterans' benefits that are available, using television, radio, magazines, and posters—perhaps with artwork resembling the recruiting posters used in World War Two. The goal is to locate all Merchant Marine veterans and/or their surviving families, which can also be done through social security, income tax, and other records. As shown by the example of Dean Beaumont, a very savvy individual, he did not learn that he was eligible for veterans' benefits until more than five years after the announcement. In addition to other forms of publicity, the Veterans Administration should also send letters of information to the known addresses of those men—and their surviving families—in order to make certain that everyone who is entitled to benefits receives them.

Two hundred fifteen thousand seamen served on U.S. Merchant Marine vessels during World War Two. According to a Veterans Administration memorandum dated January 4, 2001, approximately eighty thousand merchant seamen from that war applied for and received Department of Defense Certificates of Release (Form 214), as permitted under the 1988 extension of benefits to those men.[15] It is not known exactly how many Merchant Marine veterans of World War Two are still alive today, but some of the men I contacted told me they did not complete the DD 214 paperwork that was sent to them by the Veterans Administration.

•GUIDANCE FOR MERCHANT MARINE VETERANS

There is considerable confusion about the Veterans Administration among merchant seamen. Since they were granted veterans' status in 1988, Merchant Marine men qualify for payments for injuries they suffered in World War Two. One realm of confusion concerns whether those payments are labeled "disability" or "medical," so there is an area of overlap that needs to be made clear to the veterans.

The Veterans Administration should assign trained counselors to help these men, and explain to them how to obtain assistance. Extra effort will be needed to make such a program work, since the veterans are elderly and some of them might have trouble understanding. Each veteran should be given a booklet (and perhaps a videotape or computer disk) that explains the details. Because of the age of the primary recipients, it is especially important to streamline paperwork requirements and to provide extra counseling in this area.

•FUNDING OF MERCHANT MARINE ASSOCIATIONS

The U.S. government should adequately fund Merchant Marine associations, such as the U.S. Merchant Marine Veterans of World War Two and the American Merchant Marine Veterans of World War Two. Such groups can aid the Veterans Administration in communicating with World War Two merchant seamen.

Fund-raising efforts should be organized on behalf of merchant seamen and their families. One way to accomplish this would be for the United States Congress to commission the U.S. Postal Authority to issue Merchant Marine postage stamps. This could involve a set of designs depicting Liberty ships, a torpedoed vessel sinking, or an actual World War Two recruiting poster for merchant seamen. Uncle Sam "wanted" these men, and now these men need Uncle Sam.

Such funding projects can also be used to pay for the lump-sum benefits that are owed.

•MERCHANT MARINE MEMORIALS

Funds should be allocated for the continued maintenance and operation of certain Liberty ships, Victory ships, and other merchant marine vessels from World War Two. One of those ships, the SS *Lane Victory*, was declared a National Historic Landmark in 1991. In large part it was created as a memorial to the thousands of Merchant Marine men who died at sea in World War Two, and still lie in unmarked, watery graves. The *Lane Victory* is the flagship of U.S. Merchant Marine memorial ships, and is moored in San Pedro, California, where surviving family members can go to honor their loved ones.[16]

The *Lane Victory* project stems from Congressional Bill H.R. 2032, which was signed by President Reagan in 1988. One of the strongest supporters of this bill was the late California governor Pat

Brown, who pressed the two U.S. Senators from his state—Pete Wilson and Alan Cranston—to push it through.[17]

Much of the restoration work on the *Lane Victory* was completed by volunteer labor, and today it is manned by retired Merchant Marine veterans. But the future of this memorial vessel—and the handful of others that are still in operation—is in grave doubt. The need for additional funding was highlighted by Claude Gammel, one of the volunteers on the *Lane Victory*, who said, "The question is, what's going to happen when we're gone? There are no young people aboard."[18]

Two Liberty ships are still in operation, the SS *John W. Brown* in Baltimore and the SS *Jeremiah O'Brien* in San Francisco, the latter of which was named after a Revolutionary War hero who led a successful raid on a British warship.[19] The ships are available for special events and tours.

In addition, Merchant Marine and Navy Armed Guard veterans set up a memorial at Tampa, Florida, in 1999, with the SS *American Victory* as their centerpiece.[20] All of these groups, and others, need funding.

U.S. Merchant Marine veterans have been demanding recognition, and have received some success. But progress is slow—somewhat like trying to melt an iceberg with a cigarette lighter. Recently, armed-forces veterans set up a statue in memory of World War Two veterans in California, at the Marin County Civic Center. When merchant seamen discovered that the U.S. Merchant Marine was not listed as one of the armed forces, they protested—vehemently. They were met with opposition from the other veterans, but a compromise was finally reached in which the U.S. Merchant Marine got a separate plaque, off to one side.

Following the success of the movie *Saving Private Ryan*, the actor Tom Hanks has been campaigning for a national World War

Two memorial for veterans of the American armed forces who served in that conflict. He's made no mention of the U.S. Merchant Marine in his public appeals so far, but such a memorial should honor *all* veterans of the war, including merchant seamen. These men were made "veterans" in 1988, but that was only a formality. They have always been veterans.

In lieu of that, it might be appropriate for the government to fund a U.S. Merchant Marine Memorial in New York City's Battery Park—and to list the names of the thousands of merchant seamen who died in World War Two. At the present time, there is a privately funded bronze memorial in that park, but it needs more attention, and recognition.[21]

The memorial depicts a sinking merchant ship—a symbolic gravestone for thousands of American men who died at sea and were never seen again. There should be many more memorials to the valiant merchant seamen of World War Two, but efforts to obtain them are often torpedoed.

•CEMETERY RIGHTS FOR U.S. MERCHANT MARINE VETERANS

Martha Haroldson, wife of U.S. Merchant Marine veteran Donald C. Haroldson, had difficulty getting the records straightened out at the national cemetery where her husband was buried. Mr. Haroldson served in the U.S. Merchant Marine for fifty years, reaching the rank of "Master." He also held a rank in the U.S. Navy. After he died, the acting cemetery director allegedly told his widow, "No Merchant Marine should be in this cemetery"—apparently because of the military veterans who were buried there. Mrs. Haroldson also claimed that the Visitors' Information computer for the cemetery showed her husband's U.S. Merchant Marine rank listed incorrectly, with an inexplicable "CM"—which she was allegedly told meant "chief metalworker." Mrs.

Haroldson said she couldn't get this straightened out, despite repeatedly providing documentation to the cemetery officials.[22]

Veterans of the U.S. Merchant Marine in World War Two should receive *full* military honors when they die—and something should be done to correct the records of the thousands of merchant seamen who died and were buried without honors.

•MEDALS

The U.S. government should issue medals to the men of the Merchant Marine who served in World War Two. The medals should be of the same quality that servicemen receive. They should not be *cardboard*, and the seamen should not have to pay for them.

Wilson J. Taylor, president of the Oregon Chapter of American Merchant Marine Veterans, put it this way, in a letter to the editor of a newspaper:

> And still (we) are being penalized in the Congress who simply ignore our efforts to receive free medals we have won more than a half century ago. We have to buy from retail outlets at such an exorbitant fee we cannot afford on our meager income. We as seamen all applaud the heroics of the active armed men but let us reflect in the interest of "fair play" to give honor and appreciation to those who served in the entire global events fighting undersea boats, marauding surface ships, and, yes, from the air as well.[23]

Ben Hammer, executive director of the Battle of the Atlantic Historical Society, said that Cadet-Midshipman Edwin J. O'Hara should be posthumously awarded the highest honor this nation can bestow—the Congressional Medal of Honor. Fresh out of the Merchant Marine Academy in 1942, the eighteen-year-old undergraduate O'Hara manned a 4-inch aft gun on the Liberty ship SS *Stephen Hopkins* and helped sink a heavily armed German auxiliary cruiser, the *Stier*—(See chapter 7, "Valor at Sea," page 76.) While the Allied armed forces sank many German U-boats in the Battle of the Atlantic, this was the only time in the entire war that a German *surface warship* was sunk in those waters—and this brave young merchant seaman deserves much of the credit, after taking over the gun from his dead shipmates and then losing his life defending his ship.

Ben Hammer said that the U.S. Armed Forces have treated the Merchant Mariners like "bastard children," and that it is an example of "old-fashioned bigotry." During the war, American merchant seamen were routinely denied access to USO and Red Cross clubs.[24] All through the war, American military men commonly referred to merchant seamen as their "poor country cousins"—as if they were all uneducated hicks or bumpkins from the hills. And, as has been noted, this was one of the kinder things that military personnel and others have had to say about the U.S. Merchant Marine.

The eminent historian also pointed out that around 20 percent of American merchant seamen in World War Two were black, and another 20 percent were Jewish. In comparison, Ben Hammer said that blacks also served in the U.S. Navy, but the vast majority of them were assigned to menial mess details, performing food-service duties. As for Jews, Hammer said that in the Navy, only about 8 percent of servicemen were Jewish, and only rarely were these men given leadership positions.

As the war went on, the U.S. Navy and other service branches broadened their recruitment bases, and began to admit blacks to more and more positions of rank. Even in the U.S. Army, however, which was ahead of the other branches in its recruitment of blacks, there was a reticence to place them in combat positions overseas. Out of 467,000 black troops in the Army, less than 54,000 were stationed in the war zones of Europe, Africa, and the Pacific. General Eisenhower said this was because of problems in foreign countries, which would not welcome them—but other officers said quite openly that they were "too dumb to fight," or were unfit for some other reason.[25]

In this regard, it is interesting to note that there is a long history of service by black men in the U.S. Merchant Marine, going all the way back to the American Revolution, when black slaves served on privateers in order to fulfill the military obligations of their white colonial masters. Some of the merchant seamen I interviewed expressed the view that bigotry against the men of the Merchant Marine can be traced all the way back to that first war in our nation's history, when George Washington and others treated Merchant seamen poorly, as if they were of lesser value than soldiers or sailors. (See appendix 2, "Seamen of the American Revolution," page 241.)

• **RECOGNITION**

As part of the healing process—since so many merchant seamen have been deeply wounded over what has been denied to them—it is important for the United States to recognize the contributions of these men. This can be done, quite simply, by declaring a *one-time* U.S. Merchant Marine Day to honor them, with festivities that would include parades in major cities. Give them their own day. Just one. A day of celebration for these men, and a day of healing. Call it "National Merchant Marine Day."

This could be done in conjunction with National Maritime Day, which takes place on May 22 of every year, but this is not a holiday well known to the American public: They do not get time off from work to celebrate it. And how many people know that this day was decreed in honor of the SS *Savannah*, the first vessel ever to cross the Atlantic under steam power, on May 22, 1819?[26]

It would be far better to select a day specifically to honor the U.S. Merchant Marine veterans of World War Two—a date when merchant seaman showed great gallantry. The saga of the Liberty ship SS *Stephen Hopkins* stands out brilliantly in Merchant Marine history—a day when a lightly armed merchant ship fought back and sank a much more powerful German raider: on September 27, 1942. So perhaps September 27th would be the proper day on which to celebrate the accomplishments of merchant seamen, to give them the recognition they deserve. The sooner the better, because these men are elderly, and are dying—they are "crossing the bar," as the seamen say.

Just one day in one year. A one-time September 27th event.

Please: Give these men happy memories. Don't let any more of them die in bitterness, thinking their country abandoned them. I'm not being melodramatic here. I'm simply telling the truth, speaking from my own heart. For these men, I refuse to do any less. If it were not for their contributions during the war, I might not even be able to write these words. If not for them, our lives would be vastly, drastically, different.

The merchant seamen of World War Two gave many of their own days for this country, and the United States of America should grant them one in return.

I am not talking about adding another national holiday. For long-term recognition, Merchant Marine veterans should be featured in Veterans Day, the Fourth of July, and other military celebrations—events they have not customarily been invited to; or where they have been overshadowed by armed-forces veterans, as if the seamen of the United States Merchant Marine were no more than second-class citizens.

Ian A. Millar, whose father Adrian E. Millar served in the American Merchant Marine, has written extensively and passionately about the plight of merchant seamen. In *The Anchor Light*, a U.S. Merchant Marine periodical, he wrote, "Given the combat record of the Merchant Marine there is no reason for the merchant seamen to march behind anyone in a parade."[27]

The armed forces—and this nation—need to recognize the merchant seamen of World War Two for their tremendous accomplishments and *personal* sacrifices. The men of the Merchant Marine need to be invited to participate in events and organizations that have been made off-limits to them in the past.

Americans are an aggressive, ambitious people, a nation of achievers, of winners. However, the self-professed "Manifest Destiny" of this country has too often justified steamrolling over entire groups of people—the Native Americans whose land was taken, the blacks who were enslaved, the Japanese-Americans who were interned during World War II, and the merchant seamen of the U.S. Merchant Marine, who were treated so unfairly during the armed conflict and in the decades afterward. Considering what the Merchant Marine accomplished for America, it seems petty to deny them a place in military parades, museums, veterans organizations, and exhibitions. Those men should be given the recognition and respect that they deserve. It is important to the elderly merchant seamen who are still alive, to their families, and to the families of those who have passed away.

•EXTEND BENEFITS TO OTHER MERCHANT MARINE VETERANS

There may be a handful of World War One merchant seamen still alive, so they also should be given some recognition. In addition, the "civilian" sailors who served the United States in other wars, especially the Korean War and the Vietnam War—were not included in the 1988 extension of "veterans" status. Those men have been denied benefits entirely, and were also forgotten by their nation. Their contributions to the United States should be recognized in the same manner as the Merchant Marine veterans of World War Two.

With respect to the veterans of World War One, the Korean War, and the Vietnam War, our government must also give consideration to the families of living and deceased merchant seamen who served in those conflicts, families who suffered alongside them for years.

•TELL THE STORY

The U.S. Merchant Marine has been an essential component of American history since the Revolutionary War, when they comprised the nation's first Navy and supplied Washington's troops. (See appendix 2, "Seamen of the American Revolution," page 239, and appendix 3, "Two Centuries of Service to America," page 247.) Captain Frank Medeiros spoke to me about a plaque in the U.S. Merchant Marine Academy (at Kings Point, New York) that reads, TELL AMERICA. He feels the Merchant Marine has not fulfilled this admonition, and that their public-relations efforts have been dismal.

"We *should* tell America," he says, in an emotion-filled voice. "And we should never forget that the Merchant Marine has a proud heritage."

In recognition of this, the story of the Merchant Marine should be included in American history books used in public schools all over the country, and the U.S. government should fund official "Merchant Marine historians," just as there are official historians for the American armed forces.[28]

As Ian A. Millar (a merchant seaman himself) said to me: "Our history has been suppressed. The Navy and every other branch of the armed forces wanted their story told—and each of them won the war on their own."

In addition to the passive actions taken against merchant seamen by the U.S. government, overt action was also taken by denying benefits to these men, and by neglecting or getting rid of old service records. Bureaucrats in the U.S. Maritime Commission, the Army Transportation Corps, and National Archives destroyed many wartime shipping records that they thought were taking up too much storage space. Documents were burned, shredded, or moved and lost.[29] The remaining records need to be treated with respect and carefully archived under one administrative jurisdiction.

I cannot help but come away with a feeling of deep respect for the valiant, dedicated Merchant Marine seamen who have contributed the best years of their lives to this nation, without sufficient recognition, appreciation, or honors. They have contributed to every major war the United States has fought.

We have not yet heard all of these accounts, and never will, because so many thousands of the participants were lost at sea and never returned home to tell their stories. I think we can be certain, however, that wherever the souls of those brave veterans are, they are exchanging exciting tales of the sea in the time-honored tradition of all mariners.

GOD BLESS THE MERCHANT MARINE

—INSCRIPTION ON THE GRAVESTONE

OF A UNITED STATES MERCHANT MARINE VETERAN

CONTACT INFORMATION

FOR MORE INFORMATION ON SOME OF THE GROUPS MENTIONED IN THIS book, contact:

U.S. MERCHANT MARINE VETERANS OF WORLD WAR II
P.O. Box 629
San Pedro, CA 90733
Phone: (310) 519-9545
Fax: (310) 519-0265

**SONS AND DAUGHTERS OF U.S. MERCHANT MARINE
VETERANS OF WORLD WAR II**
c/o Ian A. Millar
1806 Bantry Trail
Kernersville, NC 27284

AMERICAN MERCHANT MARINE VETERANS OF WORLD WAR II
P.O. Box 151205
Cape Coral, FL 33915-1205
Phone: (239) 549-1010
Fax: (239) 549-1990

AMERICAN MERCHANT MARINE VETERANS OF WORLD WAR II
"Just Compensation" executive board
Henry Van Gemert, cochairman
800 25th Avenue West
Palmetto, FL 34221
(941) 722-1194

U.S. NAVY ARMED GUARD WORLD WAR II VETERANS
115 Wall Creek Drive
Rolesville, NC 27571
(919) 570-0909
clloyd@nc.rr.com
bowerman@armed-guard.com
Web site: www.armed-guard.com

U.S. NAVY HISTORICAL CENTER
865 Kidder Brieze Street
Washington Navy Yard
Washington, DC 20374

NAVAL HISTORICAL DETACHMENT (NAVHISDET)
P.O. Box 15021
Arlington, VA 22215

PROJECT LIBERTY SHIP
P.O. Box 25846
Highland Town Station
Baltimore, MD 21224-5214
(410) 661-1550

UNIVERSITY OF THE NATIONS
75–5851 Kuakini Highway
Kailua-Kona, HI 96740
(808) 326-4447

MERCY SHIPS INTERNATIONAL
P.O. Box 2020
Garden Valley, TX 75771-2020
(903) 882-0887 or 1-800-MERCYSHIPS

U.S. DEPARTMENT OF VETERANS AFFAIRS
(FORMERLY THE VETERANS ADMINISTRATION)
Washington, DC 20111
Head Office
810 Vermont Avenue
Washington, D.C. 20420
(202) 273-5400
Web site info: www.va.gov and http://vabenefits.vba.va.gov/
Regional Offices
Buffalo, New York (Eastern region)
St. Louis, Missouri (Central region)
Muskogee, Oklahoma (Western region)
Atlanta, Georgia (Southern region)

For additional information on applying for veterans' status or
benefits, contact the Merchant Marine Web site at
www.usmm.org/update.html, or write to:
American Merchant Marine Veterans of World War II
P.O. Box 151205
Cape Coral, FL 33915-1205
Phone: (239)-549-1010
Fax: (239) 549-1990

NATIONAL LIBERTY SHIP MEMORIAL
GGNRA Fort Mason
San Francisco, CA 94123

PUGET SOUND MARITIME HISTORICAL SOCIETY
2700 24th Avenue East
Seattle, WA 98112
(206) 324-1126
Fax: (206) 324-1326

SEAMEN OF THE AMERICAN REVOLUTION

WHEN CREWMEN SAILED LIBERTY SHIPS AND OTHER MERCHANT VESSELS IN World War Two, some of the old salts told their shipmates about the proud history of the U.S. Merchant Marine, how seafaring men had contributed their gallant efforts to the United States for more than two centuries, all the way back to colonial times and the founding of the nation.

Unfortunately the merchant seamen who served so heroically in Revolutionary times have been forgotten by most writers of history, to such a shameful degree that today many Americans have no idea what really happened in those days. It is a pattern of neglect that has continued throughout the entire course of American history.

Since roads were so bad in eighteenth-century America, the primary highways connecting the colonies were the Atlantic shipping lanes that ran north and south along the eastern coast of North America. Colonial merchants made fortunes from seaborne commerce—much of it through smuggling operations—but in the latter half of the century the oppressive policies of Great Britain began to cut into their profits, setting the stage for the Revolutionary War.[1]

After 1775, many of the colonial governments outfitted their own navies, sending armed, converted merchant ships out to prey on the shipping of the British and their Tory sympathizers. These transformed vessels were known as "privateers" if they were commissioned as warships and carried no cargo, or as "letters of marque" if they were armed, cargo-carrying ships.[2]

In common parlance, both types are frequently called privateers, but there is a fine distinction between the two. In both cases they carried documents authorizing them to capture enemy ships and cargo, and bring them back to prize agents in the colonies for distribution of the proceeds. Many of the British came to view the crews of such vessels as pirates, but there was a legal difference—one that legally entitled privateering crews to be treated as prisoners of war under international law, and not as pirates,[3] who were summarily hung from the nearest yardarm or run through with a sword and pitched into the churning sea.

As the noted naval historian Nathan Miller put it, so succinctly, "The privateer had a license to steal; the pirate did not."[4] Another historian, Ernest E. Barker, had this colorful comment concerning those dangerous times: "[Privateering was] an art-form, the practice of capturing prizes at sea, just as in the case of the Old West [when] an artful gunslinger took what he wanted at the point of a six-shooter."[5]

In 1775, Pennsylvania, South Carolina, Massachusetts, and Connecticut formed their own navies, and most of the other states followed suit.[6] For a while, General Washington had his own naval force as well, known as "George Washington's Navy." His small seagoing fleet was augmented and then supplanted by the Continental Navy, formed by act of Congress on October 13, 1775, "to be employed for the protection and defense of the united Colonies." The new Navy of thirty-one ships was, in the words of congressional delegate Samuel Chase, "the maddest idea in the world"—and suicidal, since the enemy's Royal Navy was so large and powerful.[7] (The Continental Navy existed from 1775 through 1783, and predated the U.S. Coast Guard and the U.S. Navy, which were created by Congressional acts in 1790 and 1798, respectively.)

Through privateering commissions and letters of marque issued by the colonies and Congress, merchant-ship captains were given the legal authority to intercept and destroy or commandeer British ships and cargoes. Much of the booty went to supply George Washington's fledgling Continental Army with gunpowder and other necessary war matériel. It was dangerous work. More seamen died in the Revolutionary War than did soldiers who fought for the Continental Army.

The seagoing men came from every nationality. Many were Portuguese immigrants, whose ancestors had sailed for centuries, while others were black slaves fulfilling the military obligations of their white colonial masters, or serving so that their masters could receive a bounty of land from the government.[8] Both the Portuguese and the black slaves served with great distinction, but because of national and racial prejudice, did not receive the recognition they deserved.

One of the World War Two merchant seamen that I interviewed for this book, Captain Frank Medeiros, is of Portuguese descent, and was born in the whaling town of New Bedford, Massachusetts. He survived one of the hellacious merchant-ship convoys that provided war supplies to Russia during the "Murmansk Run" in 1942. (See chapter 9, "The Russian Gauntlet," page 95.) A career seaman, today he runs a chapter of Merchant Marine veterans near San Francisco, and calls his group the "Minutemen of the Sea." That catchy name is based upon his knowledge of the important role of the Merchant Marine in the founding of the United States. Some of the most important things that the merchant crews provided for the Continental Army were warm clothing and shoes, enabling them to survive harsh winter conditions. Similarly, World War Two convoys later provided the Russians with clothing and millions of insulated boots that kept them from freezing on the Stalingrad front against the German invaders.

Captain Medeiros speaks passionately of his own experiences more than half a century ago, and of the courage and heroism of his predecessors in the Revolutionary War. Many of those eighteenth-century seamen gave their lives for the United States—just as Medeiros put his own life on the line in World War Two.

Some of the bravest merchant seamen in colonial times were the captains of privateer vessels. One, Jonathan Haraden, was in command of the 16-gun privateer *General Pickering*. Coming upon a larger British ship in the middle of the night, Haraden took them by surprise and announced that he was a frigate of the highest class and would blow them out of the water if they didn't surrender. In darkness, his bluff worked, and he captured the vessel, a 22-gun British privateer.[9]

A short while later, the *General Pickering* faced off against a much larger, 42-gun British privateer in the harbor of Bilbao, Spain. During the battle thousands of Spaniards lined the shores to see the spectacle, as if it were a naval battle staged in the flooded arena of the Roman Coliseum. One witness said that the American vessel "looked like a longboat by the side of a ship," the difference in their size was so striking. When Haraden ran short of ammunition, he had his cannons loaded with crowbars that had been taken from another ship. Fired into the opponent ship, the crowbars tore through sails and rigging, and sent the gun crews scrambling for safety. Embarrassed and unable to continue the fight, the English captain sailed out of the harbor to get away. Ashore, Haraden was mobbed by cheering Spaniards and carried aloft on their shoulders. Before retiring to Salem, Massachusetts, Captain Haraden had captured British ships that had carried, in all, more than one thousand guns.[10]

Working side by side with the privateers, the first Navy of the United States—the Continental Navy—undertook its inaugural military mission in early 1776. Under the command of Commodore Esek Hopkins, a squadron of eight converted merchant ships set sail from Philadelphia on a wintry February morning. Aboard the modest 24-gun flagship *Alfred* (formerly the London packet the *Black Prince*), a lieutenant raised a flag. There is some disagreement over what that flag looked like. It may have been a red-and-white–striped Navy Jack or a plain yellow flag—either of them with a rattlesnake on it, and perhaps including the legendary words, "Don't Tread On Me." Or it may have been the Grand Union flag, with red-and-white stripes, and a Union Jack in the top left corner where stars are today. It may even have been a broad red pennant, which was Commodore Hopkins's regular command flag. One thing is known for certain: The flag lieutenant on the *Alfred* was John Paul Jones, who later became the greatest naval hero of the Revolutionary War.[11]

The tiny fleet set sail for the Bahamas. On March 3, 1776, Commodore Hopkins landed men on the island of New Providence in the Bahamas. Marching against the fort of Nassau with 220 marines and 50 sailors, they attacked from the rear and forced a surrender. This amphibious assault—led by a Philadelphia tavern owner named Samuel Nicholas—was the first by United States forces, and marked the origin of the U.S. Marine Corps. The Americans took so much booty in the venture—including 24 barrels of precious gunpowder, along with 88 cannon and 15 mortars—that it required two weeks to load the ships for the voyage back home. On the way back, Hopkins and the *Alfred* also captured two small British ships, carrying a total of 18 guns.[12]

The motley American ships and their crews—including the Continental Navy and mosquito fleets of privateers hired by the colonies and their congress—racked up impressive wartime totals. With small naval units that were not able to face the powerful Royal Navy in direct battles, the Americans instead employed guerrilla tactics against their adversaries, attacking and running. In the process they seized or destroyed more than two thousand British ships and took sixteen thousand British seamen into custody, close to the twenty-two thousand redcoats the Continental Army captured.[13]

John Adams, one of the Founding Fathers of the United States of America, described the use of privateers as "a short, easy, and infallible method of humbling the British."[14] His tactic worked, to a remarkable degree. The loss of ships, men, and supplies caused such a stir in England that it was treated as a crisis on the floor of Parliament. In 1776, Lord Admiral Richard Howe of Great Britain wrote: "[However] numerous our Cruisers may be or however attentive our Officers to their Duty, it has been found impossible to prevent some of our Ordnance and other valuable stores, in small Vessels, falling into the hands of the Rebels. . . ."[15]

In the Revolutionary War, thousands of American seamen were

captured and incarcerated by the British. These prisoners were given the opportunity to get out of prison, but only if they signed up for the Royal Navy or one of the British regiments—subject to the promise that they would never have to fight against the colonists. An astounding 92 percent of the captured men refused the offer, and chose the likelihood of death instead. (Of those who did enlist, many had been born in Great Britain.)[16]

"Talk about volunteers," Captain Medeiros said to me. "They were brave men, true patriots."

The British treated their captive colonial seamen cruelly, especially those who were incarcerated on floating, decommissioned ships anchored at Wallabout Bay on Long Island. The most notorious of these prison boats was the HMS *Jersey*, a 64-gun ship of the line that was nicknamed "Hell Afloat."[17] Its spars were removed, leaving only her bowsprit and flagstaff.[18] The gun-ports were closed and nailed shut, and square holes were cut along the length of the hull to let in some air and light—but not enough.[19] American prisoners were crowded onto the lower decks—as many as twelve hundred at a time, in stifling quarters without bunks, benches, or tables.[20]

These unfortunate men received no fresh foods or medical care, so scurvy, dysentery, smallpox, yellow fever, and other diseases ran rampant.[21] Each morning the guards opened the hatches and shouted down to the prisoners, "Turn out your dead!" The Americans would then haul corpses up and sew them into their ragged clothing. Thusly attired, they were buried on the beaches and mudflats around the bay[22]—treated more like animals than human beings.

William Russell, a prisoner on the HMS *Jersey*, described it as "one of the worst places in the world" and a "horrid pit."[23] Another prisoner, Ebenezer Fox, wrote:

> I now found myself in a loathsome prison, among a collection of the most wretched and disgusting looking objects that I have ever beheld in human form . . . cov-

ered with rags and filth . . . visages pallid with disease, emaciated with hunger and anxiety. . . . They were shriveled by a scant and unwholesome diet, ghastly with inhaling an impure atmosphere, exposed to contagion, in contact with disease, and surrounded with the horrors of sickness and death.[24]

For those American seamen unlucky enough to be incarcerated on the HMS *Jersey* or any of its companion vessels anchored nearby, the mortality rate was a frightful 47 percent, in comparison with a figure one-tenth of that—just 4.7 percent in a British facility on land, Mill Prison. Recently, a British researcher reported that Americans in captivity on the ships "were allowed gently to rot, and more than eleven thousand expired."[25] The vast majority of them were merchant seamen, and thousands more died at sea in unmarked graves.

Those British military officers, while agreeing that American seamen were not pirates, still considered them to be rebels and traitors, and not "belligerents" under international law. Hence the English justified treating other prisoners—particularly the Spanish and Dutch—much better.[26]

Even General George Washington did not treat colonial seamen with the respect they deserved. Whenever prisoner exchanges were discussed between the parties, Washington refused to trade any of the British soldiers and sailors he had in custody for American seamen. He used the legalistic argument that most of the Americans in captivity were civilian privateersmen rather than military men—but he was in fact making a cold, hard choice: judging that the British in his custody were in better physical condition than the sickly, emaciated American seamen held by the redcoats, and thus would not be an equal exchange.[27]

It may also have been a decision influenced by racial bigotry, as some modern merchant seamen believe—since so many of the Revolutionary War merchant seamen were black slaves serving for their masters' benefit. It must always be remembered that many of the captured sailors were Portuguese, and indentured slaves. Some historians have suggested that there was a degree of discrimination against these seamen on the part of the American government, since they were not considered "gentlemen"—not even by the high-minded founders of the United States.

But, even in their motley assortment of ships, the men of the colonial merchant marine were the first actual seagoing force of the United States. They sailed the first "liberty" ships—vessels that were directly responsible for the eventual freedom of the American people.

TWO CENTURIES OF
SERVICE TO AMERICA

*Merchant Marine ships have always answered the
call to duty in every conflict in which we have been
engaged.*

—NORMAN Y. MINETA,

U.S. SECRETARY OF TRANSPORTATION[1]

IN THE YEARS IMMEDIATELY FOLLOWING THE AMERICAN WAR OF INDEPENDENCE,
thousands of British seamen deserted the repressive conditions on
their own ships in order to sign on to American vessels, which
offered more attractive working conditions.[2] In response, the
British government instituted a policy known as "impressment,"
under which they stopped American ships, searched them for
deserters, and took men into custody, forcing them to work on
British naval and merchant ships. Many of these men were forced to
fight in the ongoing war between Great Britain and Napoléon Bona-
parte of France. This method of "hiring" was a variation on the old
"press-gangs," which the British had been using for years to obtain
seamen from their own ports—except that now they were seizing
men at sea, from American ships.[3]

From 1802 to 1812, between five and ten thousand American
seamen were "impressed"—in large part because it was difficult to

distinguish Americans of British heritage from actual Englishmen. The British government did have a policy of returning men who were wrongly taken, but this required extensive documentation on the part of those seeking to be released, and could take as long as two years to straighten out. No reparations were ever paid for the inconvenience, or for the forced-labor conditions. Some men were *never* released from custody.[4]

On June 1, 1812, U.S. president James Madison delivered a war message to Congress, outlining American grievances against Great Britain. Impressment was first on his list. It was an affront against American sovereignty, and against individual freedoms. Hearkening back to the documents written by the Founding Fathers, Madison called for a second "war of independence."[5]

The British were also inhibiting free trade, and instituted a number of policies to deny Americans the rights of a neutral state to trade with France, Britain's mortal enemy. This issue—and that of impressment—caused the Americans to go into battle with the slogan, "Free Trade and Sailors' Rights." These were indeed matters of intense national pride for both the Americans and the British.[6]

The War of 1812, therefore, was fought partially over the issue of impressment of merchant seamen, and was fought *by* merchant seamen. Since the United States had almost no Navy to speak of in the war—only seven frigates—many privately owned vessels did the fighting instead, manned by merchant seamen.[7]

While the British instituted an effective blockade of American ports, it left its own homeland unprotected—and this became a fertile hunting ground where more than five hundred American privateers captured thirty thousand British prisoners and more than thirteen hundred ships and cargoes, valued at almost forty million dollars. The most effective privateers carried crews of 150 to 160 men, and were often armed with a pivot gun known as a "Long Tom."[8]

One vessel, purchased by an American in France, was christened the *True-Blooded Yankee*, and made raids off the coasts of Ireland and Scotland. In one 37-day period it took twenty-seven

British vessels as prizes and conquered a Scottish town, where the crew burned seven enemy ships in the harbor. Another noted privateer was the *Chausseur*, which took more than thirty "prizes" in the war.[9]

One young Army officer who fought in the war was Winfield Scott, who became the most influential American military thinker in the first part of the nineteenth century. Winfield Scott showed great heroism throughout the War of 1812, and again, later as a general in the Mexican-American War (1846–1848). During the Civil War (the "War between the States," 1861–1865), the strategy Scott recommended to President Abraham Lincoln was one that led, ultimately, to victory.

Winfield Scott was a controversial figure. Back in 1810, as a young Army captain, he was court-martialed and suspended for a year, charged with "ungentlemanly" and "unofficer-like" conduct for insulting his superior officer, General James Wilkinson, referring to him as a traitor on the level of Aaron Burr.[10]

After serving the 1810 suspension, Scott quickly rose to the rank of lieutenant colonel in the Second Artillery. In the spring of 1813 he led a successful amphibious assault at the British-held Fort George, on the Niagara front, just over the Canadian border. Wounded in the battle, Scott chomped at the bit, wanting to get back into action. Two months later, the highly aggressive officer was in uniform again, and led a victorious assault at Lundy's Lane—this time against a British force nearly twice the size of his own.[11]

Scott was complex, however. Despite his earlier insubordinate behavior, he later became a stickler for military order and formalities, to the point where his soldiers nicknamed him, affectionately, "Old Fuss and Feathers."[12]

He was also a man who recognized the tremendous value of the merchant marine. A great military strategist, Scott had studied the successful amphibious assault on the Bahamas by American forces in 1776, and further developed this technique himself—a powerful combination of naval and ground forces. It was a technique he employed in the War of 1812 and, on a larger scale, during the Mexican-American War.

By the time of the outbreak of the Mexican-American War in 1846, General Winfield Scott—well known as a hero of the War of 1812—had high political aspirations that threatened to hold back his military career. For a time, President James Polk kept Scott out of the war because of their differing politics: Polk was a "Jackson Democrat" and Scott was a Whig (who would eventually run for president in 1852). However, when it looked as if General Zachary Taylor—who had been leading the American ground forces against the Mexicans—would not be able to complete the job satisfactorily, Scott was permitted to go in. He won several decisive battles that would end the war.[13]

Scott began with a flanking invasion from the east, making an amphibious landing of ten thousand men on the Gulf coast of Mexico, at Antón Lizardo, in 1847. This required the use of chartered, oceangoing merchant ships to transport troops and military supplies—vessels that were operated by merchant seamen. Now the American invasion force was just twelve miles south of the fortress city of Vera Cruz Llave (later renamed Veracruz), and its nearly impregnable seaward castle of San Juan de Ulúa; at the time, this was considered the strongest fortress in the Western Hemisphere.[14]

After a one-week siege by U.S. land and naval batteries, the Mexicans surrendered the fortress and the city. Now Scott turned his attentions to an inland march on Mexico City, but he was inhibited by the mountain barrier of Cerro Gordo. Robert E. Lee—then a captain under Scott's command—found a path through the ravines and jungle, which enabled the American Army to get through and capture Mexico City. As Scott's Army marched into the Mexican capital, his military band played "Hail, Columbia!" "Washington's March," "Yankee Doodle," and "Hail to the Chief." It was a victory made possible only because of the mighty contribution of the United States' merchant marine.[15]

The amphibious landing near Veracruz—jointly planned by General Winfield Scott and Navy Commodore David Conner—was considered a model military operation that was later studied in detail by the U.S. Marine Corps for their amphibious landings during World War Two.[16]

At the commencement of the American Civil War in 1861, General Winfield Scott—the decorated hero of two earlier wars—provided President Lincoln with a comprehensive strategy to defeat the Confederacy. The only aspect of his plan that Lincoln adopted, however, was to blockade key rebel seaports, to "starve out" the South by cutting off the import of supplies, and ruining their economy by preventing exports. The Union Navy had only ninety warships at the time, and more than half of them were obsolete. They did not have nearly enough naval power to enforce an effective blockade on over thirty-five hundred miles of Confederate-controlled coastline—from South Carolina to Texas. This made it necessary for the Union Navy to take control of six hundred merchant marine vessels, manned by seventy thousand civilian seamen.[17]

The North did it in a hurry, assembling the most eclectic collection of vessels in the annals of military history. Virtually anything that could float and carry a gun was put to sea, where they took up stations outside Southern harbors—including whaling and fishing boats, coastal steamers, decrepit clipper ships, and even ferryboats. While these vessels were being pressed into service, the Union Navy undertook a construction program to produce new, shallow-draft, lightly armed vessels known as "ninety-day gunboats"—since that was how long it took to commission and construct them.[18]

To counter this strategy, the Confederacy showed surprising ingenuity, especially considering the fact that they did not have a strong maritime tradition of their own. The South had no Navy—and no industrial facilities to build large ships—but in an enterprising, imaginative fashion they contracted with shipbuilders in England, to construct warships, including armor-clads.

The British, however, had laws against building warships for "belligerents." To get around this, the South made arrangements under the names of phony purchasers, ordering unarmed merchant vessels. A number of these ships were then sailed to friendly ports, where they were armed and sent into battle against the North, as "commerce raiders."[19] Their military assignment, as one captain put it, was "brief and to the point, leaving much to discretion, but more to the torch."[20]

The first English-built raider ship—the steam-engine corvette CSS *Florida*—sailed from Liverpool, England, in 1862, and began attacking Northern shipping lanes in the Atlantic Ocean and in the Gulf of Mexico. Upon learning of the origins of the vessel, Northern political leaders began protesting to the British government, and built a case against a possible second ship—referred to only as "Number 290"—that was under construction in Liverpool.[21]

On July 29, 1862, that ship went out on what was supposed to be a trial run, but Captain Raphael Semmes—a daring skipper who would soon have his name written indelibly in military history books—ordered all visitors onto tugs, and then steamed for the Azores, where his ship was retrofitted with armaments and recommissioned as the CSS *Alabama*. The *Alabama*, a single-screw "sloop-of-war," became the most successful and notorious of all the Confederate raiders. Over a twenty-three-month period, Semmes and his crew destroyed fifty-eight unarmed merchant ships (valued at almost seven million dollars), captured nine more, and sank a Federal warship: the USS *Hatteras*. Another raider, the CSS *Shenandoah*, kept destroying Northern merchant ships for two months after the end of the war, unaware that it had ended.[22]

In the end, Confederate raiders and privateers destroyed 257 Union ships, forcing Northern shipowners to register more than seven hundred of their remaining vessels in foreign countries, principally in Great Britain. The merchant-marine industry in the United States would not recover, or begin to increase the number of American ships involved in foreign trade, until 1918—more than half a century later.[23]

Other Confederate vessels would become unarmed, privately

owned "blockade runners"—fast ships that could get in and out of Southern ports quickly, carrying important cargoes. Not enough blockade runners got through, however, so the Confederate economy was eventually strangled by the Northern blockade. Confederate gold reserves were being drained, too, since the blockade-running companies began to demand payments in gold. Ultimately, the South was reduced to bartering with the only valuable commodity it had left: cotton.[24]

In the Spanish-American War, the merchant marine—while not recovered from the devastation of the industry during the Civil War—still made important contributions. On May 1, 1898, Commodore George Dewey, commanding the Asiatic squadron of the U.S. Navy, attacked and destroyed the Spanish fleet at Manila Bay in the Philippines. Dewey then occupied the Spanish naval station Cavite on the bay, while the U.S. Department of War prepared an Army to take control of Manila, the capital city of the Philippines.

Over the next two months, American military authorities commissioned a fleet of nineteen chartered and purchased steamers, which were then modified to troop carriers in San Francisco. The converted merchant ships—carrying eleven thousand U.S. troops—were sent across the Pacific Ocean to the Philippines in five convoys. On August 13, 1898, they took control of the city of Manila, effectively ending Spanish control of the Philippines.[25]

In World War One, the conflict had raged on for almost three years before the United States entered it, on April 6, 1917. At that time, Congress ordered a massive merchant-fleet shipbuilding program. More than 160 shipyards were put to work, constructing more than thirty-three hundred vessels. But the war ended the following year, before most of these ships had been finished and put to use. For that reason, the contributions of the U.S. Merchant Marine to the war were limited.[26] Just before the next worldwide conflagration—World War Two—the United States started building at a much faster pace, so that we had ships up and sailing by the time the nation entered the war in 1941.

Following World War Two, the U.S. merchant fleet was drastically reduced. Most of the ships that had been so valuable during the war were sold to other nations, mothballed, or scrapped. Nonetheless, the U.S. Merchant Marine went on to make significant contributions in the Korean War (1950–1953). In particular, there are two stories of heroism in which merchant seamen put their own lives in danger.

One involved a ship that is still operated by Merchant Marine veterans, the SS *Lane Victory*. In December 1950, the merchant ship was delivering 3,834 American troops to the Korean war zone, along with 1,146 vehicles and 10,013 bulk tons of war cargo. Then, while a U.S. cruiser and two destroyers laid down covering fire, the Lane Victory evacuated 7,009 civilians from Wonsan, North Korea, *in one day*, including women and children.[27]

The second major rescue occurred around the same time, on December 22, 1950. In the North Korean harbor of Hungnam, the temperature was frigid, with howling winds. Thousands of Korean refugees stood on the docks and the shore, carrying their meager personal possessions. The people were terrified, because the Chinese communists had threatened to behead them.

The SS *Meredith Victory*, a five-year-old American freighter, had recently transported military tanks, trucks, machine guns, ammunition, and land mines to the war zone, and now had a highly explosive cargo of aviation fuel in its hold, stored in 52-gallon drums. The U.S. Marine Corps and Army had already evacuated, under pressure from Chinese forces, and there had been no opportunity to unload all of the fuel. A blanket of snow lay on the ground, and a glow of fire ringed the city, from the bombs dropped by U.S. Navy pilots.

The captain of the *Meredith Victory*, Leonard LaRue, had visited St. Mary's Church in San Francisco before departure, to say a prayer for his ship and his crew. Now, as he steamed into the North Korean harbor, he would need all of God's help. Although he was not required to do so, Captain LaRue began accepting the Korean refugees onto his ship. Ragged and dirty, the refugees streamed over a makeshift wooden causeway from the beach to the ship—at least fourteen thousand men, women, and children. It was probably the greatest number of people ever taken onto a freighter of any size—even more than the much larger *Queen Mary* took when it transported troops.

Remembering this later, Captain LaRue wrote:

> Koreans do not show emotion readily, but as I stood on the bridge, I saw expressions on faces that, even now, bring a warm glow to my heart. Our passengers, waving gaily, gave us all glances of profound gratitude.

With people standing shoulder-to-shoulder in the holds, and with the decks crowded with shivering passengers, the *Meredith Victory* steamed out of the harbor. Captain LaRue said:

> I cannot possibly describe the nightmarish quality of that journey. We had no food and almost no water for the refugees—they ate only what they could bring aboard. There were no extra blankets, no clothes to warm them.

They also had no sanitary or medical facilities, but made it—by the grace of God—through a gauntlet of enemy mines and submarines, without any means of detecting or fighting their adversaries.[28]

By the time the United States became involved in the Vietnam War, in the mid-1960s, the U.S. Merchant Marine was a shadow of its former self, with only a small number of ships and seamen. Even so, every available merchant vessel was drawn in—to transport armaments, munitions, fuel, food, and other military supplies, for the five hundred thousand American troops stationed in Vietnam. Most of the U.S. soldiers were deployed by air, but at least 98 percent of their supplies went by sea.[29]

As Lane C. Kendall, a commercial shipping advisor during the war, wrote in one report:

Use of the American Merchant Marine to support the operations in Vietnam has served to point up significantly . . . that ships still provide transportation at a fraction of the cost of air delivery. The Military Airlift Command estimated in December 1966 that the cost of transporting a short ton of cargo in a C-141 cargo aircraft from Dover, Delaware, to Tan Son Nhut, Vietnam, is $709. The ocean freight rate from an East Coast port of the United States to any port in Vietnam for a similar quantity of cargo is approximately $73.50, exclusive of stevedoring costs.[30]

To compensate for the shortage of civilian seamen, the Maritime Commission moved up by a year the graduation dates of the classes of 1966 and 1967 at the U.S. Merchant Marine Academy in Kings Point, New York—shortening the requirements for licensed deck and engineering officers and apprentices, so that they could work on ships bound for Vietnam.[31]

These were dangerous waters, where merchant ships and their crews were subject to destruction by gunfire or mines. Sometimes enemy "sappers"—frogmen—attached mines or bombs to the anchor-chains, screws, or hulls. Mines could be rigged onto small rafts and then floated into merchant ships moored in harbors, or at anchor. A number of ships were hit by one form of attack or another, especially as they approached the city of Saigon. The SS *Baton Rouge Victory*, for example, was sunk by a mine in Vietnamese waters.[32]

Fortunately for the United States, its merchant ships were not attacked on the high seas during the war. North Vietnam did not have the naval capacity to do this, and the Soviet Union did not elect to commit their powerful fleet of submarines to that task, either.[33] Nonetheless, this did not prevent disaster.

The SS *Badger State* was a C-2–type cargo ship, built at the tail end of World War Two. In those days, it had been one of the faster vessels that could elude German U-boats, better than Liberties or Victories. Now the *Badger State* was just old and worn, with a lot of sea miles and storms recorded in its logbooks. It was originally christened the SS *Florence Luckenbach*, but its name had since been changed, an act that most experienced seamen consider bad luck.

In early December, 1969, the *Badger State* was docked at the U.S. Navy base in Bangor, Washington, on the Hood Canal. Navy crews loaded bombs onto the ship for five days—5,330 long tons of bombs on pallets. There were 500-pound, 750-pound, and 2,000-pound bombs. The one-ton bombs were loaded two per pallet, banded together on a frame. They were positioned in rows athwartship, with wedges and blocks in between. This method of loading, however, meant that if one wedge gave way, a whole row of pallets and torpedoes would slide along with it.

The Chief Mate, Leonard Cobbs, complained that the cargo was not shored securely enough. He was also concerned because the loading had been done in the rain, with no hatch tents to keep the cargo holds dry, which meant the wedges could shrink if they dried out. But nothing could be done about this, it was the way things were done then. They did bring along extra four-by-fours, to help with shoring-up if necessary, and these were lashed to the deck.

Captain Charles Wilson was also concerned about the light-weight load, since the ship could hold much more. He asked for more cargo, but this request was refused by the U.S. Navy authorities. He then asked for better vertical distribution of the cargo, which was granted.

On December 14, 1969, the ship sailed for the Pacific. According to directions given to them by MSTS (the "Military Sea Transportation Service," a Defense Department agency), they were supposed to steer a course close to the Aleutians, then veer southwest past the Marianas, through the strait between Taiwan and Luzon, and then on through the South China Sea to Vietnam.

Two days later they got into very bad weather, and the crew

heard the sounds of something loose in the number 3 cargo hold. Merchant crewmen scrambled down into the hold with the extra four-by-fours, to do more shoring-up, but they were not trained in this dangerous work. For the next week the crew kept shoring up the cargo holds, replacing and adding wedges, but the fixes didn't hold. It was winter in the North Pacific; the *Badger State* was taking on swell systems from different directions, and rolling from 40 to 50 degrees. The weather got worse and worse, and finally Captain Wilson radioed to the Navy that he needed a port of refuge. They assigned him Pearl Harbor, a thousand miles away, but it was the closest. The ship was caught in a hurricane that the weather forecasters had not anticipated, however, and they had trouble holding course.

Through all of this, there were mechanical problems with the old ship. The steering was leaking hydraulic fluid, a chronic ailment that the engineers fixed in an hour and a half. Then a nipple on the superheater of the port boiler started leaking. The boiler had to be shut down for twelve hours, so they had to steam slowly through bad seas. And they discovered the hull plating in the propeller shaft had sustained nickel-sized leaks, so now the shaft alley was taking on a lot of water. The First Engineer patched this, but they had to further slow the ship.

The *Badger State* also had stability problems in the rough seas. It had originally been built with bilge keels which would have increased stability, but these had been removed in 1966. The cargo, as stated, was already light, and, to make matters worse, they had expended a lot of fuel so far—which had been acting as ballast. The index of stability had become too large, a serious situation in itself—in addition to all the other problems.

On Christmas Eve, they faced mountainous seas, and still could not hold course. They needed to follow a westerly, or southerly route, to reach calmer seas—but they could not do either.

By Christmas Day, all cargo in every compartment was loose and shifting around. The crew kept working desperately in rough seas. In the crew areas, a refrigerator and a chart table broke loose. Captain Wilson radioed for an escort ship, presumably to take them to Pearl

Harbor. Now the Navy changed their port of refuge to Midway and sent a vessel to bring them in, but that was still a long ways off. It wasn't turning out to be much of a holiday for the crew.

The next day, the *Badger State* hit the second unpredicted hurricane. The ship was rolling 50 degrees, and on one roll went over 52 degrees, destroying the port lifeboat as it smashed against the side of the ship. Everything broke loose, especially on the number 5 upper 'tween deck, where the 2,000-pound bombs were stored. Bombs were slithering around, hitting the sides of the ship.

The captain radioed an S.O.S., which was picked up by a Greek ship forty miles away—the *Khian Star*. That ship stayed in radio contact, and hurried to the rescue.

But, when the *Khian Star* was two miles away, a 2,000-pound bomb exploded—in what investigators later would call a "low-order explosion"—since all of the bombs had been defused. It was still powerful enough to blast a 12- by 8-foot hole through the hull.* There were no injuries, though—not yet.

The captain gave the order to "abandon ship." Since the port lifeboat was ruined, the starboard boat was lowered, with thirty-five men in it. Captain Wilson and four others were still on the *Badger State*, all wearing life jackets and life rings. Just then, the ship lurched and the painter holding the boat broke loose, causing the boat to land roughly in the water. A 2,000-pound bomb shot through the hole in the hull of the ship, flying over the heads of the startled men in the lifeboat. Moments later another bomb went through the hole and landed on the lifeboat, killing many men and capsizing the boat.

Other seamen, exhausted from the struggle they had already faced at sea, couldn't keep their heads out of the water, and drowned. Other men had trouble climbing the Jacob's ladders on the *Khian Star*, and tumbled back into the stormy sea. When the ordeal was

---

*Doug Fleming, who provided me with information on the SS *Badger State*, said that it was a mystery why a defused bomb exploded. Originally he'd thought that the 2,000-pound bomb must have split open when it banged around on the 'tween decks, causing powder to come out of the sealed bomb, which in turn was ignited by sparks created by all of the metal clanging around. But Captain Charles Wilson told him that experiments were conducted afterward, to answer this very question. They took defused bombs up in an airplane and dropped them from a couple of thousand feet. Approximately 5 percent of them exploded, even without fuses.

over, only fourteen out of a crew of forty were rescued, including Captain Wilson and Chief Mate Cobbs. The ship's log—commonly known as the "bridge log"—was lost. Captain Wilson remembered placing it into a watertight package and handing it to the Third Mate as the mate climbed into the lifeboat. The mate had been one of the men killed.

Each morning when Captain Wilson awoke afterward, for more than thirty years, he asked himself the same question: "What could I have done differently to have prevented this from happening?" His friend Doug Fleming, an expert on the tragedy of the *Badger State*, assured him he had done everything possible, everything that an intelligent, experienced officer would have done.

Unfortunately, a combination of factors—"a chain of malevolent circumstances"—had worked against the ill-fated ship and its crew. Similar vessels that had sailed from Bangor, Washington—one of them two days before the *Badger State*, and the other, two days afterward; the *Elwell* and the *Empire State*, respectively—made it to Vietnam, carrying their cargoes of bombs without incident.

Doug Fleming served in the U.S. Navy during World Two, and took part in the battle of Iwo Jima and in the invasion of Okinawa, where his naval picket ship faced kamikaze attacks. Thinking back on his own experiences, it seemed miraculous to Fleming that he and his fellow crewmen ever made it through.[34]

The twenty-six crewmen who died in the disaster of the SS *Badger State* did not receive military burial or cemetery honors because they were considered civilians, even though they'd been transporting war supplies to Vietnam—and died because of the dangers they'd faced. Similarly, the surviving crewmen today are not eligible for the G.I. Bill, since merchant seamen who served in the Korean and Vietnam Wars have never been made eligible for any benefits at all. The same is true for the civilian crews who provided transportation services in the recent Gulf War.

☆ ☆ ☆

ARTHUR BEAUMONT: "ARTIST LAUREATE" OF THE U.S. NAVY

FOLLOWING WORLD WAR TWO, ARTHUR BEAUMONT CONTINUED TO PAINT, in association with the U.S. Navy. He produced paintings as well as designs for military plaques displayed in the Pentagon, and in other important buildings. He even conducted painting classes for naval personnel, and gave away his demonstration canvases to lucky participants—works of art that eventually became extremely valuable.

In recognition of his many contributions, the Secretary of the Navy granted him the Meritorious Public Service Citation, one of the highest honors granted by the armed forces to a civilian. In 1946, Beau observed and painted the atomic-bomb tests at the Bikini atoll in the Pacific. He later journeyed to the Arctic with the International Geophysical Year expedition, and to Antarctica with a Navy task force.

For the journey to Antarctica in 1959–1960, he was a passenger on the USS *Glacier* (AGB-4). Nicknamed "The Mighty G," it was the largest icebreaker in the world and the flagship of Admiral Richard Byrd. The Americans, engaged in a race with the Soviet Union, were on a mission to claim previously unexplored territory, a 400,000-square-mile area around the Bellinghausen Sea of Antarctica. This was part of what the U.S. Navy called "Operation Deep Freeze." The venture was a resounding success, and an American flag was planted in the contested area. The Russians abandoned their effort.[1]

Arthur Beaumont was only the second artist to paint the geographic features of the South Pole, and he was the first to paint at both the North and South Poles. He risked his life repeatedly in order to complete his work, riding in helicopters, bombers, and huge cargo planes over the frozen wastelands. On one trek across the ice, in a group that was roped together, he tumbled into a crevasse and was pulled to safety by his companions. Another time he suffered broken ribs during a huge storm at sea.

At every opportunity, Beau painted, but his efforts were especially challenging in extremely cold weather, since he preferred to use watercolors. It was so cold in the polar regions that he had to mix his paints with 30 percent medicinal alcohol, or bourbon, in order to keep them from freezing in temperatures that reached as low as 70 degrees (Fahrenheit) below zero.[2]

Each drawing or painting that Beau made in severe arctic conditions was a supreme effort, a fight against the elements. He would wear several layers of clothing while he was at work; including a thick parka, two pairs of socks and underwear, a heavy woolen cap (with earflaps), thermal inner boots, mukluks, and woolen mittens cut open so that two fingers of his painting hand were bare and exposed.

He quipped, "I felt like a knight in armor, and weighed about the same."

His silver-blond beard would freeze when it was exposed to the elements, and so did his breath in front of his face. Under the most extreme conditions, he wore a face mask. To avoid snow blindness, he always had to wear dark glasses. If he remained in one place for too long a time, ice would crack off his clothing when he began to move around. He held a hand-warmer in his teeth, along with a brush, and often had a pair of fleece-lined mittens draped around his neck, into which he had to thrust his hands every thirty to sixty seconds.

"Once a finger is frozen," he wrote in a journal, "it's very painful trying to get it back to normal."[3]

Sometimes, despite his best efforts, it was just too cold to complete the paintings, and the artist left them as is, choosing not to touch them up, since that would detract from their integrity. He did not like to paint from photographs, and always preferred to see his subjects in person, for authenticity.

To honor their eminent naval artist, the U.S. Navy named a mountainous island in the Bellinghausen Sea after him, calling it "Beau's Butte." After looking at the island on a map, Arthur Beaumont smiled and quipped to the captain of the USS *Glacier*, "Be sure to put an *e* on the end of 'Beau's Butte'."[4]

In the 1950s, Mrs. Dwight D. Eisenhower commissioned Beau to paint a picture of the USS *Nautilus*, the first nuclear-powered submarine. She displayed the painting in the White House and later presented it to the crew of the *Nautilus*, where it was hung in the wardroom of the vessel. The painting was on board when the submarine made its highly publicized voyage under the ice cap at the North Pole.[5]

From his early years in England, to his stint as a cowboy in California, and his great naval art and adventures—Arthur Beaumont led a diverse, fascinating life. He has left a lasting legacy of his artistic talents. Following a highly productive lifetime in which Beau traveled all over the world on naval vessels, he died in 1978 at the age of eighty-seven.[6]

As a tribute to the important contributions he made to naval art and history, the U.S. Navy staged a memorial service for Arthur Beaumont aboard a nuclear-powered missile cruiser just outside of San Diego Harbor. With hundreds of family and friends aboard, along with naval officers and chaplains, a number of tributes were spoken for him, with an emphasis on how accurate his renditions had been, and how they would be admired for generations to come.[7]

The artist's paintings have become extremely valuable, and much sought after. Just one of the fourteen paintings he completed of Antarctica—*South Pole Station*—sold for $350,000. That was years after his death—Arthur Beaumont never received great monetary riches from his work during his lifetime. He painted because he loved the work, loved the challenges the craft presented for him, and he loved the critical acclaim he did receive.

(Note: Please refer to the "Bibliography" for a detailed list of reference works.)

INTRODUCTION

1. U.S. Merchant Marine Veterans, World War Two. *Booklet of SS Lane Victory.* Also copyrighted by Leeds Music Corporation. Seaman Jack Laurance wrote the USMM Anthem in 1942.

Note: There are slight variations in different versions of the anthem. Some refer to the "Merchant Marines" (plural), which is not strictly correct spelling. As a veteran of World War II told me, he and his comrades were merchant seamen in the organization known as the United States Merchant Marine.

2. World Almanac Books, *The World Almanac and Book of Facts*, pp. 705, 821.

3. Armed Forces statistics: World Almanac (1999), p. 209; Merchant Marine statistics: Web site, "American Merchant Marine in World War Two" (page 1 of 12 on the U.S. Merchant Marine Web site www.usmm.org as of October 5, 2001); also see *The Anchor Light*, March 2001, p. 5.

In addition to 7,280 Merchant Marine deaths at sea, there were 12,000 wounded—according to congressional testimony—and 1,100 of them died from their wounds. Thus the total number of deaths was 8,380. According to the American Merchant Marine Veterans, the number of missing and dead among merchant seamen was more than 9,200—and this figure did not include men who died long after the war from asbestos exposure and other injuries while serving on board the ships (AMMV "Progress Report on Just Compensation," by Henry Van Gemert, cochairman, in *Salty Dog*, December 2002).

For decades, it has been common knowledge that the U.S. Merchant Marine suffered a high casualty rate, and it was thought that only the U.S. Marine Corps took more casualties. Recent statistics indicate that the USMM was, in fact, at the top of the list. However, I received a letter from the noted maritime author Charles Dana Gibson, in which he said that "comparisons with losses of U.S. Armed Forces is statistically impossible to arrive at."

Statistics are notoriously subject to interpretation and manipulation, and additional information may be developed in the future to adjust these figures. Even if that were to occur, however, it would be *moot*. What earthly difference would it make whether the USMM was first or second in casualty numbers? Either way, the merchant seamen deserved much more credit—instead of the pathetic, shameful excuses and twisted justifications they received instead of respect.

It must also be noted that the U.S. Navy Armed Guard serving on American merchant ships suffered 1,810 deaths in World War Two (Bob Galati, *A Winning Team!* . . . , p. 3). The merchant shipping losses and deaths suffered by our allies were also high—more than 30,000 British merchant seamen died during World War Two. (Also see epigraph for chapter 10, page 101.)

The sinking of the *Cynthia Olson*: Peter Stanford, "Seamen's Recognition Day," in *Sea History*, Spring 1985, p. 12; Captain Arthur R. Moore, *A Careless Word* . . . , p. 67.

4. Denis Hamill, "Merchant Marines [*sic*] Deserve Credit," in *Daily News*, September 29, 2002.

5. Refer to appendix 2, "Seamen of the American Revolution," page 239.

6. Web site, Dan Horodysky and Toni Horodysky, "U.S. Merchant

Marine in World War Two: Casualties," www.usmm.org, March 5, 2001 (cited by Gerald Reminick, *Nightmare in Bari*, p. 41).

7. Women in the Merchant Marine: During World War Two, Admiral Emory S. Land, the head of the War Shipping Administration, announced that there were "no provisions on wartime ships for women crewmembers." Groups of women disputed this and fought for their jobs, but to little avail. Only a handful of women served on merchant ships during the war. One of those people was Mrs. Edna T. Johansson, who was a stewardess on the SS *Sixaola*, a passenger liner that was torpedoed and sunk in the Caribbean Sea on June 12, 1942.

In addition to the 108 passengers on board—along with 87 merchant crew and 6 members of the Navy Armed Guard—the ship was transporting military trucks and war cargo. Johansson survived to tell her story, but 29 of her Merchant Marine comrades did not. Other Allied merchant fleets prohibited women as well, with the exception of the Norwegian Merchant Navy (where women served as radio officers), and perhaps the merchant fleet of the Soviet Union. It was not until the 1970s that the U.S. Merchant Marine Academy at Kings Point, New York, began accepting female candidates.

Toni Horodysky, "Women Mariners in World War Two," p. 8; Allen Thronson, "Kings Point Women Graduates Honored," p. 1; Ian A. Millar, "A Canadian Girl in the Norwegian Merchant Navy," p. 3; Captain Arthur R. Moore, *A Careless Word . . . A Needless Sinking*, pp. 260–61.

Additional information has recently come to light, from Ian A. Millar, that two women—stewardesses on passenger ships in the U.S. Merchant Marine—died when their vessels were torpedoed by German submarines in World War Two. One of the women was Mary C. Kimbro, on the SS *City of Birmingham*, torpedoed off the coast of North Carolina on June 30, 1942. The other known victim was Winifred Gray, on the SS *Robert E. Lee,* torpedoed in the Gulf of Mexico on July 30, 1942. Undoubtedly, there were others—untold stories that may surface one day.

Ian A. Millar, "When America Forgets Her Heroes," p. 7; Captain

Arthur R. Moore, *A Careless Word . . . A Needless Sinking*, pp. 56, 238.

8. Studs Terkel, *The Good War . . .* (oral account of David Milton), p. 104.

9. Peter Stanford, "Seamen's Recognition Day," *Sea History*, Spring 1985, p. 13.

CHAPTER 1: DREAMS OF GLORY

1. Peter H. Spectre, *The Mariner's Book of Days*, page for April 16, 2001.

2. James E. Scott (JO2), "Arthur Beaumont Hall Opens at MID-PAC," *Fleet News*, September 6, 1996.

3. Chuck Hartle, "Arthur Beaumont: He Mastered the Sea with Watercolors," p. 40.

4. JFC, "Arthur E. Beaumont, 1890–1978: First American Artist in Antarctica," p. 14.

5. Ibid.

CHAPTER 2: ALL THE SHIPS AT SEA

1. Don McCombs and Fred L. Worth, *World War II: Strange and Fascinating Facts*, p. 327.

2. Hans-Joachim Braun, "Advanced Weaponry of the Stars," pp. 10–16.

3. Ian A. Millar, "A Very Fine Line," pp. 11–12.

4. Trevor N. Dupuy, *The Naval War in the West: The Wolf Packs*, p. 53; Peter Young, *The World Almanac of World War II*, p. 450; Don McCombs and Fred L. Worth, *World War II: Strange and Fascinating Facts*, p. 129; Robert Gannon, *Hellions of the Deep: The Development of American Torpedoes in World War Two*, pp. 99–100, 133.

5. Gerald Reminick, *Nightmare in Bari*, p. 39; Richard B. Morris, *Encyclopedia of American History*, p. 354.

6. *Naval History,* Fall 1988, p. 73.

7. Maria Brooks (video), *The Men Who Sailed the Liberty Ships*; Neal Gabler, *Winchell*, pp. 295–96.

CHAPTER 3: STORMY WATERS

1. John Bartlett, *Bartlett's Familiar Quotations*, p. 919.

2. Felix Riesenberg, Jr., *Sea War*, p. 95 (citing a *Washington Post* article).

3. Maria Brooks (video), *The Men Who Sailed the Liberty Ships*.

4. Malcolm F. Willoughby, *The U.S. Coast Guard in World War II*, p. 131.

5. Felix Riesenberg, Jr., *Sea War*, pp. 188–91.

Note: According to Peter Stanford, this event occurred at Guadalcanal (rather than Midway), and a story about it was printed in Hearst newspapers in 1943. He said that the National Maritime Union filed suit for libel, and settled six years later for a small amount. A court then ordered the newspapers to publish retractions, but many of them never did (Peter Stanford, "Seamen's Recognition Day," p. 13).

6. Felix Riesenberg, Jr., *Sea War*, pp. 188–191.

7. Ibid., p. 286.

8. Thomas Parrish and S. L. A. Marshall, *The Simon and Schuster Encyclopedia of World War II*, p. 434.

9. Bob Galati, *A Winning Team!* . . . , p. 171.

10. The History Channel (video), *Modern Marvels*: "Liberty Ships of World War II."

11. Ibid.

12. Atlas Video, Inc. (video), *"War Stories: The Merchant Marine."*

13. Malcolm F. Willoughby, *The U.S. Coast Guard in World War II*, p. 132; The History Channel (video), *Battle Stations: Liberty Convoy*; Bob Galati, *A Winning Team!* . . . , p. 3.

Note: The information about adding straps at key structural points was obtained from interviews with merchant seamen.

14. Martin Middlebrook, *Convoy: The Battle for Convoys SC.122 and HX.229*, p. 27; James MacGregor Burns, *Roosevelt: The Soldier of Freedom*, p. 245.

15. I. C. B. Dear, ed., *Oxford Companion to World War II*, p. 1202; Martin Middlebrook, *Convoy: The Battle for Convoys*

SC. 122 and HX.229, p. 26; Gerald Reminick, *Nightmare in Bari*, pp. 39–41; James MacGregor Burns, *Roosevelt: The Soldier of Freedom*, p. 245.

16. Bob Galati, *A Winning Team!* . . . , p. 5; The History Channel (video), *Modern Marvels*: "Liberty Ships of World War II"; Robert T. Young, "The Lessons of the Liberties," p. 3; Don McCombs and Fred L. Worth, *World War II: Strange and Fascinating Facts*, p. 332; The History Channel (video), *Battle Stations: Liberty Convoy*.

17. Peter Kemp, *Decision at Sea: The Convoy Escorts*, p. 31.

18. Peter Young, ed., *The World Almanac of World War II*, p. 446; Jack LeVien and Jack Lord, *Winston Churchill: The Valiant Years*, pp. 76–77; Felix Riesenberg, Jr., *Sea War*, pp. 165–66.

19. Trevor N. Dupuy, *The Naval War in the West: The Wolf Packs*, pp. 31–33.

20. Bob Galati, *A Winning Team!* . . . , p. 170; Maria Brooks (video), *The Men Who Sailed the Liberty Ships*; The History Channel (video), *Battle Stations: Liberty Convoy*.

21. Ian A. Millar, "In an Act of Historic Ingratitude, America Forgot Those Who Made Possible the Final Victory," p. 7.

22. Bob Galati, *A Winning Team!* . . . , pp. 42–45; Ian A. Millar, "Tankers At War!" pp. 22–27.

23. Ian A. Millar, "We Thought She Was Scandinavian," p. 16.

24. Ian A. Millar, "Tankers at War!" pp. 22–24.

25. Captain Arthur R. Moore, *A Careless Word . . . A Needless Sinking*, p. 30.

26. Felix Riesenberg, Jr., *Sea War*, pp. 115–16 (citing the account of Junior Engineer Ira C. Kenny, by Marjorie Dent Candee of *The Lookout*—a publication of the Seamen's Church Institute).

CHAPTER 4: REPORTING FOR DUTY

1. Web site, "American Merchant Marine in World War II" (page 1 of 12 on the U.S. Merchant Marine Web site as of 10/5/01).

2. Captain Peter Chelemedos, *Peter: The Odyssey of a Merchant Mariner*, pp. 11–45.

3. Don McCombs and Fred L. Worth, *World War II: Strange and Fascinating Facts*, p. 521.

4. Captain Richard Britton, "A U.S. Merchant Marine Seaman's Memory of His World War II Experiences," *The Anchor Light*, October 2001, p. 9.

5. Bob Galati, *A Winning Team!* . . . , pp. 47–49.

6. Ibid., pp. 135–40.

7. Excerpt of undated letter from Lincoln R. Masur, on file with the Puget Sound Maritime Historical Society, Seattle, Washington; Captain Arthur R. Moore, *A Careless Word . . . A Needless Sinking*, p. 306.

8. Bob Galati, *A Winning Team!* . . . , pp. 92–95; Ian A. Millar, "Tankers at War!—Part Two Conclusion," pp. 67–68.

9. Robert M. Browning Jr., *U.S. Merchant Vessel War Casualties of World War II*, p. 206.

Note: I also interviewed William C. Crozier.

10. Felix Riesenberg, Jr., *Sea War*, p. 97.

11. Captain Arthur R. Moore, *A Careless Word . . . A Needless Sinking*, p. 537.

12. Harold J. McCormick, "After Forty Years: I Find Out How My Ship Was Sunk in World War II . . . ," *Sea History*, Spring 1985, p. 17.

13. Carl B. Wall, "Captain of His Fate," *Reader's Digest*, July 1994. (Cited in *The Pointer*, October/November/December 2001, pp. 13–15. Also cited in Captain Arthur R. Moore's *A Careless Word . . . A Needless Sinking*, pp. 319–321.)

CHAPTER 5: WAR CRIMES

1. Captain Arthur R. Moore, *A Careless Word . . . A Needless Sinking*, p. 70.

2. Ibid., p. 44.

3. Samuel Eliot Morison, *The Atlantic Battle Won: May 1943–May 1945*, pp. 300–301.

4. Ibid., pp. 276, 298–300; Bob Galati, *A Winning Team!* . . . , pp. 78–88; Bernard Edwards, *Blood and Bushido*, chapter 13; John Berger, "Tjisalak."

Note: Various reports on the atrocities of Mr. Ariizumi spell his given name as Tatsunosuke, Tetsunosuke, or Tatsunoseke. His rank is shown as either commander or lieutenant commander.

5. Samuel Eliot Morison, *The Atlantic Battle Won: May 1943–May 1945*, pp. 276–77.

6. Anonymous, "Just When Pacific Coast Sailing Looked Calm, Japanese Sub Sunk Ship and Strafed Survivors," pp. 3–4; Anonymous, "Jap Raiders Rove Pacific, Ram Lifeboat" and "American Convoys Are Alerted After Ship Is Sunk, Crew Strafed," p. 9; Maria Brooks (video), *The Men Who Sailed the Liberty Ships*; Captain Arthur R. Moore, *A Careless Word . . . A Needless Sinking*, p. 148; John Costello, *The Pacific War*, p. 562; Raymond A. Booth, "My Knowledge of the Sinking of the SS *John A. Johnson*"; Captain Peter Chelemedos, *Peter: the Odyssey of a Merchant Mariner*, pp. 89–93, 137.

Note: I also interviewed Peter Chelemedos, one of the survivors of the SS *John A. Johnson*, who was Chief Mate on the ill-fated voyage. His poetic words about the murdered ship's carpenter, Jim Brady, were part of a longer poem that he wrote in tribute to his fellow merchant seamen.

7. Felix Riesenberg, Jr., *Sea War*, pp. 259–62; Samuel Eliot Morison, *The Atlantic Battle Won: May 1943–May 1945*, pp. 298–300; Captain Arthur R. Moore, *A Careless Word . . . A Needless Sinking*, pp. 146–147, 569; Maria Brooks (video), *The Men Who Sailed the Liberty Ships*; Bernard Edwards, *Blood and Bushido*, chapter 13.

Note: On page 84 of *A Winning Team! . . .* , by Bob Galati, he describes an earlier incident involving these sadistic Japanese submariners. They tied twenty or thirty crewmen from the Dutch freighter *Tjisalak* to the deck of the submarine and then dove into the sea, drowning most of them. This same cruel punishment was inflicted upon the crew of the SS *Jean Nicolet*, with a variation—the Japanese reportedly spotted a British plane before diving.

CHAPTER 6: THE BATTLE OF SAIPAN

1. U.S. Department of Transportation news bulletin, May 22, 2001, remarks of Norman Y. Mineta, U.S. Secretary of Transportation.

2. Chuck Hartle, "Arthur Beaumont: He Mastered the Sea with Watercolors," p. 39.

3. *The (Orange County, Calif.) Register Leisurtime*, February 9, 1975, p. 6; *Orange County (Calif.) Illustrated*, September 1977, p. 118.

4. *National Geographic*, September 1941.

5. Chuck Hartle, "Arthur Beaumont: He Mastered the Sea with Watercolors," p. 42.

6. Don McCombs and Fred L. Worth, *World War II: Strange and Fascinating Facts*, pp. 521, 587.

CHAPTER 7: VALOR AT SEA

1. Ian A. Millar, "A Very Fine Line," p. 10.

2. Ian A. Miller, "*Virginia Dare* Was a Fighting Lady," pp. 19–20; Felix Riesenberg, Jr., *Sea War*, pp. 149–50, 152; Robert M. Browning Jr., *U.S. Merchant Vessel War Casualties of World War II*, p. 490; Ian A. Millar, "All They Had for Norway," pp. 102–07.

3. Bob Galati, *A Winning Team! . . .* , pp. 65–71, 141–43; Captain Arthur R. Moore, *A Careless Word . . . A Needless Sinking*, pp. 346, 364.

4. Felix Riesenberg, Jr., *Sea War*, p. 124; Captain Arthur R. Moore, *A Careless Word . . . A Needless Sinking*, pp. 46–47, 82.

5. Walter Karig, Earl Burton, and Stephen L. Freeland, *Battle Report: The Atlantic War*, p. 84.

6. Barbara W. Tuchman, *The First Salute*, p. 47; Richard B. Morris, *The American Navies of the Revolutionary War*, p. 17.

7. Felix Riesenberg, Jr., *Sea War*, pp. 167–68; Don McCombs and Fred L. Worth, *World War II: Strange and Fascinating Facts*, pp. 559, 561; Walter Karig, Earl Burton, and Stephen L. Freeland, *Battle Report: The Atlantic War*, pp. 124–25; Robert T. Young, "The Lessons of the Liberties," *The Anchor Light*, January 2001, p. 3; Captain Arthur R. Moore, *A Careless Word . . . A Needless Sinking*, pp. 269–70, 552; Samuel Eliot Morison, *The Two-Ocean War . . .* pp. 240–41; Peter Stanford, "How an Ugly Duckling

Fought Back and Sank Her Assailant," p. 22; Robert M. Browning, Jr., *U.S. Merchant Vessel War Casualties of World War II*, pp. 221–22; L. A. Sawyer and W. H. Mitchell, *The Liberty Ships*, p. 130; William D. Sawyer, "A Tough Breed Hangs In There—Last of the Libertys [*sic*]," in *Sea History*, p. 28.

Note 1: While the crew of the *Tannenfels* respected their enemies who fought so heroically, other German raiders were ruthless predators, not unlike their Japanese allies in the Pacific Ocean. After torpedoing the SS *William Humphrey*, the crew of the German raider *Michel* shelled lifeboats, killing hapless, unarmed crewmen as they sought to escape their sinking ship. At the Nuremberg trials in 1946, the captain of the *Michel*, Hellmuth von Ruckteschell, was convicted of war crimes. He died in prison while serving a ten-year sentence. (William N. Wallace, "The Saga of the SS *William F. Humphrey*," *The Pointer*, October/November/December 2001, pp. 15–16.) In addition, Michael Gannon wrote that "the *U-852*, commanded by Kapitänleutnant Heinz Eck, machine-gunned both survivors and debris in an attempt to leave no trace of its sinking of the Greek ship SS *Peleus* in the Indian Ocean on 13 March 1944" (Michael Gannon, *Operation Drumbeat*, p. xx of Prologue).

Note 2: The conviction of von Ruckteschell was controversial. According to Ian A. Millar, he was made a scapegoat by the Allies after the war, and the evidence did not actually support a conviction. On the contrary, Millar described him as a man who "fought gallantly, spared lives when that could be done, and put his ship and crew in grave danger to rescue survivors" (Ian A. Millar, "Homecoming Denied: The Cruise of the Sea Raider *Michel*," pp. 34, 117).

8. Ian A. Millar, "Remembering a Friend," *Nautical Brass*, March/April 1995, pp. 11–12.

CHAPTER 8: TORPEDO RUN

1. Ian A. Millar, "The Type of Man Your Brother Was . . . ," p. 22; Ian A. Millar, "The Stephen Hopkins Epilogue . . . ," pp. 29–31, 77; Ian A. Millar, "California's Gallant Ship," pp. 38–39.

2. Maria Brooks (video), *The Men Who Sailed the Liberty Ships*.

3. Captain Arthur R. Moore, *A Careless Word . . . A Needless Sinking*, p. 536.

4. Atlas Video, Inc. (video), *War Stories: The Merchant Marine*.

5. Bob Hope, "A Christmas Broadcast to Merchant Seamen Everywhere." (See Chapter 12, footnote 1.)

6. Don McCombs and Fred L. Worth, *World War II: Strange and Fascinating Facts*, p. 471; Captain Arthur R. Moore, *A Careless Word . . . A Needless Sinking*, pp. 397–98.

7. Bob Galati, *A Winning Team! . . .* , pp. 72–77.

8. Donald R. Wellington, "My WWII Adventures on the SS *Ames Victory*," p. 3.

9. Felix Ricsenberg, Jr., *Sea War*, pp. 36–37.

CHAPTER 9: THE RUSSIAN GAUNTLET

1. Jack LeVien and John Lord, *Winston Churchill: The Valiant Years*, p. 72.

2. Felix Riesenberg, Jr., *Sea War*, pp. 151–52.

3. American Mail Lines, *History of the American Mail Lines, 1850–1946*, pp. 46–47.

4. Robert T. Young, "The Lessons of the Liberties," p. 3.

5. Trevor N. Dupuy, *The Naval War in the West: The Wolf Packs*, p. 11.

6. Richard B. Morris, *Encyclopedia of American History*, pp. 367–68.

7. I. C. B. Dear, ed., *Oxford Companion to World War II*, p. 47.

8. *Orange County (Calif.) Register*, May 18, 2001, p. News-3; Trevor N. Dupuy, *The Naval War in the West: The Wolf Packs*, p. 11.

9. Robert T. Young, "The Lessons of the Liberties," p. 3; Trevor N. Dupuy, *The Naval War in the West: The Wolf Packs*, p. 15; Atlas Video, Inc. (video), *War Stories: The Merchant Marine*.

10. Bob Galati, *A Winning Team! . . .* , p. 155.

11. Bernard Edwards, *Blood and Bushido: Japanese Atrocities at Sea, 1941–1945*, Chapter 13.

12. Atlas Video, Inc. (video), *War Stories: The Merchant Marine*; Maria Brooks (video), *The Men Who Sailed the Liberty Ships*; Trevor N. Dupuy, *The Naval War in the West: The Wolf Packs*, p. 15; Richard Hough, *The Longest Battle: The War at Sea, 1939–45*, p. 75.

13. Maria Brooks (video), *The Men Who Sailed the Liberty Ships*.

14. I. C. B. Dear, ed., *Oxford Companion to World War II*, p. 47; Trevor N. Dupuy, *The Naval War in the West: The Wolf Packs*, pp. 13–15; Atlas Video, Inc. (video), *War Stories: The Merchant Marine*; Maria Brooks (video), *The Men Who Sailed the Liberty Ships*.

15. Richard Hough, *The Longest Battle: The War at Sea, 1939–45*, p. 75.

16. Maria Brooks (video), *The Men Who Sailed the Liberty Ships*; Captain Arthur R. Moore, *A Careless Word . . . A Needless Sinking*, pp. 555–58.

17. Felix Riesenberg, Jr., *Sea War*, p. 144; Don McCombs and Fred L. Worth, *World War II: Strange and Fascinating Facts*, p. 470; Maria Brooks (video), *The Men Who Sailed the Liberty Ships*; I. C. B. Dear, ed., *Oxford Companion to World War II*, p. 47; Captain Arthur R. Moore, *A Careless Word . . . A Needless Sinking*, pp. 29–30.

18. Trevor N. Dupuy, *The Naval War in the West: The Wolf Packs*, p. 16; Don McCombs and Fred L. Worth, *World War II: Strange and Fascinating Facts*, p. 475.

19. Studs Terkel, *The Good War . . .* (oral account of David Milton), p. 106.

20. Felix Riesenberg, Jr., *Sea War*, pp. 131–50.

21. Richard Hough, *The Longest Battle: The War at Sea, 1939–45*, pp. 311–12; Peter Kemp, *Decision at Sea: The Convoy Escorts*, pp. 113–15.

22. Captain Arthur R. Moore, *A Careless Word . . .* (account of William L. Smith), pp. 557–58.

23. Studs Terkel, *The Good War . . .* (oral account of David Milton), pp. 104–05.

24. Ian A. Millar, "The Big Roll," pp. 89–90.

CHAPTER 10: THE SUBMARINE PARADE

1. See endnote 3 for "Introduction," page 265, for the sources of fatalities statistics.

2. Don McCombs and Fred L. Worth, *World War II: Strange and Fascinating Facts*, p. 593; Peter Kemp, *Decision at Sea: The Convoy Escorts*, p. 71.

3. Edward L. Beach, *The United States Navy*, pp. 437–39.

4. George Weller, *The Story of Submarines*, pp. 127–30; Don McCombs and Fred L. Worth, *World War II: Strange and Fascinating Facts*, p. 356.

5. Ibid., p. 596.

6. Ibid., pp. 413–14, 609; U.S. Naval History Division, *United States Submarine Losses/World War II* (map, inside back cover).

7. U.S. Navy pamphlet, *USS O'Kane (DDG 77)*; U.S. Naval History Division, *United States Submarine Losses/World War Two* (map, inside back cover); James F. DeRose, *Unrestricted Warfare*, p. 213; Captain Frazee, ——— "When We Ran Out of Torpedoes," *Naval History*, pp. 49–51.

8. Theodore Roscoe, *United States Submarine Operations in World War II*, p. 262; Edward L. Beach, *Submarine!*, p. 178.

9. Bob Galati, *A Winning Team! . . .* , pp. 90, 159–60.

CHAPTER 11: THE HELPING HANDS

1. Atlas Video, Inc. (video), *War Stories: The Merchant Marine*.

2. *Orange County (Calif.) Register*, May 18, 2001, p. News-3; *Congressional Record*, HCON 109 RFS, 107th Congress, May 22, 2001.

3. Cargo information based upon personal interviews con-

ducted by the author, along with various books in the Bibliography, including an analysis of the cargoes of ships listed in *U.S. Merchant Vessel War Casualties of World War II*, *A Careless Word . . . A Needless Sinking*, *Sea War*, and *Nightmare in Bari*, in particular. (Also see John Costello, *The Pacific War*, p. 564.)

4. Studs Terkel, *The Good War . . .* (oral account of David Milton), p. 103.

5. Captain Arthur R. Moore, *A Careless Word . . . A Needless Sinking*, p. 31.

6. Ibid., pp. 179–80.

7. Ernest E. Barker, "Where Was the U.S. Merchant Marine?" p. 3.

8. Gerald Reminick, *Nightmare in Bari*, pp. 82–83, 165–66.

9. John Mitchell, "Cargo Ship Visits Port of Hueneme," pp. B-1, B-2.

10. Ian A. Millar, "He Survived the *Junyo Maru*," pp. 24–27.

11. U.S. Department of Transportation news bulletin, May 22, 2001, remarks of Norman Y. Mineta, U.S. Secretary of Transportation.

12. *Daily Breeze*, May 4, 2001, p. B-1; *Seattle Times*, January 22, 2003, p. A-10.

Note: A 1999 California law granted the right of former POWs to file suit against Japanese and German companies who forced them to work as slave laborers during World War Two. However, this lawsuit was dismissed in 2003 by a federal appeals court in San Francisco, since treaties signed by the U.S. after the war barred restitution.

13. Robert M. Browning Jr., *U.S. Merchant Vessel War Casualties of World War II*, pp. 446–47; Captain Arthur R. Moore, "Never Seen or Heard From Again," pp. 1, 11.

Note: Captain Moore wrote that sixteen men had originally been in the number 4 lifeboat of the SS *Fort Lee*, including ten merchant seamen and six members of the Navy Armed Guard. Evidence indicates that the man who "died shortly after landing" was probably a member of the Armed Guard, Robert Franklin Lanning. It is not known who the other two men were, or what happened to the rest of the men who originally had made it into the lifeboat.

14. Captain Arthur R. Moore, *A Careless Word . . . A Needless Sinking*, p. 540.

15. Marvin Ettinger, "These 'Ducks' Carried Cargo!" pp. 3–4.

16. Carl E. Nelson, "On Borrowed Time," p. 5; Captain Arthur R. Moore, *A Careless Word . . . A Needless Sinking*, pp. 337–38; Felix Riesenberg Jr., *Sea War*, p. 272.

17. Richard Newcomb, "Kuribayashi's Last Stand," *The United States Marine Corps in World War II*, edited by S. E. Smith, pp. 812–13.

18. Thomas Parrish and S. L. A. Marshall, *The Simon and Schuster Encyclopedia of World War II*, p. 367.

19. Felix Riesenberg, Jr., *Sea War*, pp. 274–75.

20. Ibid., pp. 207–09.

21. Ibid., pp. 260–61.

22. A. G. Hansler, "The *Knute Nelsen*," p. 6.

23. Captain Arthur R. Moore, *A Careless Word . . . A Needless Sinking*, p. 551.

24. Maria Brooks (video), *The Men Who Sailed the Liberty Ships*.

Note: According to this documentary, the Merchant Marine needed only one-third as many men to operate a typical Liberty ship, compared with Liberty ships operated by the U.S. Navy.

CHAPTER 12: THE LEAKY LIFEBOAT

1. Bob Hope, "A Christmas Broadcast to Merchant Seamen Everywhere"; Captain Arthur R. Moore, *A Careless Word . . .* , pp. 178, 570.

2. Captain Arthur R. Moore, *A Careless Word . . .* , pp. 75–76, 494, 533.

3. Ian A. Millar, "All They Had for Norway," p. 106.

4. Ian A. Millar, "The Third Mate Stuck."

CHAPTER 13: PASSAGE TO INDIA

1. Walter Karig, Earl Burton, and Stephen L. Freeland, *Battle Report: The Atlantic War*, p. 126.

2. Jim Higman, "A Fish Story," p. 2.

3. John Costello, *The Pacific War*, p. 563.

4. Captain Arthur R. Moore, *A Careless Word . . . A Needless Sinking*, pp. 12, 150, 234–35.

5. Michael Gannon, *Operation Drumbeat . . .* , p. 365; Felix Riesenberg Jr., *Sea War*, pp. 104–05.

6. Captain Arthur R. Moore, *A Careless Word . . . A Needless Sinking*, pp. 42, 114, 174.

7. William J. Koenig, *Over the Hump: Airlift to China*, pp. 7, 17–25; Kenneth Scott Latourette, *China*, p. 141.

CHAPTER 14: INVASION FORCES

1. John Costello, *The Pacific War*, p. 564.

2. George W. Baer, *One Hundred Years of Sea Power*, p. 229.

3. I.C.B. Dear, ed., *Oxford Companion to World War II*, p. 1202.

4. Felix Riesenberg, Jr., *Sea War*, pp. 210–11; Captain Arthur R. Moore, *A Careless Word . . . A Needless Sinking*, p. 23.

5. Samuel Eliot Morison, *The Two-Ocean War . . .* , p. 382; Captain Arthur R. Moore, *A Careless Word . . . A Needless Sinking*, p. 217.

6. Andrew Wineke, "Remembering the *Rohna*," pp. D1–2.

7. Don McCombs and Fred L. Worth, *World War II: Strange and Fascinating Facts*, p. 437.

8. Trevor N. Dupuy, *The Naval War in the West: The Wolf Packs*, pp. 16–18.

9. Don McCombs and Fred L. Worth, *World War II: Strange and Fascinating Facts*, p. 413; John MacDonald, *Great Battles of World War II*, pp. 61–62.

10. Felix Riesenberg, Jr., *Sea War*, p. 208; Captain Arthur R. Moore, *A Careless Word . . . A Needless Sinking*, pp. 382, 551;

American Mail Lines, *History of the American Mail Lines, 1850–1946*, p. 48.

11. Felix Riesenberg, Jr., *Sea War*, pp. 207–09; Captain Arthur R. Moore, *A Careless Word . . . A Needless Sinking*, p. 281; Bob Galati, *A Winning Team! . . .* , p. 173.

12. Don McCombs and Fred L. Worth, *World War II: Strange and Fascinating Facts*, p. 543.

13. Richard B. Morris, *Encyclopedia of American History*, p. 377.

14. Gerald Reminick, *Nightmare in Bari*, p. 33.

15. Don McCombs and Fred L. Worth, *World War II: Strange and Fascinating Facts*, pp. 498, 595.

16. Gerald Reminick, *Nightmare in Bari*, pp. 12, 66–68, 75, 119.

17. Ibid., pp. 4, 7, 51, 63–64; Don McCombs and Fred L. Worth, *World War II: Strange and Fascinating Facts*, p. 290.

18. Gerald Reminick, *Nightmare in Bari*, pp. 12, 75.

19. Don McCombs and Fred L. Worth, *World War II: Strange and Fascinating Facts*, p. 40; Gerald Reminick, *Nightmare in Bari*, pp. 125, 128–29.

20. Gerald Reminick, *Nightmare in Bari*, pp. 13, 54.

21. Ian A. Miller, "For Military Merit—The Award of the Purple Heart Medal to Crew Members of the SS *Lyman Abbott*."

22. Ian A. Millar, "In the Crosshairs of 'Anzio Annie,'" pp. 16–17.

23. I. C. B. Dear, ed., *Oxford Companion to World War II*, p. 1202.

24. U.S. Maritime Coalition in association with Gardy-McGrath International, Inc. (video), *The Last Convoy*.

25. Don McCombs and Fred L. Worth, *World War II: Strange and Fascinating Facts*, pp. 388, 463, 643; Captain Arthur R. Moore, *A Careless Word . . . A Needless Sinking*, pp. 65, 133.

26. U.S. Maritime Coalition in association with Gardy-McGrath International Inc. (video), *The Last Convoy*.

27. The History Channel (video), *Modern Marvels*: "Liberty Ships of World War II."

28. Frank F. Farrar, "Delivering the Goods to the Normandy Beaches in 1944," p. 47.

29. Richard A. Freed, "Sub-Ordinary Seaman," pp. 137–39.

CHAPTER 15: HURRICANE AT SEA

1. Peter H. Spectre, *The Mariner's Book of Days*, page for April 30.

2. Samuel Eliot Morison, *The Atlantic Battle Won: May 1943–May 1945*, pp. 301–02.

3. Captain Arthur R. Moore, *A Careless Word . . . A Needless Sinking*, p. 44.

4. Ibid., pp. 51–52.

5. Don McCombs and Fred L. Worth, *World War II: Strange and Fascinating Facts*, p. 300; Michael Gannon, *Operation Drumbeat . . .* , p. 168; Bob Galati, *A Winning Team! . . .* , p. 85.

6. Michael Gannon, *Operation Drumbeat . . .* , p. 365.

7. Ian A. Millar, "At His Post to the End," pp. 18–20.

CHAPTER 16: THE DARKEST DAYS

1. U.S. Maritime Coalition in association with Gardy-McGrath International, Inc. (video), *The Last Convoy*.

2. Cornelius A. ("Pete") Burke, "Liberty Ship Signalman," p. 144.

3. Thomas P. Lowry and John W. G. Wellham, *The Attack on Taranto: Blueprint for Pearl Harbor*, pp. 1, 21, 88; Don McCombs and Fred L. Worth, *World War II: Strange and Fascinating Facts*, pp. 575–76.

4. Ian A. Millar, "In the Crosshairs of 'Anzio Annie,'" p. 16.

CHAPTER 17: THE CIGARETTE SALESMAN

1. Peter H. Spectre, *The Mariner's Book of Days*, page for August 6.

CHAPTER 18: NOT COVERED!

1. James B. Simpson, *Contemporary Quotations*, p. 68.

2. *The Honolulu Advertiser*, June 9, 2001, p. A2.

3. Maria Brooks (video), *The Men Who Sailed the Liberty Ships*.

4. Ian A. Millar, "In an Act of Historic Ingratitude, America Forgot Those Who Made Possible the Final Victory," p. 7.

5. Don McCombs and Fred L. Worth, *World War II: Strange and Fascinating Facts*, p. 389.

6. Ibid., p. 389.

7. I. C. B. Dear, ed., *Oxford Companion to World War II*, p. 1203; *Collier's Encyclopedia*, volume 12, p. 643.

8. Don McCombs and Fred L. Worth, *World War II: Strange and Fascinating Facts*, p. 212.

9. Ian A. Millar, "Brave Men Denied," p. 47.

10. John C. Burley, biographical information.

CHAPTER 19: THEY EARNED OUR RESPECT

1. James B. Simpson, *Contemporary Quotations*, p. 66.

2. Maria Brooks (video), *The Men Who Sailed the Liberty Ships*.

Note: When President Franklin D. Roosevelt signed the G.I. Bill of Rights, he said, "I trust Congress will soon provide similar opportunities for members of the Merchant Marine who have risked their lives time and time again during this war." (Quoted by National Maritime Union in *Sea History*, Spring 1985, p. 5.)

3. Felix Riesenberg, Jr., *Sea War*, p. 103.

4. Anonymous, "Extract from the Log of the SS *The Dalles*," p. 9.

5. Felix Riesenberg, Jr., *Sea War*, pp. 25, 100–103; Maria Brooks (video), *The Men Who Sailed the Liberty Ships; Federal Benefits for Veterans and Dependents*, Veterans Administration pamphlet 80-00-1, P94663, p. 11; *Compton's Pictured Encyclopedia . . .* , volume 14, p. 466a.

6. Excerpt of undated letter from Lincoln R. Masur, on file with the Puget Sound Maritime Historical Society, Seattle, Washington.

7. Maria Brooks (video), *The Men Who Sailed the Liberty Ships*.

8. Donald C. Metz, Department of the Air Force letter, January 11, 1988. (Cited by Captain Arthur R. Moore in *A Careless Word . . . A Needless Sinking*, p. 591.)

9. *Boston Globe*, January 21, 1988, pp. 1, 5. (Cited by Captain Arthur R. Moore in *A Careless Word . . . A Needless Sinking*, p. 592.)

10. Maria Brooks (video), *The Men Who Sailed the Liberty Ships*.

11. U.S. Navy Armed Guard WWII Veterans, *The Pointer*, July/August/September 2001, p. 12.

12. Ian A. Millar, "Merchant Seamen in the VFW—Some Thoughts to Ponder," pp. 1, 6; Ian A. Millar, "Well Done, Norway," pp. 69–71.

CHAPTER 20: LAST MAN TO STAND

1. Captain Peter Chelemedos, *Peter: The Odyssey of a Merchant Mariner*, pp. 71–78. (Some information is also from my personal interviews with Mr. Chelemedos.)

Note: The survivors of the the MS *Cape Decision* used the lifeboat sail to make a balloon jib for the trip to Barbados. Peter Chelemedos wrote this poem afterward, which was published on p. 75 of his book *Peter: The Odyssey of a Merchant Mariner*, and is reprinted here with the permission of the author:

The Sun
The warm trade winds scudded
The lifeboat
At a good clip
Across the empty tropic sea.
There was no shade for the forty men
Sitting uncomfortably as they had to do
Except for those fortunate few
Who sat in the shadow of the sail

On the hard wooden benches along the rail
And thwarts of the open boat.

The men used anything,
Handkerchiefs,
Undershirts,
Even torn cuffs from their trousers
To make covering
For their heads from the merciless rays
Of the burning sun.
But when the cool night came,
A shiver
Would wrack the bodies
Of the forcibly chilled men.
They would once again
Be looking forward to morn
And the rising
Of the warming sun.

2. Ian A. Millar, "Murmansk Run Veterans Honored by Russia," p. 73.

3. Ian A. Millar, "Merchant Seamen in the VFW—Some Thoughts to Ponder," p. 1.

4. Ian A. Millar, "So Little Remembered: Merchant Marine Vets Have to Buy Their Own Medals," p. 39.

5. Fox News (television), *Oliver North's "War Stories,"* December 23, 2001; The History Channel (television), December 24, 2001.

CHAPTER 21: THE QUEST FOR JUSTICE

1. Fox News (television), *Oliver North's "War Stories,"* December 23, 2001.

2. Maria Brooks (video), *The Men Who Sailed the Liberty Ships.*

3. Ian A. Millar, "Merchant Seamen in the VFW—Some Thoughts to Ponder," p. 1.

4. Cathy Ingalls and Erik Peterson, "Award Is First for Merchant Marines [*sic*]."

5. Felix Riesenberg, Jr., *Sea War*, p. 286.

6. Ibid., p. 97.

7. Captain Warren G. Leback, "A Bittersweet Discovery," p. 8.

8. Michael Gannon, *Operation Drumbeat . . .* , p. 168.

9. Maria Brooks (video), *The Men Who Sailed the Liberty Ships*.

10. *Collier's Encyclopedia*, volume 19, p. 164.

11. Clifton Daniel, ed., *Chronicle of America*, p. 655; John Mack Faragher, ed., *The American Heritage Encyclopedia of American History*, p. 100; Lorraine Glennon, ed., *Our Times: The Illustrated History of the Twentieth Century*, p. 238.

CHAPTER 22: MAN ON A MISSION

No footnotes.

CHAPTER 23: HEALING THE WOUNDS

1. Ian A. Millar, "Under the Gun at Sea: An Appeal to the Sons and Daughters."

2. Denis Hamill, "Merchant Marines [*sic*] Deserve Credit," *Daily News*, September 29, 2002.

3. The information on asbestos injuries is based upon legal documents and letters, and on interviews with injured merchant seamen who were claimants in the various lawsuits. The written documentation includes allegations of trust-fund theft against a deceased attorney.

4. July 26, 2001, letter from Patsy T. Mink, with a copy of H.R. 2302 enclosed.

5. August 31, 2001, letter from Daniel K. Akaka.

6. Don McCombs and Fred L. Worth, *World War II: Strange and Fascinating Facts*, p. 279.

7. August 30, 1995, letter from Daniel K. Inouye.

8. American Merchant Marine Veterans, "Progress Report on Just Compensation," in *Salty Dog*, December 2002.

9. Keith Milton, "Canadian Merchant Seaman Update—An Update," p. 12.

10. Anonymous, "Louisiana Merchant Marine Bonus Deadline Nears," p. 2.

11. American Merchant Marine Veterans, "Progress Report on Just Compensation," in *Salty Dog*, December 2002.

12. *Congressional Record*, H.R. 679, testimony of Ian A. Millar, p. 106.

13. Raymond A. Booth, "My Knowledge of the Sinking of the SS *John A. Johnson*."

14. American Merchant Marine Veterans, "Progress Report on Just Compensation," in *Salty Dog*, December 2002.

15. Department of Veterans Affairs memorandum dated January 4, 2001, from the office of Thomas L. Garthwaite, M.D.

Note: A "Dear Abby" column showing only the date "2001," provided by a retired merchant seaman, indicates that as many as 95,000 Merchant Marine veterans may have applied for benefits by the year 2001.

16. Brian Brannon, "Victory Ship Offers History, Memorial, and One-Day Cruises," p. 10.

17. U.S. Merchant Marine Veterans World War II, *Booklet of SS Lane Victory*; Joseph B. Vernick, "Governor Pat Brown: A True Friend to the USMMV, WWII," p. 1.

18. *Orange County (Calif.) Register*, May 18, 2001, p. News-3.

19. Nathan Miller, *The U.S. Navy: A History*, p. 15.

20. U.S. Navy Armed Guard WWII Veterans, *The Pointer*, July/August/September 2001, pp. 7–8.

21. Denis Hamill, "Merchant Marines [*sic*] Deserve Credit," *Daily News*, September 29, 2002.

22. "Letters to the Editor," *The Anchor Light*, March 2001, p. 11.

23. Wilson J. Taylor, letters to the editor, August 14, 1992.

24. Denis Hamill, "Merchant Marines [*sic*] Deserve Credit," *Daily News*, September 29, 2002.

25. John P. Davis, ed., *The American Negro Reference Book*, pp. 632–38.

26. City of Bellingham [Washington] mayoral proclamation, May 10, 2000.

27. Ian A. Millar, "Merchant Seamen in the VFW—Some Thoughts to Ponder," *The Anchor Light*, March, 1999, p. 6.

28. Ernest E. Barker, "Where Was the U.S. Merchant Marine?" p. 3.

29. Charles Dana Gibson, "In Clio's Cause: Is the History of the Mariners of World War Two to Go Missing Without Trace?" *Sea History*, Spring 1985, p. 10.

APPENDIX 1: CONTACT INFORMATION

No footnotes.

APPENDIX 2: SEAMEN OF THE AMERICAN REVOLUTION

1. Nathan Miller, *The U.S. Navy: A History*, pp. 13–14.

2. Edward L. Beach, *The United States Navy*, pp. 20–21; Jack Coggins, *Ships and Seamen of the American Revolution*, p. 66.

3. Edward L. Beach, *The United States Navy*, pp. 20–21.

4. Nathan Miller, *Sea of Glory: A Naval History of the American Revolution*, p. 256.

5. Ernest E. Barker, "Where Was the U.S. Merchant Marine?" p. 3.

6. Jack Coggins, *Ships and Seamen of the American Revolution* pp. 99–106; Nathan Miller, *The U.S. Navy: A History*, p. 19.

7. Nathan Miller, *The U.S. Navy: A History*, pp. 13, 15; Jack Coggins, *Ships and Seamen of the American Revolution*, p. 23; Barbara W. Tuchman, *The First Salute*, p. 45; American Merchant Marine Veterans, "The Merchant Marine in War and Peace."

8. John P. Davis, ed., *The American Negro Reference Book*, p. 594.

9. Jack Coggins, *Ships and Seamen of the American Revolution*, p. 69; Nathan Miller, *Sea of Glory: A Naval History of the American Revolution*, p. 269.

10. Jack Coggins, *Ships and Seamen of the American Revolution*, p. 69; Nathan Miller, *Sea of Glory: A Naval History of the American Revolution*, pp. 270–71.

11. Jack Coggins, *Ships and Seamen of the American Revolution*, pp. 26, 76; Samuel Eliot Morison, *John Paul Jones: A Sailor's Biography*, p. 426.

12. Nathan Miller, *The U.S. Navy: A History*, p. 12; Jack Coggins, *Ships and Seamen of the American Revolution*, pp. 27, 49; Richard B. Morris *The American Navies of the Revolutionary War*, p. 17.

13. Jack Coggins, *Ships and Seamen of the American Revolution*, p. 74; Nathan Miller, *Sea of Glory: A Naval History of the American Revolution*, p. 260.

14. Nathan Miller, *Sea of Glory: A Naval History of the American Revolution*, p. 282.

15. Jack Coggins, *Ships and Seamen of the American Revolution*, p. 25.

16. Ibid., p. 82; Nathan Miller, *Sea of Glory: A Naval History of the American Revolution*, pp. 268–69.

17. Jack Coggins, *Ships and Seamen of the American Revolution*, p. 79.

18. Barbara W. Tuchman, *The First Salute*, p. 266.

19. Jack Coggins, *Ships and Seamen of the American Revolution*, p. 79.

20. Barbara W. Tuchman, *The First Salute*, p. 266.

21. Jack Coggins, *Ships and Seamen of the American Revolution*, p. 81; Francis D. Cogliano, *American Maritime Prisoners in the Revolutionary War . . .*, p. 149; Barbara W. Tuchman, *The First Salute*, p. 267.

22. Nathan Miller, *Sea of Glory: A Naval History of the American Revolution*, p. 267; Jack Coggins, *Ships and Seamen of the American Revolution*, p. 79.

23. Francis D. Cogliano, *American Maritime Prisoners in the Revolutionary War . . .*, pp. 142, 144.

24. Barbara W. Tuchman, *The First Salute*, pp. 266–67; Jack Coggins, *Ships and Seamen of the American Revolution*, p. 82.

25. Francis D. Cogliano, *American Maritime Prisoners in the Revolutionary War* . . . , pp. 149–50, 152.

26. Jack Coggins, *Ships and Seamen of the American Revolution*, p. 83.

27. Francis D. Cogliano, *American Maritime Prisoners in the Revolutionary War* . . . , p. 164.

APPENDIX 3: TWO CENTURIES OF SERVICE TO AMERICA

1. U.S. Department of Transportation News bulletin, May 22, 2001, remarks of Norman Y. Mineta, U.S. Secretary of Transportation.

2. Harry L. Coles, *The War of 1812*, pp. 4–5.

3. Edward L. Beach, *The United States Navy*, p. 56.

4. Donald R. Hickey, *The War of 1812: A Short History*, p. 7; *Compton's Pictured Encyclopedia* . . . , volume 15, p. 11; *Funk and Wagnalls New Encyclopedia*, volume 27, p. 143; Julius W. Pratt, *A History of United States Foreign Policy*, p. 61; Paul S. Boyer, ed., *The Oxford Companion to United States History*, p. 814.

5. Harry L. Coles, *The War of 1812*, pp. 23–24, 247; Donald R. Hickey, *The War of 1812: A Short History*, p. 13; Julius W. Pratt, *A History of United States Foreign Policy*, p. 61.

6. Paul S. Boyer, ed., *The Oxford Companion to United States History*, p. 814; Donald R. Hickey, *The War of 1812: A Short History*, p. 16; Harry L. Coles, *The War of 1812*, pp. 104–05.

7. American Merchant Marine Veterans, "The Merchant Marine in War and Peace"; *Compton's Pictured Encyclopedia* . . . , volume 15, p. 13.

8. *Compton's Pictured Encyclopedia* . . . , volume 15, p. 14; American Merchant Marine Veterans, "The Merchant Marine in War and Peace"; Harry L. Coles, *The War of 1812*, pp. 95, 98.

9. Harry L. Coles, *The War of 1812*, pp. 95–97.

10. *Encyclopedia Americana: International Edition* (1997), volume 24, p. 433; *Dictionary of American Biography*, volume 8, p. 506.

11. Donald R. Hickey, *The War of 1812: A Short History*, pp. 41–42, 54–55.

12. Ernest R. May, *A Proud Nation*, p. 386; *Compton's Pictured Encyclopedia . . .* , volume 13, p. 69.

13. Margaret C. S. Christman, *1846: Portrait of the Nation*, p. 131.

14. Edward L. Beach, *The United States Navy*, p. 159; American Merchant Marine Veterans, "The Merchant Marine in War and Peace"; John Mack Faragher, general ed., *The American Heritage Encyclopedia of American History*, pp. 587–88; Richard B. Morris, *Encyclopedia of American History*, p. 205; *Encyclopedia Americana* (1948 edition), volume 18, p. 738; *Compton's Pictured Encyclopedia . . .* , volume 9, p. 186.

15. Richard B. Morris, *Encyclopedia of American History*, p. 205; Julius W. Pratt, *A History of United States Foreign Policy*, p. 135; Margaret C. S. Christman, *1846: Portrait of the Nation*, p. 133.

16. Edward L. Beach, *The United States Navy*, p. 159.

17. Richard M. Ketchum, ed., *The American Heritage Picture History of the Civil War*, pp. 62, 169–70; Colonel R. Ernest Dupuy and Trevor N. Dupuy, *The Compact History of the Civil War*, pp. 7–8; *Funk and Wagnalls New Encyclopedia*, volume 6, p. 338; *The New Encyclopedia Britannica* (2002 edition), volume 10, p. 566; American Merchant Marine Veterans, "The Merchant Marine in War and Peace."

18. Richard M. Ketchum, ed., *The American Heritage Picture History of the Civil War*, pp. 170–71.

19. Ibid., pp. 173, 260.

20. Ibid., p. 205.

21. Ibid., pp. 203, 260; Colonel R. Ernest Dupuy and Trevor N. Dupuy, *The Compact History of the Civil War*, p. 348.

22. Richard M. Ketchum, ed., *The American Heritage Picture History of The Civil War*, pp. 205, 260; Edward L. Beach, *The United States Navy*, p. 306; Colonel R. Ernest Dupuy and Trevor N. Dupuy, *The Compact History of the Civil War*, pp. 348–49.

23. Edward L. Beach, *The United States Navy*, p. 306; *The Statistical History of the United States: From Colonial Times to the Present*, pp. 444–45; Richard B. Morris, *Encyclopedia of American History*, p. 240; Colonel R. Ernest Dupuy and Trevor N. Dupuy, *The Compact History of the Civil War*, pp. 40–41, 284–85, 347.

24. Bern Anderson, *By Sea and By River: The Naval History of the Civil War*, pp. 218, 230.

25. Julius W. Pratt, *A History of United States Foreign Policy*, pp. 212–13; American Merchant Marine Veterans, "The Merchant Marine in War and Peace."

26. Edward L. Beach, *The United States Navy*, p. 494–95; American Merchant Marine Veterans, "The Merchant Marine in War and Peace."

27. U.S. Merchant Marine Veterans of World War II, *Booklet of SS* Lane Victory.

28. Bill Gilbert, *Ship of Miracles . . .*, pp. 27, 55–56, 100–102, 122, 142–44; Rosanne Fohn, "Voyage of Mercy," *USAA Magazine*, pp. 16–19.

29. Frank Uhlig, Jr., *Vietnam: The Naval Story*, p. 479; Commander R. L. Schreadley, *From the Rivers to the Sea . . .*, p. 52.

30. Frank Uhlig, Jr., *Vietnam: The Naval Story*, pp. 498–99.

31. Ibid., pp. 491–92.

32. Commander R. L. Schreadley, *From the Rivers to the Sea . . .*, p. 21; Frank Uhlig, Jr., *Vietnam: The Naval Story*, pp. 491, 499–500.

33. Commander R. L. Schreadley, *From the Rivers to the Sea . . .*, pp. 21, 52.

34. Doug Fleming, lecture on the last voyage of the SS *Badger State*; and my personal interview of him.

APPENDIX 4: ARTHUR BEAUMONT:
"ARTIST LAUREATE" OF THE U.S. NAVY

1. Anonymous, "With Navy Team: Southland Artist Has Exhibit in Antarctica," *Los Angeles Times*, March 21, 1960; *Independent*, March 3, 1960; Anonymous, "Icebreaker Crew Celebrates 40th Anniversary of Historic Mission," p. 4.

2. JFC, "Arthur E. Beaumont, 1890–1978: First American Artist in Antarctica," p. 15; Dean Beaumont, "In Profile: Arthur Beaumont," *Naval History*, Fall 1988, p. 73.

3. Anonymous, "With Navy Team: Southland Artist Has Exhibit in Antarctica," *Los Angeles Times*, March 21, 1960; *Orange County (Calif.) Illustrated*, September 1977, pp. 117–18; Dean Beaumont, "In Profile: Arthur Beaumont," *Naval History*, Fall 1988, p. 73; JFC, "Arthur E. Beaumont, 1890–1978: First American Artist in Antarctica," p. 15.

4. Dean Beaumont, "In Profile: Arthur Beaumont," *Naval History*, Fall 1988, p. 73.

5. Anonymous, "With Navy Team: Southland Artist Has Exhibit in Antarctica," *Los Angeles Times*, March 21, 1960.

6. Dean Beaumont, *Naval Battles of World War Two, 1939–1945*.

7. Dean Beaumont, "In Profile: Arthur Beaumont," *Naval History*, Fall 1988, p. 75.

BIBLIOGRAPHY

Akaka, Daniel K. August 31, 2001, letter to Dean Beaumont.

American Mail Lines. *History of the American Mail Lines, 1850–1946*. (No other publication information given.)

American Merchant Marine Veterans. "The Merchant Marine in War and Peace." Undated report distributed by San Juan Chapter, Bellingham, Washington.

———. "Progress Report on Just Compensation." *Salty Dog,* December 2002.

The Anchor Light. A publication of the U.S. Merchant Marine Veterans [of] World War II.

Anderson, Bern. *By Sea and By River: The Naval History of the Civil War*. New York: Alfred A. Knopf, 1962.

Anonymous. "Appeals Court Throws Out POW Slave-Labor Suits." *Seattle Times*, January 22, 2003, p. A-10.

———. "Extract from the Log of the SS *The Dalles*." *The Anchor Light*, October 2001, p. 9.

———. "Icebreaker Crew Celebrates 40th Anniversary of Historic Mission." *The Anchor Light*, November 1999, p. 4.

———. "Jap Raiders Rove Pacific, Ram Lifeboat" and "American Convoys Are Alerted After Ship Is Sunk, Crew Strafed." *The Anchor Light*, December 1999–January 2000, p. 9.

———. "Just When Pacific Coast Sailing Looked Calm, Japanese Sub Sunk Ship and Strafed Survivors." *The Anchor Light*, July 1996, pp. 3–4.

———. "Louisiana Merchant Marine Bonus Deadline Nears." *The Anchor Light*, February 1999, p. 2.

———. "With Navy Team: Southland Artist Has Exhibit in Antarctica." *Los Angeles Times*, March 21, 1960.

Asbestos class-action lawsuit documents, letters, and other files.

Atlas Video, Inc. (video), Military History Productions Inc. (Edwin Newman, narrator.) *War Stories: The Merchant Marine*. 1991.

Baer, George W. *One Hundred Years of Sea Power*. Stanford, Calif.: Stanford University Press, 1994.

Barker, Ernest E. "Where Was the U.S. Merchant Marine?" *The Anchor Light*, February 1996, p. 3.

Bartlett, John. *Bartlett's Familiar Quotations*. Boston: Little, Brown and Co., 1968.

Beach, Edward L. *Submarine!* New York: Henry Holt and Co., 1952.

———. *The United States Navy*. New York: Henry Holt and Co., 1986.

Beaumont, Dean. "In Profile: Arthur Beaumont." *Naval History*, Fall 1988, pp. 72–75.

———. *Naval Battles of World War Two, 1939–1945*. Illustrated by naval artist Arthur Beaumont (1890–1978), "Artist Laureate of the U.S. Navy." Santa Ana, Calif.: Radcliff Publishing Co., 1977.

Berger, John. "Tjisalak." Undated reprint of 2001 *Honolulu Star Bulletin* article.

Booth, Raymond A. "My Knowledge of the Sinking of the SS *John A. Johnson*." Seven-page account from Donnaray@fix.net.

Boston Globe. January 21, 1988, pp. 1, 5. (Cited by Captain Arthur R. Moore, *A Careless Word . . . A Needless Sinking*, p. 592.)

Boyer, Paul S., ed. *The Oxford Companion to United States History*. New York: Oxford University Press, 2001.

Brannon, Brian. "Victory Ship Offers History, Memorial and One-Day Cruises." *The Anchor Light*, September 2001, p. 10.

Braun, Hans-Joachim. "Advanced Weaponry of the Stars." *Invention and Technology*, Spring 1997, pp. 10–16.

Britton, Captain Richard. "A U.S. Merchant Marine Seaman's Memory of His World War II Experiences." *The Anchor Light*, October 2001, p. 9.

Brooks, Maria (writer, producer, director). *The Men Who Sailed the Liberty Ships*. (Ed Markmann, narrator.) KTEH/San Jose Public Television and Waterfront Soundings; distributed by PBS Home Video, 1994.

Browning, Robert M., Jr. *U.S. Merchant Vessel War Casualties of World War II*. Annapolis, Md.: Naval Institute Press, 1996.

Burke, Cornelius A. ("Pete"). "Liberty Ship Signalman." *Assault on Normandy: First-person Accounts from the Sea Services*. Edited by Paul Stillwell. Annapolis, Md.: Naval Institute Press, 1994, p. 144.

Burley, John C. Biographical information entitled "John Corwin Burley."

Burns, James MacGregor. *Roosevelt: The Soldier of Freedom*. New York: Harcourt Brace Jovanovich, 1970.

Chelemedos, Captain Peter. *Peter: The Odyssey of a Merchant Mariner*. Seattle, Wash.: Peanut Butter Publishing, 1992. (Note: This is a very well written first-person account by a veteran of World War Two. When I asked the captain if he'd developed his writing style by writing in ship's logs, he quipped, "The less you put in a log, the less they can hold against you." He said that since merchant seamen were not permitted to carry cameras during wartime, he formed relationships with several pen pals, through which he perfected his descriptive talents. He also had a good English teacher in high school. When his former teacher later saw the manuscript, he said to Captain Chelemedos, "The school of hard knocks taught you a heck of a lot more than I could ever teach you." For ordering information on this excellent book, contact: Peter Chelemedos, P.O. Box 15617, Seattle, WA 98115-0617.)

Christman, Margaret C. S. *1846: Portrait of the Nation*. Washington, D.C.: Smithsonian Institution Press, 1996.

City of Bellingham (Washington) mayoral proclamation, May 10, 2000.

Coggins, Jack. *Ships and Seamen of the American Revolution.* Harrisburg, Pa.: Stackpole Books, 1969.

Cogliano, Francis D. *American Maritime Prisoners in the Revolutionary War: The Captivity of William Russell.* Annapolis, Md.: Naval Institute Press, 2001.

Coles, Harry L. *The War of 1812.* Chicago: University of Chicago Press, 1965.

Collier's Encyclopedia. New York: P. F. Collier and Son Corp., 1960.

Compton's Pictured Encyclopedia and Fact-Index. Chicago: F. E. Compton and Co., 1956.

Congressional Record. H.R. 679, August 13, 1986. (Hearing before the Subcommittee on Merchant Marine of the Committee on Merchant Marine and Fisheries; testimony of Ian A. Millar, pp. 105–08.)

Congressional Record. HCON 109 RFS, (107th Congress), May 22, 2001.

Costello, John. *The Pacific War.* New York: Quill, 1982.

Daily Breeze. May 4, 2001.

Daniel, Clifton, editorial director. *Chronicle of America.* New York: DK Publishing, Inc., 1995.

Davis, John P., ed. *The American Negro Reference Book.* Englewood Cliffs, N.J.: Prentice-Hall, 1966.

Dear, I. C. B., ed. *Oxford Companion to World War II.* Oxford: Oxford University Press, 1995.

"Dear Abby" column (originated by Abigail Van Buren). "Merchant Marine Vets Should Enjoy Status." No date available except 2001 (from a photocopy provided by a retired merchant seaman).

Department of Veterans Affairs memorandum. From the office of Thomas L. Garthwaite, M.D. Dated January 4, 2001.

DeRose, James F. *Unrestricted Warfare.* New York: John Wiley and Sons, Inc., 2000.

Dictionary of American Biography. New York: Charles Scribner's Sons, 1935.

Dupuy, Colonel R. Ernest, and Trevor N. Dupuy (Colonel, U.S.

Army, ret.). *The Compact History of the Civil War*. New York: Warner Books, 1993.

Dupuy, Trevor N. (Colonel, U.S. Army, ret.). *The Naval War in the West: The Wolf Packs*. New York: Franklin Watts, Inc., 1963.

Edwards, Bernard. *Blood and Bushido: Japanese Atrocities at Sea, 1941–1945*. (Note: Only an excerpt—chapter 13—of this book was provided to me, by a retired merchant seaman, without publication information or page numbers. This chapter describes the tragedy of the SS *Jean Nicolet*.)

Encyclopedia Americana. New York: 1948.

Encyclopedia Americana: International Edition. Danbury, Conn.: Grolier, Inc., 1997.

Ettinger, Marvin. "These 'Ducks' Carried Cargo!" *The Anchor Light*, June 1996, pp. 3–4.

Faragher, John Mack, general ed. *American Heritage Encyclopedia of American History*. New York: Henry Holt and Co., 1998.

Farrar, Frank F. "Delivering the Goods to the Normandy Beaches in 1944." *Sea History*, Spring 1985, pp. 46–47.

Federal Benefits for Veterans and Dependents. Veterans Administration pamphlet 80-00-1, P94663 (2000 edition).

Fleming, Doug. Lecture on the last voyage of the SS *Badger State*, at a meeting of the Puget Sound Maritime Historical Society in Seattle, Washington, December 4, 2002. (I also interviewed him personally afterward.)

Fohn, Rosanne. "Voyage of Mercy," *USAA Magazine*. November/ December 2002, pp. 16–19.

Fox News (television). *Oliver North's "War Stories."* December 23, 2001.

Frazee, Captain ———. "When We Ran Out of Torpedoes." *Naval History*, July/August 1994, pp. 49–51. (Note: Given name of Captain Frazee not shown because only these excerpted pages were available.)

Freed, Richard A. "Sub-Ordinary Seaman." *Assault on Normandy: First-person Accounts from the Sea Services*. Edited by Paul Stillwell. Annapolis, Md.: Naval Institute Press, 1994, pp. 137–39.

Funk and Wagnalls New Encyclopedia. Dun and Bradstreet Corp., 1983.

Gabler, Neal. *Winchell*. New York: Alfred A. Knopf, 1994.

Galati, Bob, compiler and editor. *A Winning Team!—The Armed Guard and Merchant Marine in World War II*. Irving, Tex.: Innovatia Press, 1995.

Gannon, Michael. *Operation Drumbeat: The Dramatic True Story of Germany's First U-boat Attacks Along the American Coast in World War Two*. New York: Harper and Row, 1990.

Gannon, Robert. *Hellions of the Deep: The Development of American Torpedoes in World War II*. University Park, Pa.: Pennsylvania State University Press, 1996.

Gibson, Charles Dana. "In Clio's Cause: Is the History of the Mariners of World War Two to Go Missing Without Trace?" *Sea History*, Spring 1985, p. 10.

Gilbert, Bill. *Ship of Miracles: 14,000 Lives and One Miraculous Voyage*. Chicago: Triumph Books, 2000.

Glennon, Lorraine, editor-in-chief. *Our Times: The Illustrated History of the 20th Century*. Atlanta, Ga: Turner Publishing, Inc., 1995.

Hamill, Denis. "Merchant Marines [sic] Deserve Credit." *Daily News*, September 29, 2002. (Photocopy of article published in December 2002 issue of *Salty Dog*, which in turn said it had appeared earlier in the October 2002 edition of the *Ambrose Light Newsletter*.)

Hansler, A. G. "The *Knute Nelsen*." *The Anchor Light*, June 1996, p. 6.

Hartle, Chuck. "Arthur Beaumont: He Mastered the Sea with Watercolors." *The Retired Officer*, October 1984, pp. 38–42.

Hickey, Donald R. *The War of 1812: A Short History*. Chicago: University of Illinois Press, 1995.

Higman, Jim. "A Fish Story." *The Anchor Light*, February 1999, p. 2.

The History Channel (video). *Battle Stations: Liberty Convoy*.

The History Channel (television). December 24, 2001.

The History Channel (video). *Modern Marvels*: "Liberty Ships of World War II."

The Honolulu Advertiser, June 9, 2001.

Hope, Bob. "A Christmas Broadcast to Merchant Seamen Everywhere." (Transcript of December 23, 1944, radio broadcast.)

Horodysky, Toni. "Women Mariners in WWII." *The Anchor Light*, February 1999, p. 8.

Horodysky, Toni, and Dan Horodysky: See "Web sites."

Hough, Richard. *The Longest Battle: The War at Sea, 1939–45.* New York: William Morrow and Co., Inc., 1986.

Independent, March 3, 1960.

Ingalls, Cathy, and Erik Peterson. "Award is First for Merchant Marines [*sic*]" *Albany (Oregon) Democrat-Herald*. (Photocopy of article published in December 2002 issue of *Salty Dog*).

Inouye, Daniel K. August 30, 1995, letter to Dean Beaumont.

JFC. "Arthur E. Beaumont, 1890–1978: First American Artist in Antarctica." *All Hands* (undated photocopy), pp. 13–16.

Karig, Walter (commander, USNR), Earl Burton (lieutenant, USNR), and Stephen L. Freeland (lieutenant, USNR). *Battle Report: The Atlantic War.* New York: Farrar and Rinehart, 1946.

Kemp, Peter. *Decision at Sea: The Convoy Escorts.* New York: Elsevier-Dutton, 1978.

Ketchum, Richard M., ed. *The American Heritage Picture History of the Civil War.* American Heritage Publishing Co., 1960.

Koenig, William J. *Over the Hump: Airlift to China.* New York: Ballantine Books, 1972.

Latourette, Kenneth Scott. *China.* Englewood Cliffs, N.J.: Prentice-Hall Inc., 1964.

Leback, Captain Warren G. "A Bittersweet Discovery." *The Anchor Light*, October 1999, p. 8.

LeVien, Jack, and John Lord. *Winston Churchill: The Valiant Years.* New York: Scholastic Book Services, 1962.

Lowry, Thomas P., and John W. G. Wellham. *The Attack on Taranto: Blueprint for Pearl Harbor.* Mechanicsburg, Pa: Stackpole Books, 1995.

MacDonald, John. *Great Battles of World War II.* New York: Macmillan Publishing Co., 1986.

May, Ernest R. *A Proud Nation.* New York: McDougal, Littell and Co., 1989.

McCombs, Don, and Fred L. Worth. *World War II: Strange and Fascinating Facts.* New York: Greenwich House, 1983.

McCormick, Harold J. (lieutenant commander, USNR, ret.). "After Forty Years: I Find Out How My Ship Was Sunk in World War II—and Meet the Extraordinary Man Who Sank Her!" *Sea History*, Spring 1985, pp. 14–19.

Metz, Donald C. Department of the Air Force letter, January 11, 1988. (Cited by Captain Arthur R. Moore, *A Careless Word . . . A Needless Sinking*, p. 591.)

Middlebrook, Martin. *Convoy: The Battle for Convoys SC.122 and HX.229.* London: Penguin Books, 1976.

Millar, Ian A. "A Canadian Girl in the Norwegian Merchant Navy." *The Anchor Light*, October 1996, p. 3.

———. "A Very Fine Line." *Nautical Brass,* November/December 1993, p. 10.

———. "All They Had for Norway." *Military Collectors' Club of Canada*, Fall 1994, pp. 102–07.

———. "At His Post to the End." *Nautical Brass*, July/August 1990, pp. 18–20.

———. "The Big Roll." *Military Collectors' Club of Canada*, Fall 1989, pp. 89–90.

———. "Brave Men Denied." *Coin and Medal News*, February 1987, pp. 47–48.

———. "California's Gallant Ship," *The Californians*, September/October 1988, pp. 37–39.

———. "For Military Merit—The Award of the Purple Heart Medal to Crew Members of the SS *Lyman Abbott*." (Publication information not available.)

———. "He Survived the *Junyo Maru*." *Fighting Forces*, November/December 1987, pp. 24–27.

———. "Homecoming Denied: The Cruise of the Sea Raider *Michel*." *War at Sea*, pp. 34–39, 114–17.

———. "In an Act of Historic Ingratitude, America Forgot Those

Who Made Possible the Final Victory." *Nautical Brass*, September/October 1985, pp. 6–7.

———. "In the Crosshairs of 'Anzio Annie.'" *Nautical Brass*, July/August 1992, pp. 15–17.

———. "Merchant Seamen in the VFW—Some Thoughts to Ponder." *The Anchor Light*, March 1999, pp. 1, 6.

———. "Murmansk Run Veterans Honored by Russia." *Sea Classics*, December 1991, p. 73.

———. "Remembering a Friend." *Nautical Brass*, March/April 1995, pp. 11–12.

———. "So Little Remembered: Merchant Marine Vets Have to Buy Their Own Medals." *Sea Classics*, December 1992, pp. 38–39.

———. "The Stephen Hopkins Epilogue: A Footnote to History." *Sea Classics*, undated, pp. 29–31, 77.

———. "Tankers at War!" *Sea Classics*, July 1990, pp. 22–29.

———. "Tankers at War!—Part Two/Conclusion." *Sea Classics*, August 1990, pp. 62–69.

———. "The Third Mate Stuck." Publication information not available.

———. "The Type of Man Your Brother Was . . ." *Sea History*, Spring 1985, p. 22.

———. "Under the Gun at Sea: An Appeal to the Sons and Daughters."

———. "*Virginia Dare* Was a Fighting Lady." *The State*, February 1985, pp. 18–20.

———. "We Thought She Was Scandinavian." *Nautical Brass*, July/August 1989, pp. 16–17.

———. "Well Done, Norway." *Sea Classics*, February 1990, pp. 69–71.

———. "When America Forgets Her Heroes." *The Lookout* (published by Pennsylvania Scholarship Association), Fall 1987, pp. 7, 11.

Miller, Nathan. *Sea of Glory: A Naval History of the American Revolution*. Charleston, S.C.: The Nautical and Aviation Publishing Company of America, 1974.

————. *The U.S. Navy: A History*. Annapolis, Md.: Naval Institute Press, 1997.

Milton, Keith. "Canadian Merchant Seaman Update." *The Anchor Light*, October 2001, p. 12.

Mink, Patsy T. July 26, 2001, letter to Dean Beaumont, with a copy of HR 2302 enclosed.

Mitchell, John. "Cargo Ship Visits Port of Hueneme." *Star Oxnard and Port Hueneme*, May 10, 2002, pp. B-1, B-2 (see also www.lanevictorship.com).

Moore, Captain Arthur R. *A Careless Word . . . A Needless Sinking*. Kings Point, N.Y.: American Merchant Marine Museum at the U.S. Merchant Marine Academy, 1983. (Printed in the U.S.A. by the Knowlton and McLeary Co., Farmington, Maine 04938.)

————. "Never Seen or Heard From Again." *The Anchor Light*, September 2001, pp. 1, 11.

Morison, Samuel Eliot. *The Atlantic Battle Won: May 1943–May 1945*. Boston: Little, Brown and Co., 1984.

————. *John Paul Jones: A Sailor's Biography*. New York: Time Inc., 1964.

————. *The Two-Ocean War: A Short History of the United States Navy in the Second World War*. New York: Little, Brown and Co., 1963.

Morris, Richard B., ed. *Encyclopedia of American History*. New York: Harper and Row, 1965.

————. *The American Navies of the Revolutionary War*. (Illustrated by Nowland Van Powell.) New York: G. P. Putnam's Sons, 1974.

Naval History, Fall 1988.

Nelson, Carl E. "On Borrowed Time." *The Anchor Light*, March 1999, p. 5.

Newcomb, Richard. "Kuribayashi's Last Stand," *The United States Marine Corps in World War II*. Edited by S. E. Smith (see pp. 812–13).

The New Encyclopaedia Britannica. Chicago: Encyclopaedia Britannica, Inc., 2002.

Orange County (Calif.) Illustrated. September 1977, pp. 117–18.

The (Orange County, Calif.) Register Leisurtime. February 9, 1975, p. 6.

Parrish, Thomas, and S. L. A. Marshall. *The Simon and Schuster Encyclopedia of World War II.* New York: Simon and Schuster, 1978.

Pratt, Julius W. *A History of United States Foreign Policy.* Englewood Cliffs, N.J.: Prentice-Hall, Inc., 1965.

Reminick, Gerald. *Nightmare in Bari: The World War II Liberty Ship Poison Gas Disaster and Cover-up.* Palo Alto, Calif.: Glencannon Press, 2001.

Riesenberg, Felix, Jr. *Sea War: The Story of the US Merchant Marine in World War II.* New York: Rinehart and Co., Inc., 1956.

Roscoe, Theodore. *United States Submarine Operations in World War Two.* Annapolis, Md.: Naval Institute Press, 1988.

Salty Dog, December 2002. Published by the Oregon Chapter of the American Merchant Marine Veterans of World War II.

San Diego Union Tribune, May 16, 2001, quoted in *The Anchor Light*, May/June 2001.

Sawyer, L. A., and W. H. Mitchell. *The Liberty Ships.* Cambridge, Mass.: Cornell Maritime Press, 1973.

Sawyer, William D. "A Tough Breed Hangs In There—Last of the Libertys [sic]." *Sea History*, Spring 1985, p. 28.

Schreadley, R. L. (commander, USN, ret.). *From the Rivers to the Sea: The United States Navy in Vietnam.* Annapolis, Md.: Naval Institute Press, 1992.

Scott, James E. (JO2). "Arthur Beaumont Hall opens at MIDPAC." *Fleet News*, September 6, 1996.

Simpson, James B. *Contemporary Quotations.* New York: Thomas Y. Crowell Co., 1964.

Smith, S. E., compiler and editor. *The United States Marine Corps in World War II.* New York: Random House, 1969.

Spectre, Peter H. *The Mariner's Book of Days.* Brooklin, Maine: WoodenBoat Books, 2001.

Stanford, Peter. "How an Ugly Duckling Fought Back and Sank Her Assailant." *Sea History*, Spring 1985, p. 22.

———. "Seamen's Recognition Day." *Sea History*, Spring 1985, pp. 12–13.

The Statistical History of the United States: From Colonial Times to the Present. Stamford, Conn.: Fairfield Publishers, Inc., 1965.

Stillwell, Paul, ed. *Assault on Normandy: First-Person Accounts from the Sea Services*. Annapolis, Md: Naval Institute Press, 1994. (Includes "Sub-Ordinary Seaman," by Richard A. Freed, pp. 137–39, and "Liberty Ship Signalman," by Cornelius A. ["Pete"] Burke, p. 144.)

Taylor, Wilson J. Letter to the editor, dated August 14, 1992, entitled "Guadalcanal Victory Due to the Armed Forces and the American Merchant Mariners."

Terkel, Studs. *The Good War: An Oral History of World War Two*. New York: The New Press, 1984. (Includes oral account of David Milton, pp. 103–07).

Thronson, Allen. "Kings Point Women Graduates Honored." *The Anchor Light*, February 1996, p. 1.

Tuchman, Barbara W. *The First Salute*. New York: Alfred A. Knopf, 1988.

Uhlig, Frank, Jr. *Vietnam: The Naval Story*. Annapolis, Md.: Naval Institute Press, 1986.

U.S. Department of Transportation news bulletin. May 22, 2001. Remarks of Norman Y. Mineta, U.S. Secretary of Transportation.

U.S. Maritime Coalition in association with Gardy-McGrath International, Inc. *The Last Convoy* (video production).

U.S. Merchant Marine Veterans of World War II. *Booklet of SS* Lane Victory (for National Historic Landmark dedication ceremony). December 14, 1991.

U.S. Naval History Division (Office of the Chief of Naval Operations). *United States Submarine Losses/World War Two*. Washington, D.C., 1963.

U.S. Navy Armed Guard WWII Veterans. *The (Rolesville, North Carolina) Pointer*, August/September 2001.

U.S. Navy pamphlet. *USS* O'Kane *(DDG 77)*.

Vernick, Joseph B. "Governor Pat Brown: A True Friend to the USMMV, WWII." *The Anchor Light*, February 1996, p. 1.

Wall, Carl B. "Captain of His Fate." *Reader's Digest*, July 1944. (Reprinted in *The Pointer*, October/November/December 2001, pp. 13–15. Also in Captain Arthur R. Moore's *A Careless Word*, pp. 319–21.)

Wallace, William N. "The Saga of the SS *William F. Humphrey*." *The Pointer*, October/November/December 2001, pp. 15–16.

Web sites:

"American Merchant Marine in World War II" (October 5, 2001, edition):

www.usmm.org (Note: Also cited by Gerald Reminich in *Nightmare in Bari*, as Horodysky, Dan and Toni, "U.S. Merchant Marine in World War Two: Casualties," www.usmm.org, March 5, 2001.)

USMM medals (Federal Maritime Commission):

www.marad.dot.gov/history/medals.html

Weller, George. *The Story of Submarines*. New York: Random House, 1962.

Wellington, Donald R. "My WWII Adventures on the SS *Ames Victory*." *The Anchor Light*, March 1999, p. 3.

Willoughby, Malcolm F. (lieutenant, USCGR T). *The U.S. Coast Guard in World War II*. Annapolis, Md.: United States Naval Institute, 1957.

Wineke, Andrew. "Remembering the *Rohna*." *The (Everett, Washington) Herald*, February 17, 2002, pp. D1–2.

World Almanac Books, *The World Almanac and Book of Facts*, Mahwah, N.J.: Primedia Reference, Inc., 1999.

Young, Peter, (brigadier), ed. *The World Almanac of World War II*. New York: Pharos Books, 1981.

Young, Robert T. (chairman and president, American Bureau of Shipping). "The Lessons of the Liberties." *The Anchor Light*, January 2001, p. 3.

INDEX

★　　　★　　　★

Galati, Bob, 272n. 7
Gallant Ship Award, 77
Gammel, Claude, 226
Ganges River, 132–33
gangrene, 98
Gardner, Herbert, 40–41
General Pickering, 242
Germans
    enemy respect of, 78
    Italy attacked by, 142–45
    Russia invaded by, 93–100
    sinking tactics by, 33, 39–42,
        50–51, 55, 139–41, 151–52
    successful fights against, 73–78,
        142
"ghost ships," 39
GI Bill of Rights, 182. *See also* benefits
Gibson, Charles Dana, 266n. 3
government. *See also* benefits
    letter writing campaign to, 217–19
    neglect of, 214–16
Great Britain
    in American Civil War, 251–52
    in American Revolution, 239–46
    in American War of Independence,
        247–51
    British Admiralty of, 94–98, 122–23
    Royal Air Force of, 116
    Royal Navy of, 243
Grucci, Felix J., Jr., 218
Grunert, Hans, 77
Guadalcanal, Battle of, 82
gunners, 71, 76–77

Hammer, Ben, 228–29
Hanks, Tom, 226–27
Hansen, Howard J., 54, 85, 94–95, 120,
    182, 201
"the Happy Time," 39
Haraden, Jonathan, 241–42
Haroldson, Donald C., 227
Haroldson, Martha, 227–28

Haviland, Donald F., 125
Hays, Ronald J., 193
"Hearsteria," 29
"Hell Afloat," 244
"Hell Convoy," 93
Henry, Patrick, 36
Herbert, Frank, 20, 22, 213
Hershey, Lewis B., 204
Hewey, Hudson A., 152
Hildbreth, Stanley, 13–14
Hitler, Adolf, 39, 157
HMS *Jersey,* 244–45
HMS *Trade Wind,* 113
Hope, Bob, 81–82
Hopkins, Esek, 75, 242–43
House Un-American Activities
    Committee (HUAC), 205
Howe, Richard, 243
Hower, Bill, 130, 150–51
H.R. 1235, 217, 220
H.R. 1893, 217–18
H.R. 2032, 225–26
H.R. 2302, 218
H.R. 2442, 218
HUAC. *See* House Un-American
    Activities Committee
Hughes, Howard, 22
humor, 49–50, 200
hurricanes, 148–53, 259
"Hurry-up Henry," 35

I-8, 57, 61
I-12, 58–59
I-boats, 57. *See also* Japanese
illness
    asbestos, 215, 286n. 3
    benzene, 215–16
    faking, 67–69
    prisoner, 114, 244–45
    psychological, 110, 128–29, 159–66
impressment, 247–48
Independence Day, 95–96